Exploring
the Origins of
the Bible

Acadia Studies in Bible and Theology

Craig A. Evans and Lee Martin McDonald, General Editors

The last two decades have witnessed dramatic developments in biblical and theological study. Full-time academics can scarcely keep up with fresh discoveries, recently published primary texts, ongoing archaeological work, new exegetical proposals, experiments in methods and hermeneutics, and innovative theological syntheses. For students and nonspecialists, these developments are confusing and daunting. What has been needed is a series of succinct studies that assess these issues and present their findings in a way that students, pastors, laity, and nonspecialists will find accessible and rewarding. Acadia Studies in Bible and Theology, sponsored by Acadia Divinity College in Wolfville, Nova Scotia, and in conjunction with the college's Hayward Lectureship, constitutes such a series.

The Hayward Lectureship has brought to Acadia many distinguished scholars of Bible and theology, such as Sir Robin Barbour, John Bright, Leander Keck, Helmut Koester, Richard Longenecker, Martin Marty, Jaroslav Pelikan, Ian Rennie, James Sanders, and Eduard Schweizer. The Acadia Studies in Bible and Theology series reflects this rich heritage.

These studies are designed to guide readers through the ever more complicated maze of critical, interpretative, and theological discussion taking place today. But these studies are not introductory in nature; nor are they mere surveys. Authored by leading authorities in the field, the Acadia Studies in Bible and Theology series offers critical assessments of the major issues that the church faces in the twenty-first century. Readers will gain the requisite orientation and fresh understanding of the important issues that will enable them to take part meaningfully in discussion and debate.

Exploring the Origins of the Bible

CANON FORMATION IN HISTORICAL,
LITERARY, AND THEOLOGICAL PERSPECTIVE

Craig A. Evans and Emanuel Tov

Editors

B
BakerAcademic
a division of Baker Publishing Group
Grand Rapids, Michigan

Published by Baker Academic
a division of Baker Publishing Group
P.O. Box 6287, Grand Rapids, MI 49516-6287
www.bakeracademic.com

Printed in the United States of America

Library of Congress Cataloging-in-Publication Data
Exploring the origins of the Bible : canon formation in historical, literary, and theological perspective / edited by Craig A. Evans and Emanuel Tov.
    p.   cm. (Acadia studies in Bible and theology)
Includes bibliographical references and indexes.
ISBN 978-0-8010-3242-4 (pbk.)
1. Bible—Canon. I. Evans, Craig A. II. Tov, Emanuel.
BS465.E97 2008
220.1'2—dc22   2008019124

Contents

Preface

Exploring the Origins of the Bible is the result of a special spring session of the Hayward Lectures at Acadia Divinity College in Wolfville, Nova Scotia, that took place in April 2006. Whereas the regular Hayward Lectures occur in the fall and are delivered by a single scholar, the spring lectures provide the occasion for a group of scholars to assemble and share their respective areas of expertise.

The first spring session of the Hayward Lectures focused on the Dead Sea Scrolls and resulted in the publication of *Christian Beginnings and the Dead Sea Scrolls* (2006). Thus far, four of the fall lectures have been published: I. Howard Marshall, *Beyond the Bible: Moving from Scripture to Theology* (2004); James D. G. Dunn, *A New Perspective on Jesus: What the Quest for the Historical Jesus Missed* (2005); John G. Stackhouse Jr., *Finally Feminist: A Pragmatic Christian Understanding of Gender* (2005); and Roger E. Olson, *Reformed and Always Reforming: The Postconservative Approach to Evangelical Theology* (2007). Lectures by N. T. Wright and Christopher Seitz are in the process of being published.

The Acadia faculty wish to express their appreciation to the scholars who journeyed from afar to take part in the lectures and to the audience that came out in good numbers to hear the papers and ask insightful, clarifying questions. The editors would also like to thank the C. C. Hayward endowment, the trustees of the

Christie Fund in Amherst, Nova Scotia, and Baker Academic for providing financial support. Without this financial assistance these lectures would not be possible. A word of thanks also to Danny Zacharias for preparing the indexes.

Craig A. Evans
Acadia Divinity College

Emanuel Tov
Hebrew University

Contributors

James H. Charlesworth (PhD, Duke University) is the George L. Collord Professor of New Testament Language and Literature at Princeton Theological Seminary and the director and editor of the Princeton Dead Sea Scrolls Project. He has taught at Princeton since 1984 and has written or edited more than thirty books and two hundred articles. Some of his recent books include *Jesus within Judaism*, *The Messiah*, *Jesus and the Dead Sea Scrolls*, and *Qumran Questions*.

Stephen G. Dempster (PhD, University of Toronto) is professor of religious studies and Stuart E. Murray Chair of Christian Studies at Atlantic Baptist University. He is the author of *Dominion and Dynasty: A Biblical Theology of the Hebrew Bible*.

Craig A. Evans (PhD, Claremont Graduate University) is the Payzant Distinguished Professor of New Testament at Acadia Divinity College. He is the author or editor of more than fifty books, including *Jesus and the Ossuaries* and *Ancient Texts for New Testament Studies*.

Lee Martin McDonald (PhD, University of Edinburgh) is president of the Institute for Biblical Research and professor of biblical studies at Acadia Divinity College, where he formerly served as president. He is the author or editor of several books, including *The Formation of the Christian Biblical Canon*, *The Canon Debate*, and *Early Christianity and Its Sacred Literature*.

Stanley E. Porter (PhD, University of Sheffield) is president and dean of McMaster Divinity College, where he also serves as professor of New Testament. He is the author or editor of more than fifty books, including *Verbal Aspect in the Greek of the New Testament*, *Idioms of the Greek New Testament*, and *Early Christianity and Its Sacred Literature*.

Emanuel Tov (PhD, Hebrew University) is J. L. Magnes Professor of Bible at Hebrew University of Jerusalem. He has been the editor-in-chief of the Dead Sea Scrolls Publication Project since 1990 and is involved in the Hebrew University Bible Project and the Computer Assisted Tools for Septuagint Studies Project (University of Pennsylvania). He has written or edited more than twenty books, including *Textual Criticism of the Hebrew Bible*.

Jonathan R. Wilson (PhD, Duke University) is Pioneer McDonald Professor of Theology at Carey Theological College. He taught previously at Acadia Divinity College and Westmont College and has authored or edited more than a dozen books, including *A Primer for Christian Doctrine*, *Gospel Virtues: Practicing Faith, Hope, and Love in Uncertain Times*, and *God So Loved the World: A Christology for Disciples*.

R. Glenn Wooden (PhD, University of St. Andrews) is associate professor of Old Testament at Acadia Divinity College. He is coeditor of *"You Will Be My Witnesses": A Festschrift in Honor of the Reverend Dr. Allison A. Trites on the Occasion of His Retirement*.

Abbreviations

AB	Anchor Bible
ABD	*Anchor Bible Dictionary*. Edited by D. N. Freedman. 6 vols. New York, 1992
ABRL	Anchor Bible Reference Library
AnBib	Analecta biblica
ANF	*The Ante-Nicene Fathers*. Edited by A. Roberts and J. Donaldson. 10 vols. 1885–87. Repr. Peabody, MA, 1994
ANRW	*Aufstieg und Niedergang der römischen Welt: Geschichte und Kultur Roms im Spiegel der neueren Forschung*. Edited by H. Temporini and W. Haase. Berlin, 1972–
b.	Babylonian Talmud
BA	*Biblical Archaeologist*
BBB	Bonner biblische Beiträge
BBR	*Bulletin for Biblical Research*
BENT	Beiträge zur Einleitung in das Neuen Testament
BETL	Bibliotheca ephemeridum theologicarum lovaniensium
Bib	*Biblica*
BIOSCS	*Bulletin of the International Organization for Septuagint and Cognate Studies*
BIS	Biblical Interpretation Series
BJRL	*Bulletin of the John Rylands University Library of Manchester*
BRev	*Bible Review*

BT	*The Bible Translator*
BWANT	Beiträge zur Wissenschaft vom Alten und Neuen Testament
BZAW	Beihefte zur Zeitschrift für die alttestamentliche Wissenschaft
BZNW	Beihefte zur Zeitschrift für die neutestamentliche Wissenschaft
CahRB	Cahiers de la Revue biblique
CBQ	*Catholic Biblical Quarterly*
CJA	Christianity and Judaism in Antiquity
ConBNT	Coniectanea biblica: New Testament Series
CRBR	*Critical Review of Books in Religion*
CTM	*Concordia Theological Monthly*
DJD	Discoveries in the Judaean Desert
DSD	*Dead Sea Discoveries*
EBib	Etudes bibliques
ER	*The Encyclopedia of Religion.* Edited by M. Eliade. 16 vols. New York, 1987
ET	English translation
ExpTim	*Expository Times*
FRLANT	Forschungen zur Religion und Literatur des Alten und Neuen Testaments
GBS	Guides to Biblical Scholarship
HSM	Harvard Semitic Monographs
HTR	*Harvard Theological Review*
HUCA	*Hebrew Union College Annual*
HUT	Hermeneutische Untersuchungen zur Theologie
ICC	International Critical Commentary
IDBSup	*Interpreter's Dictionary of the Bible: Supplementary Volume.* Edited by K. Crim. Nashville, 1976
Int	*Interpretation*
JAOS	*Journal of the American Oriental Society*
JBL	*Journal of Biblical Literature*
JBLMS	Journal of Biblical Literature Monograph Series
JBS	Jerusalem Biblical Studies
JHS	*Journal of Hellenic Studies*
JJS	*Journal of Jewish Studies*
JNSL	*Journal of Northwest Semitic Languages*
JSHRZ	*Jüdische Schriften aus hellenistisch-römischer Zeit*

JSNT	*Journal for the Study of the New Testament*
JSNTSup	Journal for the Study of the New Testament: Supplement Series
JSOTSup	Journal for the Study of the Old Testament: Supplement Series
JSPSup	Journal for the Study of the Pseudepigrapha: Supplement Series
JTS	*Journal of Theological Studies*
LCL	Loeb Classical Library
LEC	Library of Early Christianity
LUÅ	Lunds universitets årsskrift
LXX	Septuagint
m.	Mishnah
MT	Masoretic Text
MTS	Marburger theologische Studien
NGS	New Gospel Studies
NHS	Nag Hammadi Studies
NIGTC	New International Greek Testament Commentary
NovT	*Novum Testamentum*
NovTSup	Novum Testamentum Supplements
NTAbh	Neutestamentliche Abhandlungen
NTG	New Testament Guides
NTOA	Novum Testamentum et Orbis Antiquus
NTS	*New Testament Studies*
NTTS	New Testament Tools and Studies
OBO	Orbis biblicus et orientalis
OTM	Oxford Theological Monographs
OTP	*Old Testament Pseudepigrapha*. Edited by J. H. Charlesworth. 2 vols. New York, 1983
RevQ	*Revue de Qumran*
RQ	*Römische Quartalschrift für christliche Altertumskunde und Kirchengeschichte*
SBLSCS	Society of Biblical Literature Septuagint and Cognate Studies
SBLSP	Society of Biblical Literature Seminar Papers
SC	Sources chrétiennes. Paris: Cerf, 1943–
ScrHier	*Scripta hierosolymitana*
SD	Studies and Documents
SecCent	*Second Century*
SJT	*Scottish Journal of Theology*

SNTSMS	Society for New Testament Studies Monograph Series
SP	Samaritan Pentateuch
SR	*Studies in Religion*
t.	Tosefta
TC	*TC: A Journal of Biblical Textual Criticism*
TLZ	*Theologische Literaturzeitung*
TNTC	Tyndale New Testament Commentaries
TU	Texte und Untersuchungen
VC	*Vigiliae christianae*
VCSup	Vigiliae christianae Supplements
VT	*Vetus Testamentum*
VTSup	Vetus Testamentum Supplements
WUNT	Wissenschaftliche Untersuchungen zum Neuen Testament
y.	Jerusalem Talmud
ZAW	*Zeitschrift für die alttestamentliche Wissenschaft*
ZNW	*Zeitschrift für die neutestamentliche Wissenschaft und die Kunde der älteren Kirche*

Introduction

CRAIG A. EVANS

Most people who read the Bible have little idea how complicated its origins, transmission, preservation, and history of compilation truly are. The word *Bible* means "book," but in reality the Bible is comprised of many books. The exact number depends on one's confessional identity. For Jews the Bible (also called Tanak or Mikra—what Christians call the Old Testament) is made up of Hebrew and Aramaic books. For Christians, the Greek New Testament is also part of the Bible. Moreover, Christians differ among themselves whether to include the books of the Apocrypha.

There are many more questions and issues. Not everyone realizes that the Jewish Bible (or Old Testament) at one time circulated not only in Hebrew/Aramaic, but also in Greek. For some, the Greek version was as authoritative as the Hebrew/Aramaic. Aramaic paraphrases (called targums) later emerged, which in some circles were also considered authoritative. In time Jerome translated the Bible into Latin, which eventually became known as the Vulgate, the official version for the Roman Catholic Church.

15

These facts are familiar to Bible scholars, but some will be new to many readers of this collection of studies. A brief survey of the basic issues will serve as a helpful introduction to this volume.[1]

Versions of the Hebrew Bible

Hebrew may have been the original language in which most of the Old Testament was written, but the Hebrew text is extant today in distinct forms: the Masoretic Text, the Samaritan Pentateuch, fragments from the Cairo Genizah (which usually agree with the Masoretic Text), and more than 200 scrolls from Qumran (which mostly agree with the Masoretic Text, but some exhibit a form of Hebrew text that corresponds with the Old Greek, or Septuagint).[2] It seems that no one of these extant texts represents the exact original form. Let's review these Hebrew texts:

The Masoretic Text. The official version of the Hebrew Bible, or Old Testament, for Judaism and Christianity since the early Middle Ages is the Masoretic Text, which derives its name from the Masoretes, the scribes who preserved, edited, and pointed the text (i.e., added vowel signs, accents, and punctuation of a sort). Their notes are called the Masora. The Masoretic tradition probably originated in the late first or early second century. The Masora provide an interesting and complex array of sigla, whereby the scribes noted their alterations of or reservations about this passage or that. Best known is *Ketib/Qere* ("written"/"spoken"): reluctant to change the written text *(Ketib)*, the scribes wrote in the margin

1. Some of the paragraphs that follow are adapted from C. A. Evans, *Ancient Texts for New Testament Studies: A Guide to the Background Literature* (Peabody, MA: Hendrickson, 2005), chaps. 4 and 6. See further E. Tov, *Textual Criticism of the Hebrew Bible* (2nd rev. ed.; Minneapolis: Fortress; Assen: Royal Van Gorcum, 2001).

2. The discovery of the Dead Sea Scrolls, both those of Qumran and those of Murabba'at and Masada, provided witnesses to the Hebrew text dating from the turn of the era. Probably best known is the Great Isaiah Scroll (1QIsaᵃ). More than two hundred scrolls (most in fragments) have been found. For an assessment of the implications of the Dead Sea Scrolls for the biblical text, see F. M. Cross and S. Talmon, eds., *Qumran and the History of the Biblical Text* (Cambridge: Harvard University Press, 1975). For an English translation and composite of the biblical scrolls of Qumran, see M. G. Abegg Jr., P. W. Flint, and E. Ulrich, *The Dead Sea Scrolls Bible: The Oldest Known Bible Translated for the First Time into English* (San Francisco: HarperCollins, 1999).

what should be read aloud (*Qere*).[3] The oldest Masoretic manuscripts date from the late ninth century CE (e.g., Codex Cairensis [C] on the Prophets). No complete manuscript is earlier than the tenth century (e.g., the Aleppo Codex, which is incomplete). Fragments from the Cairo Genizah date from the sixth (possibly fifth) to the eighth centuries. Codex Leningradensis, on which the modern critical Hebrew Bible is based, dates to 1008 CE.[4]

Samaritan Pentateuch. As a distinct recension the Samaritan Pentateuch probably owes its origin to the schism in the second century BCE. There are 150 manuscripts of the Samaritan Pentateuch, many nothing more than fragments, and most in Hebrew, though some are in Aramaic and Arabic. What makes the Samaritan Pentateuch interesting is that in approximately 1,900 places it agrees with the Greek version (the Septuagint) over against the Masoretic Text. In some places it agrees with New Testament quotations or allusions over against both the Greek and the Masoretic Text (e.g., Acts 7:4, 32). Some fragments of the Pentateuch at Qumran reflect a form of the text on which the Samaritan Pentateuch was apparently based (cf. 4QpaleoExod^{m14}; 4Q158^{15}; 4Q364; 4QNum^{b}; 4QDeut^{n19}; 4Q175).[5]

3. The Masora *marginalis* is the material written in the four margins of the page. The Masora *finalis* represents an alphabetical compilation at the end of the Old Testament. The Masora *parva* ("small Masora") is found in the side margins, while the Masora *magna* ("large Masora") is found at the top and bottom margins.

4. The principal text is that edited by R. Kittel, *Biblia Hebraica* (with P. Kahle; Stuttgart: Württembergische Bibelanstalt, 1968), and the more recent edition by K. Elliger and W. Rudolph, *Biblia Hebraica Stuttgartensia* (Stuttgart: Deutsche Bibelgesellschaft, 1983). A smaller and less expensive edition has been produced by N. H. Snaith, *Tora, Nebi'im, Ketubim* (London: British and Foreign Bible Society, 1958). For the Leningrad Codex, see A. B. Beck and D. N. Freedman, eds., *The Leningrad Codex: A Facsimile Edition* (Grand Rapids: Eerdmans, 1998). A series of volumes devoted to the textual variants is being prepared by D. Barthélemy, ed., *Critique textuelle de l'Ancien Testament* (OBO 50; Fribourg: Editions Universitaires; Göttingen: Vandenhoeck & Ruprecht, 1982–).

5. The rabbis may have known of the Samaritan Pentateuch: "Said Rabbi Eleazar ben R. Simeon, 'I stated to Samaritan scribes, "You have forged your own Torah, and it has done you no good"'" (*y. Sotah* 7.3). The text of the Samaritan Pentateuch has been edited by A. F. von Gall, *Der hebräische Pentateuch der Samaritaner* (5 vols.; Giessen: Töpelmann, 1914–18; repr., Berlin: Töpelmann, 1963–66). See also A. Sadaqa and R. Sadaqa, *The Samaritan Pentateuch: Jewish Version—Samaritan Version of the Pentateuch* (5 vols.; Tel Aviv: Rubin Mass, 1961–65).

Other Versions of the Bible

Old Greek. The Old Greek (OG), or more commonly the Septuagint (LXX, from the Latin *septuaginta,* "seventy"), is the Greek
translation of the Old Testament (including the Old Testament
Apocrypha). The name "seventy" comes from the legend found in
the pseudepigraphal *Letter of Aristeas,* in which it is claimed that
King Ptolemy II Philadelphus (285–247 BCE) commissioned seventy-
two Palestinian scribes to translate the Hebrew Pentateuch into
Greek for the royal library. In isolation on the island of Pharos the
scribes finished the task in seventy-two days. The story is recounted
by Josephus (cf. *Jewish Antiquities* 12.11–118). Philo himself accepted the story and regarded the translation as inspired, given, as
it were, by divine dictation (cf. *On the Life of Moses* 2.37), a view
that became common among many of the early church fathers.[6]

The LXX is an important witness to the Hebrew text that predates the Masoretes. Some of its variations from the Masoretic
Text agree with readings found in the Dead Sea Scrolls. Some of
its differing readings appear in the New Testament, whose authors
follow the LXX in more than half of their quotations of the Old
Testament. The diversity of the first-century Greek Old Testament
text has been documented by the discovery and publication of
8HevXII gr, a fragmentary Greek scroll of the Minor Prophets.[7]
This text differs from the LXX in a number of places, and has
several points of agreement with at least three of the recensions
(Aquila, Symmachus, and Theodotion).[8]

---

6. For several reasons the account of Aristeas is generally accepted as legendary rather
than historical. Although the date of the LXX (at least as it concerns the Pentateuch) may
be as ancient as *Aristeas* purports, the reason for the translation was to make the Bible
more readily accessible to the Greek-speaking Jews of Alexandria. The remaining portions
of the Bible were translated in succeeding generations, perhaps not being completed until
the first century CE. Evidently several translators were involved in this long process, for
the style varies from one book to another. For more on this topic, see the essays by R. G.
Wooden ("The Role of 'the Septuagint' in the Formation of the Biblical Canons") and L. M.
McDonald ("Wherein Lies Authority? A Discussion of Books, Texts, and Translations")
in the present volume.

7. E. Tov, *The Greek Minor Prophets Scroll from Naḥal Ḥever (8HevXII gr)* (DJD VIII;
Oxford: Clarendon, 1990).

8. The principal text of the LXX is A. Rahlfs, *Septuaginta* (2 vols.; Stuttgart: Württembergische Bibelanstalt, 1935). A multi-volume critical edition has been edited by A. Rahlfs,
J. Ziegler et al., *Septuaginta: Vetus Testamentum Graecum* (Göttingen: Vandenhoeck &

For various reasons, several recensions of the LXX were produced in the second and third centuries CE. The oldest was by Aquila, a possible disciple of Rabbi Aqiba who may be the Onqelos associated with the Pentateuch targum of that name (cf. *b. Gittin* 56b; *b. Megillah* 3a). Aquila's Greek recension, which is really a new, woodenly literal translation of the Hebrew text, was published ca. 130 CE. His recension survives in quotations, fragments of Origen's Hexapla, and a few sixth-century palimpsests. Symmachus produced a recension ca. 170 CE that represented a much more stylish Greek than that of Aquila. According to Eusebius and Jerome, Symmachus was a Jewish Christian, but Epiphanius claims he was a Samaritan who had converted to Judaism. Symmachus's work survives in a few Hexapla fragments. Following the Hebrew text, Theodotion revised the LXX (or at least a Greek text that was very similar) sometime toward the end of the second century. Only fragments of Theodotion's translation are extant (principally in quotations).[9]

Old Latin. The Old Latin survives in fragmentary manuscripts, liturgical books, and quotations of early Latin fathers (e.g., Tertullian, Cyprian, Ambrose). A few books survive in complete form as part of the Vulgate (Baruch, Epistle of Jeremiah, Wisdom, Sirach, 1 and 2 Maccabees). Jerome did not edit these books because he regarded them as uninspired (principally because they were not extant in Hebrew or Aramaic, and because they were not as ancient

---

Ruprecht, 1931–). This work is not yet finished, though some two dozen volumes have appeared to date. For critical study, see E. Tov, *The Greek and Hebrew Bible: Collected Essays on the Septuagint* (VTSup 72; Leiden: Brill, 1999); idem, *The Text-Critical Use of the Septuagint in Biblical Research* (2nd ed.; JBS 8; Jerusalem: Simor, 1997). A New English Translation of the Septuagint (NETS) has been launched by the International Organization for Septuagint and Cognate Studies (IOSCS) (A. Pietersma and B. G. Wright III, eds., *A New English Translation of the Septuagint and the Other Greek Translations Traditionally Included under That Title* [New York: Oxford University Press, 2007]). The first fascicle to appear was by A. Pietersma, *The Psalms: A New English Translation of the Septuagint* (Oxford: Oxford University Press, 2000). Members of the IOSCS are also preparing a commentary on the LXX.

9. For more studies of the Greek recensions, see D. Barthélemy, *Les Devanciers d'Aquila* (VTSup 10; Leiden: Brill, 1962); D. W. Gooding, *Recensions of the Septuagint Pentateuch* (London: Tyndale, 1955); K. G. O'Connell, "Greek Versions," *IDBSup* 377–81; B. M. Metzger, "Lucian and the Lucianic Recension of the Greek Bible," *NTS* 8 (1962): 189–203.

as the rest of the Old Testament). The Old Latin represents various translations of the LXX. The primary value of the Old Latin is that it provides an important witness to the text of the LXX before the influences of the Greek recensions.[10]

Vulgate. In 382 Pope Damasus I commissioned Jerome to prepare a reliable Latin translation of the Bible. Despite Augustine's protests, Jerome, who had studied Hebrew in Bethlehem, based the Old Testament translation on the Hebrew text.[11] This translation became the official Bible of the Roman Church and eventually became known as the "Vulgate" (from the Latin, meaning "common"). It was not, however, until the ninth century that Jerome's version finally displaced the popular Old Latin. Many theologians were reluctant to depart from the Old Latin because, unlike the Vulgate, it was dependent upon the LXX, which many (e.g., Augustine) regarded as divinely inspired. The major value of the Vulgate is that it represents an early witness to the Hebrew text.[12]

Targums. Produced over generations in the homiletical and liturgical setting of the synagogue, the targums constitute an Aramaic translation/paraphrase/interpretation of the Hebrew Bible. The word *targum*, from the Aramaic word *trgm*, "to translate," basically means a paraphrase or interpretive translation. The Aramaic translator was called the *meturgeman.* Targums to all of the books of the Old Testament, with the exceptions of Ezra–Nehemiah and Daniel (large portions of which were already in Aramaic), are extant in manuscripts that date, for the most part, from the Middle Ages. Until recent years New Testament interpreters have made little use

10. A multi-volume critical edition of the Old Latin has been undertaken by B. Fischer and others, *Vetus Latina: Die Reste der altlateinischen Bibel, nach Petrus Sabatier neu gesammelt und herausgegeben von der Erzabtei Beuron* (Freiburg: Herder, 1949–). The work is not yet complete. Each volume is published one fascicle at a time over a period of years.

11. See Jerome's letter to Pope Damasus (*Epistle* 18, ca. 381), where he defends the priority of the Hebrew over the Greek.

12. The principal edition of the Vulgate is by R. Weber, ed., *Biblia Sacra iuxta Vulgatam Versionem* (2 vols.; 3rd ed.; Stuttgart: Deutsche Bibelgesellschaft, 1985). There are various English translations available. An old classic is the Douay-Rheims, so called because it combines the Douay English translation of the Old Testament (1609) with the Rheims English translation of the New Testament (1582): *The Holy Bible Translated from the Latin Vulgate* (New York: P. J. Kennedy & Sons, 1914). A multi-volume critical edition has also been produced by the Benedictine Order, *Biblia Sacra iuxta Latinam Vulgatam Versionem* (16 vols.; Rome: Typis Polyglottis Vaticanis, 1926–81).

of them, primarily because it was assumed that they originated too late to be relevant. However, Paul Kahle's discovery and publication of the Cairo Genizah fragments and the discovery of targum fragments among the Dead Sea Scrolls (i.e., 4QtgLev, 4QtgJob, 11QtgJob, and possibly 6Q19, which may be a targum on Genesis) have led several scholars to reconsider this assumption.[13]

Peshitta. The Syriac version of the Bible came to be called the Peshitta (or Peshitto), which means "simple" (compare the Aramaic word *peshita'*, "plain [meaning]"). One of the oldest manuscripts is MS Add. 14,425 of the British Museum (containing the Pentateuch, minus Leviticus), which is dated 464 CE. The origin of the Peshitta is obscure. Scholars are now aware of this version's close relationship to the targums.[14]

Contents of the Hebrew Bible

The Hebrew Bible has been traditionally divided into three parts: (1) Law, or Torah, (2) Prophets, or Nevi'im, and (3) Writings, or Ketuvim. The acronym "Tanak" refers to this tripartite division (i.e., Torah [T], Nevi'im [N], Ketuvim [K]).

Torah is made up of the five books of the Law:

Genesis (or Bereshit)

Exodus (or Shemot)

13. The standard Aramaic edition is Alexander Sperber, *The Bible in Aramaic Based on Old Manuscripts and Printed Texts* (4 vols.; Leiden: Brill, 1959–68). One should also see A. Díez Macho, *Neophyti 1: Targum Palestinense ms de la Biblioteca Vaticana* (5 vols.; Madrid and Barcelona: Consejo Superior de Investigaciones Científicas, 1968–78); M. L. Klein, *The Fragment-Targums of the Pentateuch: According to their Extant Sources* (AnBib 76; Rome: Pontifical Biblical Institute Press, 1980); E. G. Clarke, *Targum Pseudo-Jonathan of the Pentateuch: Text and Concordance* (Hoboken, NJ: Ktav, 1984); M. L. Klein, *Genizah Manuscripts of Palestinian Targum to the Pentateuch* (2 vols.; Cincinnati: Hebrew Union College Press, 1986). Publisher Michael Glazier (now Liturgical Press) is currently preparing an English translation of all extant targums. This work is nearly complete.

14. The principal edition of the Peshitta is A. M. Ceriani, *Translatio Syra Pescitto Veteris Testamenti ex Codex Ambrosiano II* (Milan: Impensis Bibliothecae Ambrosianae, 1876–83). A critical edition has been sponsored by the Peshitta Institute of Leiden on behalf of the International Organization for the Study of the Old Testament. An English translation of the Syriac Bible (based on Codex Ambrosianus) has been produced by G. Lamsa, *The Holy Bible from Ancient Manuscripts* (Nashville: Holman Bible Publishers, 1957).

Leviticus (or Vayiqra)
Numbers (or Bemidbar)
Deuteronomy (or Devarim)

These books were the first to be recognized as authoritative and probably the first translated into Greek. The text of Torah is different at many places in the Samaritan version.

The Prophets are divided into two groups: the Former Prophets and the Latter Prophets. The first group (Former Prophets) is made up of four books (though normally thought of as six):

Joshua
Judges
Samuel (i.e., 1–2 Samuel)
Kings (i.e., 1–2 Kings)

The second group (Latter Prophets) is made up of four books (though usually thought of as fifteen):

Isaiah
Jeremiah
Ezekiel
The Twelve (i.e., the Twelve Minor Prophets, comprising Hosea, Joel, Amos, Obadiah, Jonah, Micah, Nahum, Habakkuk, Zephaniah, Haggai, Zechariah, and Malachi)

Christians should note that books usually thought of as "historical books" (i.e., 1–2 Samuel and 1–2 Kings) are included in the Prophets, while the book of Daniel is not.

The Writings are the most diverse body of literature in the Jewish Bible. These writings are twelve in number, though commonly thought of as thirteen:

Psalms
Proverbs
Job
Song of Songs

Ruth
Lamentations
Ecclesiastes (or Qohelet)
Esther
Daniel
Ezra
Nehemiah
Chronicles (i.e., 1–2 Chronicles)

In antiquity Ezra and Nehemiah were usually combined in a single scroll. The book of Psalms (or the Psalter) is divided into five books. The genre and character of the psalms are wide-ranging, including psalms of lament, celebration, and imprecation against enemies, to name a few. The books of Proverbs, Job, and Ecclesiastes constitute wisdom literature. Daniel presents an interesting mixture of wisdom, prophecy, narrative, and apocalyptic. Chronicles retells and updates the old stories of Samuel and Kings.

The Writings comprise the third and final portion of the Jewish Bible. Exactly when the contents of this portion became widely known and accepted is unclear and a subject of debate.[15]

Contents of the Apocrypha

The Old Testament Apocrypha (meaning "hidden books") comprise a diverse collection of literature. In all there are fifteen books (though this number sometimes varies). Some of the writings are historical (e.g., 1 Esdras, 1 and 2 Maccabees), some are romantic (e.g., Tobit, Judith, Susanna, Additions to Esther), some are didactic (e.g., Wisdom of Solomon, Ecclesiasticus), some are moralistic (e.g., Baruch, Letter of Jeremiah, Bel and the Dragon), and some

15. For discussion of the development of the Jewish Bible, see S. Z. Leiman, *The Canonization of the Hebrew Scriptures: The Talmudic and Midrashic Evidence* (Connecticut Academy of Arts and Sciences 47; Hamden, CT: Archon, 1976); L. M. McDonald, *The Biblical Canon: Its Origin, Transmission, and Authority* (Peabody, MA: Hendrickson, 2007), 73–113. See the very helpful "Appendix A: Primary Sources for the Study of the Old Testament/Hebrew Bible Canon," in L. M. McDonald and J. A. Sanders, eds., *The Canon Debate* (Peabody, MA: Hendrickson, 2002), 580–82.

are devotional (e.g., Prayer of Azariah and the Song of the Three Children, Prayer of Manasseh). One is apocalyptic (2 Esdras). Most of these books are recognized as authoritative in the scriptural canons of the Roman Catholic, Greek Orthodox, Russian Orthodox, Eastern, and Coptic Churches. Most Protestant Churches have omitted the books of the Apocrypha, though these texts enjoy a quasi-canonical status in the Anglican Church.[16]

Contents of the Pseudepigrapha

The writings of the Old Testament Pseudepigrapha are numerous and diverse. Several literary genres are represented in this amorphous collection. Their dates of composition also cover a broad period of time, with *Ahiqar* being the oldest at ca. seventh or sixth century BCE and the *Apocalypse of Daniel* the youngest at ca. ninth century CE. Many of these books were among those to which *4 Ezra* refers: "ninety-four books were written. And . . . the Most High spoke to me, saying, 'Make public the twenty-four books that you wrote first and let the worthy and the unworthy read them; but keep the seventy that were written last, in order to give them to the wise among your people. For in them is the spring of understanding, the fountain of wisdom, and the river of knowledge'" (14:44–47 [Metzger, *OTP* 1:555]). The "twenty-four" books are the books that make up the Jewish Bible, or Old Testament. The seventy books are the books of the Apocrypha and Pseudepigrapha. In addition to the sixty-six books treated in

16. The Greek text of the Apocrypha is found in the Septuagint. A very fine English translation is found in B. M. Metzger, ed., *The Apocrypha of the Old Testament, Revised Standard Version* (New York: Oxford University Press, 1977). This edition contains several helpful notes and tables. Metzger has also edited *A Concordance to the Apocryphal/Deuterocanonical Books of the Revised Standard Version* (London: Collins; Grand Rapids: Eerdmans, 1983). See also the translation in the *New Revised Standard Version* (New York: Oxford University Press, 1989). For current introductions, see D. A. deSilva, *Introducing the Apocrypha: Message, Context, and Significance* (Grand Rapids: Baker Academic, 2002), and D. J. Harrington, *Invitation to the Apocrypha* (Grand Rapids: Eerdmans, 1999). For current one-volume commentaries on the Apocrypha, see J. L. Mays, ed., *Harper's Bible Commentary* (San Francisco: Harper & Row, 1988), and W. R. Farmer et al., eds., *The International Bible Commentary: A Catholic and Ecumenical Commentary for the Twenty-First Century* (Collegeville, MN: Liturgical Press, 1998).

this chapter (many of which did not exist when *4 Ezra* was written), some fifty more apocryphal and pseudepigraphal writings were found among the scrolls of Qumran. Thus, in the time of the writing of *4 Ezra* there were probably more than seventy books in this category of those "written last."

The word *pseudepigrapha* is a Greek word meaning "falsely ascribed," or what we might call writing under a pen name. The classification "Old Testament Pseudepigrapha" is a label that scholars have given to these writings. Although some of them have been grouped together or associated in one way or another, most never had any connection to one another.

The line that divides the Old Testament Apocrypha from the Old Testament Pseudepigrapha is not clearly drawn. Two writings found in the Apocrypha, the Prayer of Manasseh and *4 Ezra* (contained within 2 Esdras), are usually assigned to the Pseudepigrapha. Three writings found in the Pseudepigrapha—3 Maccabees, 4 Maccabees, and Psalm 151—appear in some canons of Scripture as part of the Apocrypha.[17]

Some of the better known Pseudepigrapha include the following:

1 and 2 Enoch
Pseudo-Philo, *Biblical Antiquities*
Jubilees
Psalms of Solomon
Testament of Solomon
Testament of Moses
Testaments of the Twelve Patriarchs
Testament of Abraham
2 and 3 Baruch

---

17. For a convenient collection of the Pseudepigrapha, in English translation with introduction and notes, see J. H. Charlesworth, ed., *The Old Testament Pseudepigrapha* (2 vols.; New York: Doubleday, 1983–85). For discussion of the relevance of these writings for New Testament study, see J. H. Charlesworth, *The Old Testament Pseudepigrapha and the New Testament: Prolegomena for the Study of Christian Origins* (Harrisburg, PA: Trinity Press International, 1998). For extensive bibliography, see L. DiTommaso, *A Bibliography of Pseudepigrapha Research 1850–1999* (JSPSup 39; Sheffield: Sheffield Academic Press, 2001).

Omissions of Jeremiah (or *4 Baruch*)

Lives of the Prophets

Letter of Aristeas

It should also be mentioned that many writings found among the Dead Sea Scrolls exemplify the genres and themes of the Pseudepigrapha: imaginative expansions and paraphrases of Old Testament Scripture, additional psalms, apocalypses and visions, prayers, and hymns.[18] This body of material, taken together with what had been known before the discovery of the scrolls in the 1940s and 1950s, demonstrates dramatically how extensive Jewish literature was in the intertestamental and New Testament periods.

Contents of the New Testament

Although not as complicated as the formation of the Old Testament canon of Scripture, the formation of the New Testament was not without debate and struggle. Most if not all of the twenty-seven writings that make up the New Testament were composed and began to circulate in the second half of the first century. (Many scholars think the Pastoral Letters and 2 Peter were not composed until the first half of the second century.)

Several other writings were treated as authoritative by some church leaders and congregations. The second-century *Gospel of Peter* was read in the Eastern Church, until Bishop Serapion in the early third century forbade it. Several other writings enjoyed favor in the Syrian Church, such as Tatian's harmony of the Gospels (the *Diatessaron*) and the *Gospel of Thomas*. The *Didache* (or "Teaching"), Clement's letter to the Corinthian Christians, and the

---

18. For English translation of the Dead Sea Scrolls, see E. Tov and D. W. Parry, eds., *The Dead Sea Scrolls Reader* (6 vols.; Leiden: Brill, 2004–5). For introduction and discussion of their relevance, see J. C. VanderKam and P. W. Flint, *The Meaning of the Dead Sea Scrolls: Their Significance for Understanding the Bible, Judaism, Jesus, and Christianity* (San Francisco: HarperCollins, 2002); J. J. Collins and C. A. Evans, eds., *Christian Beginnings and the Dead Sea Scrolls* (Acadia Studies in Bible and Theology; Grand Rapids: Baker Academic, 2006).

interesting compilation produced by a church leader known as the *Shepherd of Hermas* commanded great respect in some circles.[19]

Other writings that did, in time, gain entry into the New Testament canon were challenged. These writings, known as the Antilegomena, or books "spoken against," included Hebrews, James, 2 Peter, and Jude. The latter book is especially interesting, for it alludes to one pseudepigraphal book (i.e., *Testament of Moses*; cf. Jude 9) and quotes another (i.e., *1 Enoch* 1:9; cf. Jude 14–15).[20]

In recent years, some scholars have argued that certain second-century Gospels, such as the *Gospel of Thomas* and the *Gospel of Peter*, may have originated as early as the first century and so in some sense may rival the Gospels of the New Testament (i.e., Matthew, Mark, Luke, and John). Recently these writings and others have gained a measure of notoriety in popular publications and television documentaries, especially in reference to study of the historical Jesus. Unfortunately, the treatment of these writings has not always been responsible.

Contributions to These Issues in This Book

The studies that comprise *Exploring the Origins of the Bible* address the questions and diverse literatures surveyed above. Each essay attempts to break new ground, or at least throw an old debate into a new light.

Emanuel Tov assesses the contribution that the Septuagint can make to the literary analysis of Hebrew Scripture. Disregarding the translator's own exegesis and focusing on those cases in which the LXX differs significantly from its Hebrew counterpart, Tov very much stresses the LXX's importance. He suggests that it reflects different editorial stages of Hebrew Scripture from that included in the MT, prior or subsequent to that text. In all these cases, the LXX should be used together with the MT and some Qumran scrolls in the literary analysis of Scripture. The relatively large

19. For an English translation of the these writings, with introduction and bibliography, see J. B. Lightfoot, J. R. Harmer, and M. W. Holmes, *The Apostolic Fathers* (rev. ed.; Grand Rapids: Baker Academic, 1989).

20. On the development of the New Testament canon, see McDonald, *The Biblical Canon*, 243–421; for Jude, see 397–98.

number of editorial differences from the MT in the LXX should probably be ascribed to the early date of the Hebrew manuscripts from which the LXX translation was made and their derivation from circles different from the ones embracing the MT.

James Charlesworth helpfully defines the word *canon* and discusses aspects of the emergence of the canons of Scripture in the various Jewish and Christian communities of faith. He traces the uncertain history of the recognition of certain writings as authoritative and asks what contribution the books traditionally identified as belonging to the Apocrypha and Pseudepigrapha can make to our understanding. He draws our attention to early forms of interpretation and adaptation of Scripture, as seen in the efforts to paraphrase and "rewrite" Scripture. Charlesworth also devotes a number of pages to the exposure of caricatures and misconceptions of Judaism and the Jewish people in the time of Jesus and the early Christian movement.

Stephen Dempster addresses the much-debated question of the emergence of the tripartite canon, that is, the form of the canon we see in the Jewish Bible, comprising the Law (or Torah), the Prophets, and the Writings. Dempster contends that the early evidence for a tripartite form of canon is stronger than many contemporary biblical scholars have allowed.

Glenn Wooden explores the role of the so-called Septuagint in the formation of the biblical canons of Scripture. After reviewing the legend of the seventy-two Jewish scribes who miraculously translated the Hebrew books of Moses into Greek, Wooden traces the history of the influence that the Greek version of Old Testament Scripture had in shaping the Christian Bible and even the Latin translation of Jerome, which attempted to return to the original Hebrew/Aramaic text. Wooden also raises questions about the significance of the fact that New Testament writers, especially Paul, mostly quote the Greek version of the Old Testament.

Craig Evans undertakes a critical investigation of the usefulness of the extracanonical Gospels for historical Jesus research. Evans focuses on four well-known texts, the *Gospel of Thomas*, Egerton Papyrus 2, the *Secret Gospel of Mark*, and the alleged *Gospel of Peter*, concluding that these texts do not take us closer to the Jesus of history than do the Gospels of the New Testament. Evans finds repeated indications of lateness and dependency on the older Gospels of Matthew, Mark, Luke, and John.

Stanley Porter explores the relationship of Paul to the process of canonization. To this end he reviews and criticizes five standard theories regarding Pauline canonical formation, which he believes are inadequate at various points. In their place Porter proposes a sixth theory, that the Pauline letter canon began as a collection of letters either initiated by the apostle himself or by one of his companions, perhaps near the end of Paul's life or when he was in prison.

Lee McDonald raises the question of authority. He finds that the earliest canon of faith for the early church was Jesus. All authority had been given to the church's Lord, and the Scriptures bear witness to that authority. In this sense we should speak of Scripture as possessing a "derived" authority. Accordingly, McDonald contends that Christians should look for their authority in a person, not in various books, versions, or translations of Scripture.

Jonathan Wilson concludes the volume with an interesting discussion of the theological implications of canon, including the nature of theology and its place in the community of faith. Wilson observes the tendency to shift theological authority away from the church to a book, which complements the point raised by Lee McDonald. Wilson closes his essay by reminding Christians that theological authority ultimately is sourced in the Holy Spirit, who leads and guides God's people.

1

The Septuagint as a Source for the Literary Analysis of Hebrew Scripture

EMANUEL TOV

In several Scripture books, the Masoretic Text displays a substantial number of major differences when compared with the LXX and, to a lesser degree, when compared with several Qumran scrolls and the Samaritan Pentateuch. The other ancient versions were translated from Hebrew texts close to the MT.

The present analysis is limited to variations bearing on literary analysis, usually found in groups of variants. A difference involving one or two words, and sometimes an isolated case of a single verse, is considered a small difference, while a discrepancy involving a whole section or chapter indicates a substantial difference, often relevant to literary criticism. However, a group of seemingly unrelated small differences might also display a common pattern, pointing to a more extensive phenomenon. This pertains to many small theological changes in the MT of Samuel, short renderings in the LXX translation of Ezekiel, and so forth.

Who created these various types of differences between ancient texts? In very broad terms, authors and editors who were involved in the composition of the texts inserted changes that we characterize today as large differences often bearing on literary criticism. At a later stage, scribes who copied the completed compositions inserted smaller changes and made mistakes while copying. However, the distinction between these two levels is unclear at both ends, since early copyists considered themselves petty collaborators in the creation process of Scripture, while authors and editors were also copyists.

While readings found in ancient Hebrew manuscripts provide stable evidence, there are many problems on the slippery road of evaluating the ancient versions, especially the LXX. One of these is that what appears to one scholar to be a safely reconstructed Hebrew variant text is for another a translator's tendentious rendering. Literary analysis of the Hebrew Bible is only interested in evidence of the first type, since it sheds light on the background of the different Hebrew texts that were once circulating. The translator's tendentious changes are also interesting, but at a different level, that of scriptural exegesis. Since a specific rendering either represents a greatly deviating Hebrew text or displays the translator's exegesis, one wonders how to differentiate between the two. For almost every variation in the LXX, one finds opposite views expressed, and there are few objective criteria for evaluating these variations. Probably the best criteria relate to external Hebrew evidence supporting the LXX, the argument from translation technique suggesting either a free or a literal approach, and the existence of Hebraisms supporting an underlying Hebrew text.

We now turn to the first proof text, the LXX of Job. The translation of Job is much shorter than its counterpart in the MT as well as in the Peshitta (S), Targum (T), and Vulgate (V). Is it possible that the translator deleted what amounts to one-sixth of the total verses in the book?[1] In the absence of external evidence such as

---

1. Some scholars substantiated the view that the translator abbreviated his underlying Hebrew text: G. Gerleman, *Studies in the Septuagint*, Vol. 1, *The Book of Job* (LUÅ 43, 2; Lund: Gleerup, 1946); D. H. Gard, *The Exegetical Method of the Greek Translator of the Book of Job* (JBLMS 8; Philadelphia: Society of Biblical Literature, 1952); H. M. Orlinsky, "Studies in the Septuagint of the Book Job, II," *HUCA* 29 (1958): 229–71. The free character of the Greek translation was analyzed in detail by J. Ziegler, "Der textkritische Wert der

Qumran manuscripts, we have to assess the translator's approach from an analysis of his techniques. If a translator represented his underlying Hebrew text rather faithfully in small details, we would not expect him to insert major changes in the text. In other words, when we find major deviations from the MT in a faithful translation, they probably reflect a different Hebrew text. On the other hand, if a translator was not faithful to his parent text in small details, even paraphrasing it occasionally, he could have inserted major changes in the translation. Translators were not consistent, but we would not expect two diametrically opposed approaches in a single translation unit.

This brings us back to the Greek text of Job. In the sample chapter chosen for this purpose (chap. 34), we find a word-for-word rendering of the MT in a very few cases.[2] There are several unusual equivalents and small changes,[3] as well as instances of rewriting on a small scale.[4] Having established the translator's free style in small elements, it is easy to accept the assumption that he also rephrased complete verses,[5] sometimes in a major way.[6] He added

---

Septuaginta des Buches Job," in *Sylloge, Gesammelte Aufsätze zur Septuaginta* (Göttingen: Vandenhoeck & Ruprecht, 1971), 9–28.

2. The following verses come closest to a word-for-word translation: vv. 10 (with one exception), 16, 34 (with one exception), and 35.

3. Verse 2 MT "give ear to me" / LXX "give ear to what is good" (influenced by v. 4); v. 10 MT "wickedness // wrongdoing" has been made into an antithetic parallelism in the LXX "impiously . . . to pervert what is right" (by adding a verb "to pervert" [for the phrase cf. v. 11]; the translator made his translation more lively); v. 15 MT "human being" / LXX "mortal"; v. 21 MT "his eyes are upon" / LXX "he is one that views"; v. 22 MT "darkness nor gloom" / LXX "place"; v. 34 MT "to me . . . to me" / LXX "to me . . . my word."

4. Verse 6 MT "I declare the judgment against me false" / LXX "and [the Lord] played false in my judgment"; v. 13 MT "Who placed the earth in His charge? Who ordered the entire world?" / LXX "He that created the earth! And who is it that created what is under heaven and all it contains?"; v. 21 MT "He observes his every step" / LXX "and nothing of what they do has escaped him."

5. Verse 9 MT "For he says, 'Man gains nothing when he is in God's favor'" / LXX "For do not say, 'There will be no visitation of a man'—when there is visitation to him from the Lord!" In the MT, this verse explains the previous one ("For . . ."). In the MT, Job socializes with impious men assuming that pleasing God will not pay off. The translator probably did not understand *yiskon*, added a negation ("For do *not* say . . ."), and completely changed the idea of this verse to a positive thought (men are looked upon by God).

6. Verse 19 MT "He is not partial to princes; the noble are not preferred to the wretched; for all of them are the work of His hands." / LXX "(It is) he who felt no reticence before a person of worth, nor knows how to accord honor to the prominent, so that their persons be

some elements,[7] but more frequently shortened the text. Usually,
we can only guess at the reason for the abbreviation.[8] The main
argument for assuming that the translator abbreviated and did not
find an already shorter Hebrew text[9] is his free translation style.[10] A
major factor in the translator's abbreviation of his Hebrew *Vorlage*
may well be the latter's verbosity and repetitiveness.[11] The transla-

respected." In the MT, this verse speaks about God's impartiality to people. In the LXX, the
verse probably refers to the impious of v. 18 (or is it Job?) who do not honor the great. The
Greek does not speak of God, and the last words are completely different. Verse 20 is likewise
rephrased in the MT: "Some die suddenly in the middle of the night; people are in turmoil
and pass on; even great men are removed—not by human hands." / LXX "But crying out
and begging a man will prove to be of no use to them, for they used people lawlessly, when
the powerless were being turned aside." The MT continues the thought of the preceding
verse, stressing the power of God who can take away life in the middle of the night. The LXX
likewise continues the thoughts of the preceding verse in that version, possibly implying that
God needs to be honored. Verse 27 MT "Because they have been disloyal to Him and have
not understood any of His ways." / LXX "because they turned aside from God's law, and did
not recognize his requirements." The LXX made the formulation of the MT more specific by
presenting "disloyalty" as moving away from God's law (*nomos*), as in v. 37, and "His ways"
as *dikaiōmata* (that is, requirements, referring to the *mitsw̄ot*). The tendency of stressing the
adherence to God's *nomos* reflects late biblical as well as postbiblical periods.

7. Verse 15 MT "All flesh would at once expire, and mankind return to dust" / LXX
adds "whence too he was formed."

8. Verses 3–4 (v. 3 does not advance the main argument and v. 4 contains merely general
thoughts introducing Job's contentions); 6b–7 (v. 6b contains only general thoughts and v. 7
contains a comparison); 11b (superfluous after v. 11a?); 23a (the verse that comes in its stead
in the LXX, v. 23b, presents a second translation of v. 21); v. 25b (considered as repeating
v. 24?); the largest group of verses omitted in the LXX of this chapter is 28–33 (stylistic abbreviation or considered repetition of 33:14–33, or deleted because of obscure Hebrew?).

9. This is the view of E. Hatch, *Essays in Biblical Greek* (Oxford: Clarendon, 1889),
215–45, esp. 244–45. According to Hatch (p. 244), after the LXX translation was completed,
the MT was expanded "by a poet whose imaginative power was at least not inferior to that
of the original writer."

10. For a judicious contextual analysis of the translator's major changes, see C. E.
Cox, "Elihu's Second Speech according to the Septuagint," in *Studies in the Book of Job*
(ed. W. E. Aufrecht; SR 16; Waterloo, ON: Wilfred Laurier University Press, 1985), 36–53.
For an earlier collection of examples, see E. P. Dhorme, *Le livre de Job* (Paris: Gabalda,
1926), clx; ET: *A Commentary on the Book of Job* (trans. H. A. Knight; London: Nelson,
1967), cxcvi–cxcvii.

11. Dhorme, *Le livre de Job*, clxii (ET, ccii–cciii) and Cox, "Elihu's Second Speech,"
39, point to the fact that the amount of abbreviating usually increases from one group of
chapters to the next. Thus in chaps. 1–15 the percentage of abbreviation is 4%, in chaps.
15–21 it is 16%, in chaps. 22–31 it is 25%, in chaps. 32–37 it is 35%, and in the epilogue
(chaps. 38–42) it is 16%. Upon the first occurrence of an idea or argument, the translator does not know that it will recur later. When reaching the recurrence, the translator

tor's shortening thus bears on the history of exegesis and not on our understanding of the Hebrew composition.

After this negative example, we now turn to positive ones in which the LXX yields important data for literary analysis supported by a literal translation technique or external Hebrew evidence. Examples are given of evidence from the LXX when its reconstructed parent text either predated (sections A, B, D) or postdated (section C) the editorial stage presented in the MT. In section E the sequence cannot be determined easily. The translated text presented in sections A, B, D, E is that of the MT.[12] In section C the analysis is based on a translation of the LXX.[13]

A. The Two Editions of Jeremiah

The three main versions of Jeremiah that have survived from antiquity are the MT (followed quite closely by S, T, V), LXX, and 4QJer[b,d]. The LXX version differs from the MT in two central matters: the order of the chapters and verses[14] and the length of the text. The translator rendered in a relatively literal fashion a Hebrew text similar to that contained in the two Qumran scrolls. The existence of literary differences between the MT on the one hand and the LXX and 4QJer[b,d] on the other thus almost becomes

---

remembers and shortens. This logic implies that the amount of abbreviation increased as the translator proceeded.

12. *JPS Hebrew–English Tanakh: The Traditional Hebrew Text and the New JPS Translation* (2nd ed.; Philadelphia: Jewish Publication Society, 1999).

13. A. Pietersma and B. G. Wright III, eds., *A New English Translation of the Septuagint and the Other Greek Translations Traditionally Included under That Title* (New York: Oxford University Press, 2007).

14. For example, MT 23:7–8 is found in the LXX after 23:40. See further Jer. 10, to be discussed below. The most striking difference in this regard pertains to the chapters containing the prophecies against the nations, which in the MT (S, V, T) are found at the end of the book in chaps. 46–51, before the historical "appendix," chap. 52, whereas in the LXX they occur in the middle, after 25:13. This verse serves as an introduction to these prophecies: "And I will bring upon that land all that I have decreed against it, all that is recorded in this book—that which Jeremiah prophesied against all the nations" (MT). Usually, the location of the prophecies against the nations in the LXX is taken as original, but strong arguments in favor of the secondary character of that location were provided by A. Rofé, "The Arrangement of the Book of Jeremiah," *ZAW* 101 (1989): 390–98; G. Fischer, "Jer 25 und die Fremdvölkersprüche—Unterschiede zwischen hebräischem und griechischem Text," *Bib* 72 (1991): 474–99.

a fact, while their interpretation is subjective. The literal translation technique of LXX-Jeremiah and its near-identity with 4QJer^bd
facilitate the use of the data in the LXX. The LXX is shorter than
the MT by one-sixth. It lacks words, phrases, sentences, and entire sections of the MT. The shortness of this text was considered
enigmatic throughout the scholarly inquiry of the Greek text, but
is now supported by the Hebrew 4QJer^bd.

The differences between the two text forms, which are not characteristic of scribal intervention, were created at an early stage
when the book of Jeremiah was still being composed. The text
forms reflect different editions; the LXX and the two scrolls probably contain the earlier, short edition I, while the MT presents an
expanded, late edition.

Edition II, created during one stage of the book's literary growth,
contains many additional sections to edition I, the largest of which
are 33:14–26 and 39:4–13. The date of the textual witnesses of
edition I does not bear on its own date, because presumably it was
composed long before the time of the LXX translation and was not
discarded when edition II was created. Edition I was still known in
the second century BCE in Egypt, when it served as the base for the
LXX translation, and was present (along with manuscripts close to
ed. II) at Qumran in the first half of the second century BCE.

Most of the additions in edition II reflect editorial expansions of
ideas and details in the context, stylistic changes, and theological
and other concerns of that revision. It is remarkable how well the
editor of edition II managed to insert the new elements (sometimes
whole sentences) into the earlier text without introducing significant changes in that text. These expansions are exemplified by an
analysis of chapters 10, 43, and 27.[15]

Jeremiah 10:1–11

The prophecy in edition II (MT) contains both mockery of the
idols and praise of the Lord. The disdain of the idols refers to their

---

15. For background material, see E. Tov, "The Literary History of the Book of Jeremiah
in the Light of Its Textual History," in *Empirical Models for Biblical Criticism* (ed. J. H.
Tigay; Philadelphia: University of Pennsylvania Press, 1985), 211–37; revised and repr. in
The Greek and Hebrew Bible—Collected Essays on the Septuagint (VTSup 72; Leiden:
Brill, 1999), 363–84.

inability to walk, speak, and move around, as well as the fact they are man-made. The mockery is included in verses 2–5, 8–9, 11, while the remaining verses 6–7 and 10 praise the Lord. The verses containing this praise are lacking in the LXX and 4QJer[b], dating to the first half of the second century BCE.

It is often assumed that the short edition I (the LXX and 4QJer[b]) reflects the original text of this chapter, and that edition II (MT) reflects a later tradition in which the praise of the Lord has been added in order to stress the futility of the idols. The addition of these verses in edition II[16] went together with the splitting up of verse 5 into two parts.

When comparing the two traditions, we must consider: Is it more logical that the praise of the Lord was added in edition II, or that these elements were deleted by edition I? In the development of Scripture, elements were usually added, not deleted.[17] Moreover, it is intrinsically more plausible that verses of praise were added than omitted.[18]

Verses lacking in the LXX and 4QJer[b] are printed in bold in parentheses (slight differences are indicated by italics):[19]

1. Hear the word which the LORD has spoken to you, O House of Israel!
2. Thus said the LORD: Do not learn to go the way of the nations, and do not be dismayed by portents in the sky; let the nations be dismayed by them!

16. The added layer of the MT, probably deriving from the prophet himself, was added during one of the book's composition stages. It may have been influenced by diatribes against idols in Deutero-Isaiah, such as 44:9–20, which is extremely close to Jer. 10. Cf. Isa. 44:12 with Jer. 10:3b; 44:9 with Jer. 10:5b; etc. However, the argument can also be made the other way, as Jeremiah may have influenced the later Deutero-Isaiah. See W. L. Holladay, *Jeremiah 1: A Commentary on the Book of the Prophet Jeremiah, Chapters 1–25* (Hermeneia; Philadelphia: Fortress, 1986), 326.

17. For an isolated instance of shortening, see Deut. 32:43, analyzed below.

18. Such additions are paralleled by the so-called doxologies at the ends of the first four of the five divisions of the book of Psalms, probably added when the book was divided into these segments (41:14 MT [41:13 Eng.]; 72:18–20; 89:53 MT [89:52 Eng.]; 106:48; cf. 150). See further the addition of Jer. 9:22–23 in the LXX after 1 Sam. 2:10, analyzed below.

19. The sequence of the LXX (and probably of 4QJer[b]) is vv. 5a, 9, 5b.

3. For the laws of the nations are delusions; *for it is the work of a craftsman's hands. He cuts down a tree in the forest with an ax,*
4. He adorns it with silver and gold, He fastens it with nails and hammer, so that it does not totter.
5a. *They are like a scarecrow in a cucumber patch,* (5b) they cannot speak. They have to be carried, for they cannot walk. Be not afraid of them, for they can do no harm; nor is it in them to do any good.
6. (O LORD, there is none like You! You are great and Your name is great in power.
7. Who would not revere You, O King of the nations? For that is Your due, since among all the wise of the nations and among all their royalty there is none like You.
8. But they are both dull and foolish; their doctrine is but delusion; it is a piece of wood,)
9. Silver beaten flat, that is brought from Tarshish, and gold from Uphaz, the work of a craftsman and the goldsmith's hands; their clothing is blue and purple, all of them are the work of skilled men.
10. (But the LORD is truly God: He is a living God, the everlasting King. At His wrath, the earth quakes, and nations cannot endure His rage.)
11. Thus shall you say to them: Let the gods, who did not make heaven and earth, perish from the earth and from under these heavens.

Jeremiah 43 (LXX 40):4–6

The major difference between the sources in chapter 43 pertains to the forms of names. Some names have two components such as "Jeremiah the prophet" as opposed to just "Jeremiah" or "the prophet," while others have three, such as "Gedaliah son of Ahikam, son of Shaphan," as opposed to just "Gedaliah" or "Gedaliah son of Ahikam." The long names are found in edition II, and the short ones in the LXX and 4QJer^d (ed. I).[20] Hundreds of

---

20. As well as in the parallel 2 Kings 25 MT and LXX, e.g., Jer. 52:16 = 2 Kings 25:12.

similar personal names appear elsewhere in edition I in their short form, while in edition II they appear in full. Edition II typically fills in personal names, mainly in the prose sections, including the name of the father, sometimes also the grandfather, a title (king or prophet), and so on. The data must be analyzed not only for the book as a whole but also for individual units. Often edition I mentions the full name or title of the person when introduced in a given unit, but in all or most subsequent references uses a shortened form. In this manner, edition I follows the practice of biblical narrative. Edition II fills in the details of the complete formula in many (sometimes in most or all) occurrences of the name.[21]

> ⁴So Johanan (son of Kareah) and all the army officers and the rest of the people did not obey the LORD's command to remain in the land of Judah. ⁵Instead, Johanan (son of Kareah) and all the army officers took the entire remnant of Judah—those who had returned from all the countries to which they had been scattered and had sojourned in the land of Judah, ⁶men, women, and children; and the daughters of the king and all the people whom Nebuzaradan (the chief of the guards) had left with Gedaliah son of Ahikam (son of Shaphan), as well as the prophet Jeremiah and Baruch son of Neriah.

Jeremiah 27 (LXX 34):19–22

Chapter 27 tells of Jeremiah prophesying to a group of kings meeting in Jerusalem with King Zedekiah. The prophet calls for the complete submission to Nebuchadnezzar in accordance with God's plans. At the end of this episode, Jeremiah speaks out against the false prophets who prophesy optimistically to the Israelites, telling them that they need not surrender to Nebuchadnezzar. Among other things, he opposes the claim of these prophets that the exiled temple vessels will be returned. Jeremiah says that this

21. A good example of this procedure is "Ishmael son of Nethaniah son of Elishama," introduced in its full form in ed. I in 41:1, but in its short form, "Ishmael," in vv. 2, 6, 7, 8, 9 (2x), 10, 11, 13, 15, 16, 18. The MT left the short name in vv. 3, 10, and 14, but expanded it to "Ishmael son of Nethaniah" in vv. 2, 6, 7, 9, 11, 15, 16, 18. Likewise, in ed. I, Johanan is introduced in chap. 43 as "Johanan son of Kareah" (41:11), but the next verses refer to him as "Johanan" only (13, 14, 16); in ed. II, he is presented in all four verses with the long form. The same pertains to chap. 43 presented here.

will not happen, and that these prophets should implore God that the temple vessels remaining in Jerusalem not be exiled. Most of the expansions by the MT to the short LXX text are based on ideas or details in the context, or reflect stylistic and theological concerns. The MT shows a great interest in the fate of the temple vessels, adding details from the context in Jeremiah and 2 Kings.

> [19]For thus said the Lord (**of Hosts concerning the columns, the tank, the stands and**) concerning the rest of the vessels (**which remain in this city**), [20]which (**Nebuchadnezzar**) the king of Babylon did not take when he exiled Jeconiah (**son of Jehoiakim, king of Judah**) from Jerusalem (**to Babylon, with all the nobles of Judah and Jerusalem**—[21]**thus said the Lord of Hosts, the God of Israel, concerning the vessels remaining in the House of the Lord, in the royal palace of Judah and in Jerusalem**): [22]They shall be brought to Babylon (**and there they shall remain until I take note of them**)— declares the Lord—(**and bring them up and restore them to this place**).

According to edition I of verse 22, Jeremiah threatens that the temple vessels left in Jerusalem will be carried off to Babylon in the future. Edition II carries the same message, but according to that version, they will be returned to Jerusalem (v. 22 "and bring them up and restore them to this place"). If Jeremiah's threat included the traditional text of Scripture (MT), his audience did not have to be concerned since they were told that the temple vessels would be returned. However, this idea is not consistent with the spirit of the surrounding verses, which focus on the false prophets and not on the fate of the temple vessels. More significantly, if the temple vessels are to return to Jerusalem, Jeremiah's threat becomes forceless and anticlimactic. Historically, the statement by the false prophets was correct since the temple vessels did return from the exile to Jerusalem (see Dan. 5:2–3; Ezra 1:7, 11; 6:5). Edition II added these words without taking into consideration the implications of tensions in the context. In this case, there is no external Hebrew evidence supporting the LXX, but since this version is supported by Qumran evidence elsewhere in the book, it is probably reliable in this chapter as well. Besides, the literal translation of the chapter gives it further credence.

B. Two Editions of Deuteronomy 32:43

In Deuteronomy 32:43 also, external evidence (4QDeut[q]) and literal translation technique support the assumption of a major literary discrepancy between texts.

Moses's Song focuses on the relationship between God and his people until the end of Moses's life. It starts out inviting heaven and earth to listen to the poet, after which it depicts God's justice, Israel's disloyalty, and God's punishment of Israel and its enemies. The joyous ending of the poem (v. 43) draws on motifs mentioned at its beginning and describes God's vengeance on Israel's enemies.

This festive ending differs in the various versions. In the MT, the poem concludes with an invocation calling upon the nations to rejoice with God for his punishment on Israel's enemies. On the other hand, according to additional colons of verse 43 found only in the LXX and 4QDeut[q], the heavens and divine beings are called upon to rejoice with God, as in verse 4, "Give ear, O heavens, let me speak; Let the earth hear the words I utter." It seems that the MT shortened the long version of the LXX and the Qumran scroll. One detail supporting this assumption is the incomplete poetic structure of verse 43 in the MT, rendering the additional colons necessary.[22]

The text presented here is that of the MT. The LXX colons additional to the MT are printed in bold between + signs, while differences between the two are italicized. Agreements between the LXX and the Qumran scroll, 4QDeut[q], are indicated:

43 (a) Gladden/acclaim, O nations, His people MT / *Be glad, O skies, with Him* LXX = 4QDeut[q]
(b) **+and let all the sons of God do obeisance to Him.+** = 4QDeut[q]
(c) **+Be glad, O nations, with His people,+**
(d) **+and let all the angels of God prevail for Him.+**
(e) For he'll avenge the blood of his servants MT / *sons* LXX

22. Usually the verses in this Song consist of colons followed by parallel colons. However, the first and last colons of the MT (a and g) are not matched by parallel colons, but the alternative text of the LXX does contain such parallels, namely colons b and h.

(f) wreak revenge on His foes MT / *and take revenge and
repay the enemies with a sentence* LXX
(g) +**and he will repay those who hate,**+ = 4QDeutᑫ
(h) and the Lord shall cleanse the land of his people. MT

The non-Masoretic witnesses represent a few remarkable
readings:
In v. 43a, LXX (= 4QDeutᑫ) reads "Be glad, O skies, with Him"
instead of MT "Be glad (JPS: acclaim), O nations, His people."
In the MT, the "nations" (*goyim*) are invoked to "gladden His
people" in contrast to the invitation to the heavens to "be glad
. . . with Him" in the LXX. It would not be an unusual scriptural
thought if the poet were to address the nations in this way, but in
this particular poem the invocation seems out of place. The essence
of this poem is that God helped Israel to survive its wars by killing
these very nations, and the poem is full of expressions of vengeance
against them (e.g., v. 35: "To be My vengeance and recompense,
at the time that their foot falters. Yea, their day of disaster is near,
and destiny rushes upon them"). It would therefore be unusual
if the same nations were invoked to be or make glad. Assuming
that the MT reflects a later text, it probably inserted the following
changes: (1) "skies" (LXX) to "peoples," (2) "be glad" (as in Ps.
32:11; 81:2) to "make glad," (3) *mw* read as *'immo* ("with Him")
in the LXX to *'ammo* ("His people").[23]
In v. 43b, the LXX reads "and let all the sons of God do obeisance to Him." This colon, occurring also in the Qumran scroll
4QDeutᑫ, while lacking in the MT, is paralleled by other verses
in the MT in which the "sons of God," also named "divine beings," are mentioned: Psalm 82:1 "God stands in the divine as-
sembly; among the divine beings He pronounces judgment"; and
Psalm 29:1 "Ascribe to the LORD, O divine beings, ascribe to the
LORD glory and strength." In Deuteronomy the "sons of God"
are mentioned only in the LXX (twice) and 4QDeutᑫ, but not in
the MT. This colon was probably removed from the MT as theo-

23. That the MT cannot reflect the original text becomes clear from the continuation:
"For He'll avenge the blood of His servants" in the next colon implies the mentioning of
a subject in the preceding colon ("with Him" as in the LXX rather than "His people" as
in the MT).

logical censorship when the phrase "sons of God" was considered an unwelcome polytheistic depiction of the world of the divine. Tendentious changes are never consistent, and indeed such "sons of God" are mentioned elsewhere in the Bible, as quoted above. A similar polytheistic phrase was likewise removed from verse 8 in the same Song where the MT now reads, "When the Most High gave nations their homes and set the divisions of man, He fixed the boundaries of peoples in relation to *Israel*'s numbers" (emphasis added). The presumed earlier text of that verse referring to "the number of the sons of *El*" is reflected in the LXX and the Qumran scroll 4QDeutᵖ.[24]

C. The Rewritten Book of 1 Kings

Our analysis so far has provided examples of chapters reflecting different editorial stages of Scripture as presented in the MT and LXX. In the two preceding examples (Jeremiah and Deuteronomy), the LXX reflects an earlier stage than the MT. First Kings exemplifies a situation in which the underlying Hebrew text represents a later stage than the MT.

The Greek version of 1 Kings (3 Kingdoms in the LXX) differs recensionally from the MT to a great extent. The tendencies visible in the Greek translation display a late[25] layer in the development

24. For an analysis, see J. H. Tigay, *The JPS Commentary: Deuteronomy* (Philadelphia: Jewish Publication Society, 1996), 314–15, 513–18.

25. On the other hand, A. Schenker believes that the MT changed an earlier edition contained in the LXX (*Septante et texte Massorétique dans l'histoire la plus ancienne du texte de 1 Rois 2–14* [CahRB 48; Paris: J. Gabalda, 2000]). Schenker dates the MT edition to between 250 and 130 BCE, probably closer to the later end of this spectrum (see pp. 36–37, 152–53). Among other things, Schenker's view is based on the Greek version of 1 Kings 2:35. According to the MT of this verse, Solomon appointed "Zadok the priest" instead of Abiathar, while according to the LXX, Zadok was appointed as "the first priest." Schenker considers the LXX the earlier version reflecting the appointment of the high priests by the kings, while the MT reflects a later reality that was initiated with Simon Maccabee in 140 BCE when kings could no longer make such appointments. Likewise, the singular *bet habamot* of MT 1 Kings 12:31 and 2 Kings 17:29, 32 replaced the earlier plural reading of *oikous eph' hypsēlōn* (and similar) in the LXX. According to Schenker (144–46), the plural of the LXX reflected the earlier reality of more than one sanctuary in Shechem, while the changed text of the MT reflects a single Samaritan sanctuary. Therefore, this correction (also reflected in the Old Greek version in Deut. 27:4 reconstructed from the Vetus Latina)

of that book, composed in Hebrew after the time of the editorial stage contained in the MT.[26] Gooding describes the first ten
chapters as being rewritten around Solomon's wisdom, including
the whitewashing of his sins, chapters 11–14 as presenting a more
favorable account of Jeroboam, and chapters 16–22 as whitewashing Ahab.[27] The revision also reorganizes the book's chronology.
One of the literary devices used for this purpose is the adding of
two "theme summaries" in chapter 2 repeating various verses in
1 Kings around the theme of Solomon's wisdom.[28] Another device
is the addition of an alternative account of the rise to power of
Jeroboam in 3 Kingdoms 12:24a–z juxtaposed with the original
account in 1 Kings 12:1–24.[29]

The differences between the LXX and the other witnesses in
1 Kings are extensive, much greater than anywhere else in Samuel–
Kings (with the exception of 1 Sam. 16–18), and among the largest
in the LXX. It is safe to say that the changes, especially the three
mentioned additions, are based on a different Hebrew version. In
this book the translation is faithful to the Hebrew and accordingly, the major discrepancies of the LXX from the MT are based
on a different Hebrew composition. The Hebrew background is

---

may be dated to the period of the existence of a temple on Mt. Gerizim between 300 and 128
BCE. Equally old elements are found in the LXX version of 1 Kings 20:10–20 mentioning
groups of dancing men as well as King David's dances, elements that were removed from
the MT, according to Schenker, probably in the second century BCE.

26. See E. Tov, "3 Kingdoms Compared with Similar Rewritten Compositions," in *Flores
Florentine: Dead Sea Scrolls and Other Early Jewish Studies in Honour of Florentino García
Martínez* (ed. A. Hilhorst et al.; JSPSup 122; Leiden: Brill, 2007), 345–66.

27. D. W. Gooding, "Problems of Text and Midrash in the Third Book of Reigns,"
Textus 7 (1969): 1–29.

28. The MT of 1 Kings 2 covers the end of David's reign and the accession of Solomon
(vv. 1–12), the tragic end of Adonijah (vv. 13–35), and the death of Shimei (vv. 36–46).
The parallel text of the LXX of 3 Kingdoms covers the same events, but in the middle and
end of the chapter it adds two long theme summaries relating to Solomon's wisdom. The
summaries were intended to stress the God-given (cf. v. 35a) wisdom of Solomon, just
as 1–2 Chronicles and 11QPs' XXVII stress David's wisdom. The first one, Summary 1,
inserted after v. 35, contains fourteen verses denoted 35a–o. Summary 2, inserted after
v. 46, contains eleven verses denoted 46a–l. Summary 1 is not connected to the context,
while Summary 2 is. For an analysis, see P. S. F. van Keulen, *Two Versions of the Solomon
Narrative: An Inquiry into the Relationship between MT 1 Kgs. 2–11 and LXX 3 Reg. 2–11*
(VTSup 104; Leiden and Boston: Brill, 2005), 265–75; Tov, "3 Kingdoms."

29. See Z. Talshir, *The Duplicate Story of the Division of the Kingdom (LXX 3 Kingdoms XII 24a–z)* (JBS 6; Jerusalem: Simor, 1989).

visible also in a number of Hebraisms in these chapters.[30] The special nature of the LXX of 1 Kings is exemplified in chapters 5 and 11.

1 Kings 5

The content of the last verse of chapter 4 (v. 20) and the first 14 verses of chapter 5 of the MT differs much from that of the LXX in 3 Kingdoms. In the MT, this chapter describes the extent of Solomon's realm and its internal prosperity (4:20; 5:1, 4–5), his daily consumption of food (vv. 2–3), the provisions brought to him (vv. 6–8), his wisdom (vv. 9–14), the first preparations for the building of the temple (consisting of Solomon's cooperation with Hiram relating to materials and artisans; vv. 15–26), and the forced labor (vv. 27–32).

Several of the elements of chapter 5 of the MT are included in the LXX in a different sequence, while some are lacking, and new ones have been added. The sequence in the LXX is as follows: the provisions brought to Solomon (v. 1 = vv. 7–8 MT), his daily consumption of food (vv. 2–3), the extent of his realm (v. 4), his wisdom (vv. 9–14), Solomon's marriage to Pharaoh's daughter (v. 14a = MT 3:1; 14b = MT 9:16–17a), his cooperation with Hiram (vv. 15–26), and the forced labor (vv. 27–32).

The details listed above show that the LXX added the story about Pharaoh's daughter in verses 14a–b. These verses are more appropriate here than in MT 3:1 and 9:16–17 (where they are lacking in the LXX),[31] as is the placement of MT vv. 7–8 as v. 1 in the

---

30. See E. Tov, "The LXX Additions (Miscellanies) in 1 Kings 2," *Textus* 11 (1984): 89–118; revised and repr. in *Greek and Hebrew Bible,* 549–70. This study includes a complete retroversion of the Hebrew text underlying the expansions. The Hebrew text underlying 1 Kings 12:24a–z has been reconstructed by J. Debus, *Die Sünde Jerobeams* (FRLANT 93; Göttingen: Vandenhoeck & Ruprecht, 1967), 55–65 and in Talshir, *Duplicate Story,* 38–153.

31. The story of the marriage to Pharaoh's daughter is in place here and not in MT 3:1 or 2:35c LXX. Verse 14a–b combines most of the elements relating to the first stage of the story of Solomon's marriage to Pharaoh's daughter (2:35c LXX = 3:1 MT), while not including the second stage narrated in 2:35f₆ LXX = 9:24 MT; 8:11a MT and LXX; 9:9a LXX. These elements have been carefully moved to their present place in the LXX, just before Solomon's preparations for the building of the temple. The implication of the

LXX.[32] The LXX left out 4:20–5:1 (the extent of Solomon's realm
and its internal prosperity), occurring in the added verses 2:46a–b,
and verses 5–6 (internal prosperity and Solomon's food), occurring in the added 2:46g, i. These verses did not suit the topic of the
rewritten and abbreviated form of chapter 5 of the LXX. More so
than the MT, the LXX forms a literary unity, which was probably
generated after the creation of the disharmonious text of the MT
in which diverse material is often juxtaposed.

[1](= MT vv. 7, 8) And thus the officials would supply provisions for
King Salomon (Solomon) and everything ordered for the table of
the king, each one in his month, they did not alter a thing; and they
also used to bring to the place where the king might be, barley and
straw for the horses and the chariots, each according to his charge.
[2]And these were Salomon's provisions for one day: thirty kors of
choice flour and sixty kors of ground meal [3]and ten choice calves
and twenty pasture-fed oxen and one hundred sheep besides deer
and gazelles and choice birds, grain fed. [4]For he ruled across the
river, and he was at peace on all sides round about.
   [9]And the Lord gave Salomon discernment and very great wisdom
and volume of mind like the sand that is by the sea, [10]and Salomon
was greatly multiplied, above the discernment of all ancient people,
and above all the discerning people of Egypt. [11]And he was wise
beyond all humans, he was wise beyond Gaithan (Ethan) the Ezraite
(Ezrahite) and Haiman (Heman) and Chalkal (Chalkol) and Darda,
son of Mal (Mahol). [12]And Salomon spoke three thousand proverbs,
and his songs were five thousand. [13]And he spoke of trees, from
the cedar that is in Lebanon and as far as the hyssop that comes
out through the wall, and he spoke of animals and of birds and of
reptiles and of fish. [14]And all the people used to come to hear the
wisdom of Salomon, and he would receive gifts from all the kings
of the earth who were hearing of his wisdom.
   [14a](= MT 3:1) And Salomon took the daughter of Pharao for
himself for a wife and brought her into the city of Dauid (David)

---

change is that the second stage in that story, the moving of Pharaoh's daughter to her own
house, took place only after Solomon finished building the temple.
   32. This verse describes the provisions for King Solomon by the prefects in the immediately preceding verses in the LXX (4:7–19 [v. 20 is lacking]), and its position is thus more
appropriate in the LXX than in the MT. In the MT, the position of this verse as v. 7 is
problematic as it mentions "all those prefects" even though the list of the prefects appears
at a considerable distance.

until he finished the house of the Lord and his own house and the wall of Ierousalem (Jerusalem). ¹⁴ᵇ (= 9:16–17a MT, not LXX) Then Pharao king of Egypt went up and captured Gazer (Gezer) and burned it and the Canaanite who lived in Mergab, and Pharao gave them as send-off gifts to his daughter, Salomon's wife; and Salomon built Gazer.

¹⁵And King Chiram (Hiram) of Tyre sent his servants to anoint Salomon in place of his father Dauid, for Chiram had affection for Dauid all the days.

1 Kings 11

The content of the first eight verses of chapter 11 of the MT differs from that of the LXX. Both versions depict the sins of King Solomon in marrying foreign wives and being involved in idolatry, but the LXX makes the latter sin more acceptable to the reader. In the LXX, Solomon's main sin consists of his love for foreign women,[33] which was forbidden according to Deuteronomy 7:1–4 and 17:17 ("And he [i.e., the king] shall not have many wives, lest his heart go astray"), while his other sins result from the initial one. The fact that he was married to foreign women in his old age made him easy prey for them, since they induced him to venerate non-Israelite gods. The MT of verse 1 ("King Solomon loved many foreign women") stresses Solomon's sins more than the LXX by mentioning that the king had many women and that they were "foreign." More importantly, the several variations between the two versions (change of sequence, addition/omission of details) create a slightly different image of the king. The LXX combines the first phrase of verse 1 with the beginning of verse 3a of the MT "He had seven hundred royal wives and three hundred concubines." In this way the LXX

33. The LXX has changed the emphasis in the first verse of the chapter by leaving out details and combining v. 1 with v. 3. MT: "King Solomon loved many foreign women . . . (3) He had seven hundred royal wives and three hundred concubines . . ." / LXX (1) "And King Salomon (Solomon) loved women. And he had seven hundred ruling women and three hundred concubines . . ." In the new context of the LXX, the word "many" of the MT has been left out, as well as the word "foreign." Solomon's major sin was that he loved women, which is further stressed by the move of the elements from v. 3 to their present position at the beginning of the chapter: all subsequent sins (idolatry) of Solomon derived from his love for women.

joins similar statements about Solomon's wives and further stresses that his major sin consisted of his love for women.

Furthermore the LXX omits verse 5 "For Solomon followed Astarte the goddess of the Sidonians, and Milcom the abomination of the Ammonites." By doing so, it does not portray Solomon as initiating idolatrous acts, like the MT.[34] The description of the sins of 1 Kings 11 was problematic also for the Chronicler, who omitted the chapter in his account of Solomon.

> ¹ (= MT vv. 1, 3) And King Salomon (Solomon) loved women. And he had seven hundred ruling women and three hundred concubines. And he took foreign women, even the daughter of Pharao, Moabites, Ammonites, Syrians and Idumeans (Edomites), Chettites (Hittites) and Amorites, ²from the nations that the Lord forbade to the sons of Israel: "You shall not go in to them, and they shall not go in to you, lest they turn away your hearts after their idols," Salomon clung to them for love. ⁴And it happened at the time of Salomon's old age that his heart was not perfect with the Lord his God as was the heart of his father Dauid (David), and his foreign wives turned away his heart after their gods. ⁵ (= MT v. 7) Then Salomon built a high place to Chamos (Chemosh), idol of Moab and to their king, idol of the sons of Ammon ⁶ (= MT v. 5) and to Astarte (Ashtoreth), abomination of the Sidonians. ⁷ (= MT v. 8) And thus he did for all his foreign wives, they were offering incense and sacrificing to their idols; ⁸ (= MT v. 6) and Salomon did evil before the Lord, he did not go after the Lord as Dauid his father.

D. A Combined Book Joshua–Judges?

Joshua 24 contains Joshua's speech at the end of his career. He reviewed Israel's history and invoked the people to renew the covenant with the Lord. After the tribes' renewal of that covenant the chapter narrates the deaths of Joshua and Eleazar (Josh. 24:33), at which point the LXX contains a section (vv. 33a–b) that is not found in the MT, at the very end of the book. The Hebraic diction of this passage allows for a relatively reliable reconstruction of the

---

34. For thorough analyses of this episode, see van Keulen, *Two Versions*, 202–21 and Z. Talshir, "1 Kings and 3 Kingdoms—Origin and Revision, Case Study: The Sins of Solomon (1 Kings 11)," *Textus* 21 (2002): 71–105.

Greek text into Hebrew. For example, the phrase "And it happened after these things" in the beginning of verse 33 in the LXX, but not in the MT, reflects *wayehi 'ahare hadebarim ha'eleh* (cf. Josh. 24:29) frequently occurring in Scripture.

The addition of verses 33a–b in the LXX repeats phrases found elsewhere in Joshua–Judges. Verse 33b ends with Judges 3:12, that is, with the account of the "judge" Ehud and his oppressor Eglon, bypassing the stories of Judges 1–2, and the first half of chapter 3. The added section of the LXX is not a real addition to the MT. These verses at the end of the book together with the remainder of Joshua point to the existence of a combined book Joshua–Judges. In that early version the present end of Joshua was followed directly by the story of Ehud in Judges 3.

The author of the *Damascus Document* (CD) V, 1–5, a member of the Qumran community, probably knew the Hebrew text now reflected in the LXX of verse 33a–b. This is the only known text that mentions in one context the ark, the death of Eleazar, the death of Joshua, the elders, and the worship of the heathen Ashtaroth.[35]

The sequence of events narrated at the end of the Greek book of Joshua depicts what may well have been the original sequence of events: the death of Joshua and Eleazar (24:29–33 MT), movement of the ark, service of Phinehas, beginning of the people's sin, and the first story typifying the chain of events in the book of Judges involving the oppression of the Israelites by Eglon and the miraculous saving by Ehud (vv. 33a–b LXX).

Joshua 24:33 (MT + LXX), 33a–b (LXX): [33]And it happened after these things that Eleazar son of Aaron, the high priest, died, and was buried in Gabaath of Phinees his son, which he gave him in Mount Ephraim. [33a] **+ On that day the sons of Israel took the ark of God and carried it around in their midst.** (Cf. v. 33 and Judg. 20:28.) **And Phinees served as priest in the place of Eleazar his father until he died, and he was interred in Gabaath, which was his own.** [33b] (Cf. v. 28.) **And the sons of Israel departed each to their place and to their own city.** (Cf. Judg. 2:6, 12–13; 3:12–14.) **And the**

---

35. This was suggested by A. Rofé, "The End of the Book of Joshua according to the Septuagint," *Henoch* 4 (1982): 17–36. See also E. Tov, "The Growth of the Book of Joshua in the Light of the Evidence of the LXX Translation," *ScrHier* 31 (1986): 321–39; revised and repr. in *Greek and Hebrew Bible*, 385–96.

sons of Israel worshiped Astarte, and Astaroth, and the gods of the nations round about them. And the Lord delivered them into the hands of Eglom, the king of Moab, and he dominated them eighteen years.+

E. The Three Editions of the Song of Hannah (1 Samuel 2)

The Song of Hannah is a song of praise (hymn) for God, even though in the MT it is described as a prayer (v. 1). Hannah thanks God that she has given birth after a long period of infertility (cf. v. 5 MT "While the barren woman bears seven, the mother of many is forlorn"). However, several other verses do not suit Hannah. For example, Hannah was not saved from an enemy as mentioned in verse 1. This Song may have been composed as a thanksgiving hymn applicable to different situations of salvation and subsequently placed on Hannah's lips.

The greater part of the Song (vv. 2–8) praises the absolute power of God over mortals, enabling God to bring about changes, especially from a bad to a good situation, as in the case of the barren woman. The moral of the Song as expressed in verses 9–11 differs much in the three major textual traditions: the MT, the LXX, and 4QSamᵃ (the latter dating to 50–25 BCE). The main idea of the original form of the Song—namely, the absolute power of God over mortals—has been reinterpreted in two different directions in the preserved texts. Each of these witnesses makes the Song of Hannah more relevant to its context on the theological level.

1. And (**Hannah prayed**) +she said+: My heart exults in the LORD; I have triumphed through the LORD. I gloat over my enemies; I rejoice in Your deliverance.
2. There is no holy one like the LORD, truly, there is none +righteous+ beside You; there is no rock like our God.
3. Talk no more with lofty pride, let no arrogance cross your lips! For the LORD is an all-knowing God; *by Him actions are measured.*
4. The bows of the mighty are broken, and the faltering are girded with strength.

5. Men once sated must hire out for bread; men once hungry hunger no more. While the barren woman bears seven, the mother of many is forlorn.

6. The LORD deals death and gives life, casts down into Sheol and raises up.

7. The LORD makes poor and makes rich; He casts down, He also lifts high.

8. *a* He raises the poor from the dust,
   b lifts up the needy from the dunghill,
   c setting them with nobles,
   d granting them seats of honor.
   (*e* **For the pillars of the earth are the LORD's;**
   f **He has set the world upon them.**)

9. (*a* **He guards the steps of His faithful, but the wicked perish in darkness.**)
   + *a'* **Granting the prayer to the one who prays,**
   b' **he has also blessed the years of the righteous+**
   c **For not by strength shall man prevail.**

10. *The foes of the* LORD *shall be shattered*;
    +**The Lord is holy.**
    Let not the clever boast in his cleverness,
    and let not the mighty boast in his might,
    and let not the wealthy boast in his wealth,
    but let him who boasts boast in this:
    to understand and know the Lord
    and to execute justice and righteousness in the midst of the land+ (= Jer. 9:22–23).
    He will thunder against them in the heavens. The LORD will judge the ends of the earth. He will give power to His king, and triumph to His anointed one.

11. (**Then Elkanah and Hannah went home to Ramah**) +**And they left him there before the Lord and departed to Harmathaim+**; and the boy entered the service of the LORD under the priest Eli.

The Hebrew base of the LXX can be reconstructed with relative confidence because of the partial support of 4QSamᵃ and the fairly faithful nature of the translation. A few remarks follow on the major tendencies visible in the LXX and the MT.[36]

In verse 8, the MT and 4QSam[a] add to the earlier text of the LXX—probably reflecting the original text—what is now verse 8e–f: "For the pillars of the earth are the LORD's; He has set the world upon them." The MT's addition takes the earlier text of the LXX in a completely different direction. Starting with the conjunction "for," the added verse is supposed to explain the previous colons by referring to God's cosmic powers ("pillars of the earth"), but in actuality it fails to do so. Colons 8a–d, as well as verse 9, focus on God's ability to determine the fate of individuals, while 8e–f, the added clause of MT (and 4QSam[a]), praises God's universal powers. Why would someone wish to stress God's cosmic powers in this context? The added verse 8e–f is not inappropriate in ancient Israelite thinking. However, it presents the divine from a different angle than was probably intended by the original poet.[37]

The contextual relevance of 9a–b MT ("He guards the steps of His faithful, but the wicked perish in darkness"), much different from the LXX, needs to be examined. Verses 4–5 mention unexpected changes for the better and the worse in the fate of individuals. Likewise in verses 6–8 the Song refers to God's power to change the personal fate of individuals. The implication of these two groups of verses is that the unexpected change in one's personal condition is due to God. For example, in verse 4a God determines the fate of the strong one whose power fails. Therefore, verse 9a–b MT, "He guards the steps of His faithful . . . ," seems contextually appropriate. However, in the original short version of the Song, the sudden changes described in verses 4–8 merely exemplify the strength and autonomy of God (for similar ideas cf. Ps. 113:7–8). The original ideas of the Song have been given a

36. See further E. Tov, "Different Editions of the Song of Hannah," in *Tehillah le-Moshe, Biblical and Judaic Studies in Honor of Moshe Greenberg* (ed. M. Cogan, B. L. Eichler, and J. H. Tigay; Winona Lake, IN: Eisenbrauns, 1997), 149–70; revised and repr. in *Greek and Hebrew Bible*, 433–55.

37. The universal power of God is mentioned again in v. 10, but in that verse this description fits the context of God overpowering his enemies. The juxtaposition of a description of the personal fate of individuals and God's greatness in the universe is found also in Ps. 113, which in many ways resembles the Song of Hannah, but that fact cannot be used as an argument in favor of the originality of v. 8e–f MT.

theological slant in the MT by stressing the power of loyalty to God. It is the person who is loyal to God who will experience an improvement in his or her condition. For example, the God-fearing barren woman will give birth, while the barren woman who is not loyal will not be blessed.

The presumed earlier text has been interpreted differently in the LXX (and 4QSam[a]). We name this different text verses 9a'–b'. The verse that is found in the LXX and 4QSam[a] but not in the MT mentions a person who makes a vow—a clear allusion to Hannah. After the various categories of a powerful change from a bad to a good situation and from good to bad (vv. 4–8), God's granting the vow to the person who vows in verse 9a'–b' seems a mere afterthought. This verse in the LXX may well reflect an attempt to relate the Song more closely to Hannah's situation.[38]

According to verse 9c found in all traditions, physical force does not give strength to people ("For not by strength shall man prevail"). The idea in this colon forms the logical conclusion of verses 4–8, and not 9a–b, showing that the only power determining the fate of humans is that of God. If this understanding is correct, the reconstructed original form of the Song has been reinterpreted in two directions in the preserved texts, therefore constituting different editions of the Song and its narrative framework.[39]

The Special Status of the LXX

Further analysis yields additional examples of texts in which the LXX reflects an editorial stage of the Hebrew books different from that in the MT.[40] Not all examples are equally convincing, and much

38. The mentioning of the righteous in the LXX and 4QSam[a] in v. 9b' in a way runs parallel to the mentioning of the persons who are loyal to God in v. 9a in the MT. The phrase in the LXX may be taken to imply that the persons who witness a change in their personal fate, as mentioned in vv. 4–5, are the righteous.

39. In the three main textual sources that have been preserved, these changes are evidenced either in individual witnesses or in groups of two, without any consistency. Sometimes the change is evidenced in the MT and sometimes in the LXX, and either one is sometimes joined by 4QSam[a]. The position of 4QSam[a] is thus rather peculiar, but the evidence of this scroll brings to light the true nature of the two other texts.

40. See E. Tov, "The Nature of the Large-Scale Differences between the LXX and MT S T V, Compared with Similar Evidence in Other Sources," in *The Earliest Text of the*

depends on the amount of support for the reconstruction of a variant text from the LXX. In most cases we may invoke support from external sources (Qumran scrolls, SP), the existence of Hebraisms/ Aramaisms, or a faithful translation technique, while some books remain problematic because of their free translation style.

The MT is often considered the major textual source for the study of Hebrew Scripture, but actually the LXX is equally important, the only problem being that its Hebrew parent text cannot be reconstructed easily. At the same time, of all the texts that have come down from antiquity, the LXX is not the only source differing from the MT at the literary level. Similar evidence is contained in a few Qumran scrolls,[41] but even if we allow for more such parallels on the basis of a maximalistic approach,[42] the LXX still reflects more evidence than the Qumran scrolls.[43] The "SP-group," that is the SP together with the so-called pre-Samaritan Qumran texts, also contains parallel material. The literary material embedded in these texts is of a special nature since their additions to the MT do not provide new material but duplicate verses of the MT.[44]

As we turn now to the background of the relatively numerous major deviations from the MT in the LXX, we are groping

---

Hebrew Bible: The Relationship between the Masoretic Text and the Hebrew Base of the Septuaginta Reconsidered (ed. A. Schenker; SBLSCS 52; Atlanta: Scholars Press, 2003), 121–44.

41. See the aforementioned scrolls 4QSamᵃ, 4QJerᵇ·ᵈ, probably 4QJoshᵃ, and possibly also 4QJudgᵃ.

42. A maximalistic approach would include 4QRP, a reworked Bible composition, on which see E. Tov, "The Many Forms of Scripture: Reflections in Light of the LXX and 4QReworked Pentateuch," in *From Qumran to Aleppo: A Discussion with Emanuel Tov about the Textual History of Jewish Scriptures in Honor of His 65th Birthday* (ed. J. Zsengeller; Leiden: Brill, 2008). It could also include one or two of the so-called abbreviated texts, such as 4QCantᵃ·ᵇ, on which see E. Tov, "Excerpted and Abbreviated Biblical Texts from Qumran," *RevQ* 16 (1995): 581–600.

43. Our assessment of the data is subjective, and furthermore the complexity of comparing the entire Qumran corpus with a single text, the LXX, should be kept in mind. However, such a comparison seems legitimate. The Qumran corpus is very fragmentary, but often a book's character is recognizable in a small fragment, such as the Jeremiah fragments from cave 4. If the two hundred (very) fragmentary Qumran scrolls of Scripture books are compared with the twenty-four canonical books of Greek Scripture, the latter group contains more evidence of different editorial stages of Hebrew Scripture than the Qumran corpus.

44. For details, see E. Tov, "Rewritten Bible Compositions and Biblical Manuscripts, with Special Attention to the Samaritan Pentateuch," *DSD* 5 (1998): 334–54.

in the dark. The special character of the *Vorlage* of the LXX seems to derive from two factors: (1) the Hebrew manuscripts used for the Greek translation were not embraced by the circles that fostered the MT;[45] and (2) at the time of the translation (275–150 BCE), still earlier Hebrew manuscripts were used that reflect some vestiges of earlier editorial stages.[46] Typologically late LXX texts (1 Kings, Esther, and Daniel) probably representing editorial stages subsequent to the MT[47] show that the key to unraveling the mystery is likely the fact that these manuscripts were non-Masoretic.

Any reply to the question of why texts of the MT family were not used for the LXX translation remains a matter of conjecture. The realm of MT influence may have been limited to certain circles, and we do not know from which circles the Hebrew manuscripts translated were sent or taken to Egypt. Clearly, the circle or persons who sent or took the manuscripts of the Torah to Alexandria did not include Eleazar the high priest and the sages, as narrated in the *Letter of Aristeas* 176. Any high priest would undoubtedly have encouraged the use of a text from the MT family for such an important enterprise. Incidentally, the *Letter of Aristeas* praises

45. On the socio-religious background of the MT, see E. Tov, "The Text of the Hebrew/Aramaic and Greek Bible Used in the Ancient Synagogues," in *The Ancient Synagogue: From Its Origins until 200 C.E.—Papers Presented at an International Conference at Lund University October 14–17, 2001* (ed. B. Olsson and M. Zetterholm; ConBNT 39; Stockholm: Almqvist & Wiksell International, 2003), 237–59; idem, "The Nature of the Masoretic Text in Light of the Scrolls from the Judean Desert and Rabbinic Literature," *Shnaton* 16 (2004), 119–39 (Heb. with Engl. summary).

46. When ascribing the non-Masoretic character of the Hebrew manuscripts included in the LXX to their early date, we find some support in the Qumran corpus. A few early Qumran texts, similarly deriving from the third and second centuries BCE, reflect redactional differences from the MT. Two Qumran manuscripts contain the same early redactional stage as the LXX, namely 4QJer[b] and 4QJer[d] (both 200–150 BCE), while 4QJosh[a] is relatively early (150–50 BCE). At the same time, one other manuscript probably reflecting an early literary stage is relatively late: 4QSam[a] (50–25 BCE). The evidence for Qumran is thus not clear-cut, but neither is it unequivocal for the LXX. For only some of the LXX books reflect redactionally different versions and by the same token only some of the early Qumran manuscripts are independent vis-à-vis the MT.

47. See E. Tov, "Three Strange Books of the LXX: 1 Kings, Esther, and Daniel Compared with Similar Rewritten Compositions from Qumran and Elsewhere," in *Die Septuaginta—Texte, Kontexte, Lebenswelten* (ed. M. Karrer and W. Kraus; WUNT 219; Tübingen: Mohr Siebeck, 2008), 369–93.

the abilities of the translators as well as the external features of the scrolls, but says nothing about their nature.

In summary, in this study we analyzed some large differences between the MT and the LXX. Disregarding discrepancies that were created by the translator, we turned to such differences as were likely found in the translators' *Vorlagen*. Probably only the large deviations in the LXX of Job were produced by the translator, while all other such discrepancies were already found in the manuscripts used by the translators. Most books yielded support for such assumptions (external evidence in Hebrew manuscripts, Semitisms, literal translations), but the decision is difficult in free translation units. We analyzed a few chapters in detail (Jeremiah, Deuteronomy, 1 Kings, Joshua, 1 Samuel). In all these cases, the LXX reflects different editorial stages of Hebrew Scripture from that included in the MT, prior or subsequent to that text. In all these cases, the LXX should be used together with the MT and some Qumran scrolls in the literary analysis of Scripture. The relatively large number of editorial differences from the MT in the LXX should probably be ascribed to the early date of the Hebrew manuscripts from which the translation was made and to their derivation from circles different from the ones embracing the MT.

2

Writings Ostensibly outside the Canon

James H. Charlesworth

Hillel and Jesus are the two most influential Jewish teachers in Palestine in the decades before the Roman armies burned Jerusalem in 70 CE. On that date worship in the temple ceased and the history of ancient Israel came to a violent end. When they lived there was no set or closed canon of the "Old Testament" or Hebrew Bible, and none of the books in the New Testament had been composed. The two centuries that separated the last book in the Old Testament and the first work in the New Testament are not silent. During that period the so-called Old Testament canon took recognizable shape, and many works on its fringes were composed. These numerous and sometimes lengthy and beautiful works helped shape the canon and mirror the process, and they brought God's Word to Jews living in the land promised to Abraham and his descendants.

What Is a Canon?

The English word *canon* goes back to the Greek word *kanōn* and eventually to the Hebrew word *qaneh*. This noun meant first a "reed" (1 Kings 14:15) and then a measuring reed as a standard length (Ezek. 40:5–8). After the period for the composition of the apocryphal books, the word once known only in Hebrew finally denoted in Greek and many other languages a standard for judging what is in a definitive collection of Scripture. The term *canon* was first used by Christians who had a codex (by the fourth century) and needed to know what books to include within the covers and in what order.[1] Eventually, scholars used the word *canon* for a selection of scrolls or books that were the standard collection of Scripture—the books in which the faithful could find God's Word. The word *canon* should have been, but was seldom used as the measuring standard by which to discern God's Word in other documents.

The canon of books in the Hebrew Bible, or Old Testament, was not decided in the first century CE or at Yavneh (Jamnia), as many experts assumed for centuries. The Hebrew and Aramaic scrolls of Scripture found in caves west of the Dead Sea prove that the canonical process moved along diverse and obscure tracts. The canon was not closed even, as some scholars claim, in the second century CE at Yavneh. Debates over some books continued in Judaism until the sixth century CE.[2] Eventually Sirach, which had been regarded as a canonical book by some Jews, was considered "noncanonical," and Esther was added to the canon. When one considers that global Christianity includes the Flasha and the Mormons, the concept of canon loses its inherent and traditional meaning. Of course, the canonical process continues through hermeneutics once the fluid canon becomes frozen.[3]

1. See esp. R. A. Kraft, "The Codex and Canon Consciousness," in *The Canon Debate* (ed. L. M. McDonald and J. A. Sanders; Peabody, MA: Hendrickson, 2002), 229–33. [To preserve the nature of the lecture, notes are kept to a minimum.]

2. See the definitive study by L. M. McDonald, *The Biblical Canon* (Peabody, MA: Hendrickson, 2007).

3. See J. A. Sanders, "The Canonical Process," in *The Cambridge History of Judaism: The Late Roman-Rabbinic Period* (ed. S. T. Katz; Cambridge: Cambridge University Press, 2006), 4:230–43.

The Hebrew Bible is trifurcated into Torah, Prophets, and Writings (Tanak). The Torah was closed first, most likely before the third century BCE. The books in the Prophets were defined sometime later, most likely before the defeat of Bar Kokhba (135/6 CE). The contents of the books of Samuel and Jeremiah remained unclear until at least 70 CE. Some books in the Writings were debated until the sixth century CE.

Since the study of canon should also include the documents collected much later into the "Christian Bible," notably the New Testament, additional documents must be included and the timeline extended to about 1000 CE when the Greek Orthodox Church accepted the Revelation of John (which is still not canonical according to the Syriac Church). Thus the following works must come under scrutiny in a full exploration of the highways and byways of the canon:

The New Testament

The Earliest Documents in the NT Apocrypha and Pseudepigrapha (esp. the *Gospel of Thomas*, the *Birth of Mary*, the *Gospel of Truth,* and the *Gospel of Peter*)

To discuss the shaping of the New Testament canon would demand far more space than is allotted here. It would demand assessing not only the composition and editing of twenty-seven documents but the vast world of more than eighty apocryphal works on the fringes of the New Testament canon. That task would require exploring the gnostic and related compositions, including the *Hymn of the Pearl*, which leads us also into early Syriac literature.

To avoid losing sight of "writings ostensibly outside the canon," we should focus on the shaping of the canon and the composition of hundreds of Jewish works from 300 BCE, when the first books of *Enoch* were composed, to 200 CE, when the Mishnah took definite shape. Our gaze also is focused upon Second Temple Judaism and the world of Palestinian Judaism.

The title of this chapter—"Writings Ostensibly outside the Canon"—was chosen with a unique perspective in mind. On the one hand, the Jews who wrote and found God's Word in the allegedly apocryphal compositions did not consider these writings "outside the canon." On the other hand, since about 200 CE many Jews and Christians have judged the writings in central focus to be on the fringes of canon or "outside the canon." The adverb "ostensibly" thus attempts to represent both viewpoints. Since "ostensible" can mean both "apparent" and "professed," the word may help us convey both the thought that some early Jews assumed or claimed most of these writings apparently preserved God's Word, and also that other Jews perceived these writings only professed to contain God's Word. Both sides might agree, at times, that such writings related to Scripture enhance and point to Scripture as the fundamental source of Torah.

Two books in this category are exceptional. The erudite Jews who gave us the books of *Enoch* seem to portray Enoch as the major (perhaps only) source of God's Word and as superior to all others who had lived, including Moses, through whom the authors of the Pentateuch claimed God gave Torah to Israel. The same situation applies to the author or compiler of the *Temple Scroll*. If Deuteronomy contains God's Word in a third-person indirect means of discourse, the *Temple Scroll* presents God's Word (sometimes the same words as Deuteronomy) in direct first-person discourse so that one hears God in God's own words. That is quintessential Torah.

What Texts Indicate an Emerging Jewish Canon Prior to 100 CE?

The first place to seek information about a developing "canon" is not in the archives of Yavneh or Usha; despite the impressions supplied by scholars working in this field before 1950, there are no such archives. In the Jewish documents that antedate the destruction of the temple, there are innuendoes, even references, that help us comprehend how the canon is taking shape. This information is evident if we forget the word *canon* and focus on references to the tripartite division of the Hebrew Bible. It is clear now that Torah took canonical shape first, then the Prophets, and finally the Writings (which includes the Psalms).

Virtually everyone who has read the Hebrew Bible or Old Testament knows that the Psalms preserve references to "thy law" (Ps. 40:8); almost all occurrences appear in Psalm 119 (cf. vv. 34, 51, 53, 55, 61, 70, 77, 85, 92, 97, 109, 126, 136, 142, 150, 153, 163, 165, 174). The Psalter also mentions "the law of the LORD" (Pss. 1:2; 19:7; 119:1). The Hebrew Scriptures mention "the law of Moses" (Neh. 8:1; Dan. 9:11, 13) and "the law of God" (Neh. 8:18; 10:28, 29), as well as simply "the law" (Neh. 10:34; Ps. 119:72; Dan. 7:25; esp. Prov. 28:4 [2x], 7, 9; 29:18). None of these indicate a developing canon or norm for a collection.

The situation changes in the second century BCE. The earliest references to something like a canon are in Sirach, which preserves, in edited form, the teaching of Jesus Ben Sirach (ca. 200–180 BCE, in Jerusalem). His grandson, who supplied the Prologue to Sirach sometime after 132, clearly mirrors the tripartite division of Scripture when he mentions "the law and the prophets and the other [books] that followed them." Further on he mentions "the law," "the prophecies," and "the rest of the books." About the same time the author or compiler of *Some Works of the Torah* (4QMMT) also seems to mirror a tripartite canon when he refers to "the book of Moses," "the book[s of the p]rophets," and (the works of) "Davi[d]" (composite text C 10; cf. 17–18).[4] Most likely, the same concept of "canon" is found in 2 Maccabees 2:13–15, which about 124 BCE refers to "the books of the kings and prophets," as well as the "writings of David." In the early first century CE, Philo of Alexandria added to this consensus, referring to the "laws," "oracles of the prophets," and "psalms"; but if Philo held the concept of a canon, he must have imagined it to be open since he added "and anything else which fosters and perfects knowledge and piety" (*On the Contemplative Life* 25).

As did the authors of Nehemiah and Daniel, as well as the authors of some Old Testament Apocrypha (Tob. 6:13; 7:13; 1 Esd. 8:3; 9:39; Bar. 2:2; Sus. 1:3, 62), many authors of New Testament books refer to "the law of Moses" (Luke 2:22; 24:44; John 7:23; 8:5; Acts 13:39; 15:5; 28:23; 1 Cor. 9:9; Heb. 10:28). The well-known

---

4. See J. H. Charlesworth and H. W. M. Rietz, eds., *Damascus Document II, Some Works of the Torah, and Related Documents* (Tübingen: Mohr Siebeck; Louisville: Westminster John Knox, 2006).

"the law of the Lord," known from the Psalter (cf. *4 Ezra* 2:40) reappears in the New Testament in Luke (2:23, 24, 39).

Some passages in Matthew and Luke imply that the Law and the Prophets were the two major authoritative collections, since Scripture is summarized as "the law and the prophets" (Matt. 5:17; 7:12; Luke 16:16; Acts 13:15 [cf. Acts 28:23]; cf. "the prophets and the law" Matt. 11:13). These passages suggest that the Law and the Prophets were the first parts of the canon that were closed. The tripartite division of the canon is reflected in Luke (composed about 90 CE); Jesus said to them, "these are my words which I spoke to you, while I was still with you, that everything written about me in the law of Moses and the prophets and the psalms must be fulfilled" (Luke 24:44 RSV). While we know that "the psalms" are categorized among the writings, perhaps it is not widely perceived that the Psalter—as we learn from a study of the Qumran Psalter—was not yet closed and the order of the psalms not yet established during the time of Jesus.

After 70 CE we obtain more information regarding the shaping of the canon. In the decades following 70, the author of *4 Ezra* mentions ninety-four books. Twenty-four of the books are written "first" and are for the public but seventy books are written "last" and are for "the wise among" the Jews (*4 Ezra* 14:44–48). In the seventy books, not to be published widely, "is the spring of understanding, the fountain of wisdom, and the river of knowledge" (*4 Ezra* 14:47 [Metzger, *OTP* 1:555]).

The most definitive evidence of the early shaping of the canon is found in Josephus (ca. 37–ca. 100 CE), the historian of early Judaism (ca. 300 BCE–200 CE). In his later writings composed perhaps shortly before 100 CE, Josephus seeks to stress that the Jews do not have books that are numerous, inconsistent, or conflicting. There are only twenty-two books that are sacred. These twenty-two comprise "the five books of Moses," "the Prophets," and finally the "hymns to God and precepts for the conduct of human life" (*Against Apion* 1.37–39). Surely reflecting the text established perhaps during the so-called Council of Yavneh and later, and not the fluid text of Scripture known from the Qumran scrolls, Josephus emphasizes apologetically that "no one has ventured to add, to remove, or to alter a syllable" of Scripture.

The latter contains "God's decrees" (*Ag. Ap.* 1.42). It is unwise to claim that Josephus defended a closed canon, since he mentions "the laws and the allied documents" (*Ag. Ap.* 1.43). Indeed, Josephus seems to know and cite some lost Jewish works. Among all writings, however, "the Law" is surely supreme (cf. *Ag. Ap.* 2.219).

These explorations into asides or references to books considered sacred scarcely clarifies what books were judged to be "Scripture"— that is, replete with God's Word to the elect—and according to whom and by what criteria. To obtain the answers to such issues demands that we enter the world of Hillel and Jesus. It also requires assessing the authority accorded, at least by some early Jews, to the following:

The books eventually collected into the "Old Testament" (and their versions)

The so-called Old Testament Apocrypha and Pseudepigrapha (esp. the books of *Enoch*)

The hundreds of documents found in the Qumran caves (esp. the *Temple Scroll*, *Some Works of the Torah*, and the pesharim)

Such a task would deter us from our present focus; suffice it now only to conclude that the process of canonization was not defined by any decree or conciliar decision. The shaping of the canon reflects the theological and social needs of the Jews from the Babylonian captivity in the sixth century BCE to at least the meetings in Usha in the second century CE.

We cannot discern the shape of the canon before 70 CE. Why? Not only is it misleading to use a Christian term, *canon*, for the period in Judaism before 70, but the texts of the so-called Old Testament were fluid at that time. Without a stable text, it is misleading to talk about a collection. We can imagine, however, the vast amount of works that were not eventually defined as canonical; that is our present task. Before turning to them, we need to assess one further question.

Do the Apocrypha and Qumran Scrolls Reflect a Closed Canon?

No. There is no closed canon during the time of Hillel, Jesus, Johanan ben Zakkai, Josephus, or Akiba. In fact, not only did the collection of books remain not-yet-defined, but the shape of many books, especially Jeremiah and the books of Samuel, appeared in widely different forms before 70. There were more than ten different text types (as Tov proves),[5] and many compositions were considered as scriptural as—even sometimes more scriptural than—works later deemed canonical.

Which Writings Were on the Fringes of the Canon?

This focused question may now be tentatively answered. We need not include at this time the Jewish magical papyri, the vast amount of inscriptions, or the works of Philo and Josephus. None of these vied for inclusion within the canon of sacred books. Many other virtually unknown compositions were once deemed sacred and authoritative by some Jewish groups before 135/6 CE. These may be presented in terms of their literary genre. We now know of over sixty-five books that were once considered part of the Bible (using the term anachronistically). These include apocalypses, testaments, hymns and poetry, expansions of Scripture, wisdom texts, and other related documents.

Apocalypses. In the Christian Bible are two apocalypses, Daniel and the Apocalypse of John. The Apocalypse of John is usually the text by which an apocalypse is identified and defined, but the genre cannot be defined categorically. The term *apocalypse* is given to a group of Jewish or Christian documents intended to help the reader live in a meaningful world in which God is acknowledged and

5. For E. Tov's publications, see: "The Interpretative Significance of a Fixed Text and Canon of the Hebrew and the Greek Bible," in *The Hebrew Bible/Old Testament: The History of Its Interpretation*, Vol. 1, *From the Beginnings to the Middle Ages (until 1300)* (ed. M. Sæbø; Göttingen: Vandenhoeck & Ruprecht, 1996), 1:49–66; *Textual Criticism of the Hebrew Bible* (2nd rev. ed; Minneapolis: Fortress; Assen: Royal Van Gorcum, 2001); "The Biblia Hebraica Quinta: An Important Step Forward," *JNSL* 31/1 (2005): 1–21; "The Writing of Early Scrolls: Implications for the Literary Analysis of Hebrew Scriptures," in *L'Ecrit et l'Esprit* (ed. D. Böhler, I. Himbaza, and P. Hugo; OBO 214; Fribourg: Academic Press; Göttingen: Vandenhoeck & Ruprecht, 2005), 355–71.

in control. These documents are revelatory narratives that bring meaning to a present chaotic world by disclosing eternal truths to those revealed to be God's elect. These truths are revealed from the future or the heavens above. Usually the insight or knowledge is provided by an intermediary like Uriel or one of the archangels or biblical sages, like Enoch, Abraham, Baruch, or Ezra.

Daniel is not the earliest known apocalypse. It is preceded by apocalyptic sections in the Prophets, especially Zechariah and Isaiah, and the earliest books within the books of *Enoch*, which date from around 300 BCE to the end of the first century BCE or early in the first century CE. Perhaps the high watermark for the Jewish apocalypses is found in the *Parables of Enoch* and *4 Ezra*. The following early Jewish apocalypses are now placed within the Old Testament Pseudepigrapha: the *Apocalypse of Abraham*, *2 Baruch (Syriac Apocalypse)*, *1 Enoch (Ethiopic Apocalypse)*, *2 Enoch (Slavonic Apocalypse)*, *4 Ezra*, and the *Apocalypse of Zephaniah*.

Testaments. Jews who lived during the Second Temple period (ca. 300 BCE–70 CE) were fond of Genesis 49 and the solemn last words of Jacob to his twelve sons concerning the future and the evil tendencies and sins of many of his sons. Taking this biblical text as a norm, a rough paradigm was fashioned whereby a famous father would call his sons around his deathbed, charge them with weaknesses, and reveal what is about to happen. Jewish testaments collected into the Pseudepigrapha include: the *Testaments of the Twelve Patriarchs*, the *Testament of Job*, the *Testament of Moses*, and the *Testament of Solomon*.

Hymns and Poetry. Most (or many) Jews before 70 assumed the Psalter was a collection of David's psalms; yet, other psalms were composed and sometimes attributed to David. These liturgical works often shaped and defined self-understanding within some groups.

Within the Pseudepigrapha are assembled numerous collections of psalms, odes, or hymns. The document called *More Psalms of David* is a collection of Psalms 151, 152, 153, 154, and 155. These psalms complete the allegedly closed Psalter—though they each antedate such a decision sometimes by three centuries. The Prayer of Manasseh is one of the most moving penitential prayers ever composed. The *Psalms of Solomon* are eighteen psalms used in worship services in Jerusalem synagogues from the first century BCE up until the burning of Jerusalem in 70 CE. The *Prayer of Joseph* and the *Prayer of Jacob* are prayers that indicate the varieties of piety and theology within pre-rabbinic Judaism. The *Odes of Solomon* has challenged many experts; some claim the work is Christian, others gnostic, and some Jewish.

Expansions of Scripture. The stories preserved in Torah were favorites for early Jews. Yet, sometimes these and other stories needed details or completion. How is it possible that the Greek translation of Hebrew Scriptures was so perfect? What is the Sabbath, and when and why was it created? How did Isaiah, Jeremiah, and other prophets die? How could Joseph marry a non-Jew? What occurred when Eve and Seth observed Adam was ill and aging? What was the name of Jeptha's daughter? Where are the Rechabites living now? What was the name of Noah's wife? How did death come to Abraham? To answer such questions, Scripture was expanded and rewritten; the result is the following early Jewish works: the *Letter of Aristeas*, *Jubilees*, the *Martyrdom of Isaiah*, *Joseph and Aseneth*, the *Life of Adam and Eve*, Pseudo-Philo's *Biblical Antiquities*, the *Lives of the Prophets*, the *Ladder of Jacob*, *4 Baruch*, *Jannes and Jambres*, the *History of the Rechabites*, as well as *Eldad and Modad*.

Wisdom Texts. Jewish interest in wisdom and knowledge antedates Solomon and is stressed in almost all Jewish collections. In the Pseudepigrapha are the following early Jewish collections of wise sayings: 3 Maccabees, 4 Maccabees, Pseudo-Phocylides, and the *Sentences of Syriac Menander.*

Other Related Documents. The previously mentioned compositions were known long before the discovery of the Qumran scrolls in 1947. Since then Bedouin and scholars have recovered, primarily from the eleven Qumran caves, numerous writings not composed at Qumran, psalms and compositions perhaps composed or edited at Qumran, and a large number of "Qumranic Pseudepigrapha." Surely, it is now clear that more works need to be included in the Pseudepigrapha, and this corpus should be defined broadly. These include astrological works attributed to Abraham, the *Book of the Giants*, the *Apocalypse of Elchasai*, the *Apocalypse of Pseudo-*

Methodius, the *Words of Gad the Seer*, the *Oracle of Hystaspes*, Pseudo-Jonah, Pseudo-Samson, the *Ethiopic History of Joseph*, and the early Jewish works preserved in the Mani Cologne Codex.[6] Many more writings are available if one is willing to include documents that are medieval and clearly do not preserve earlier Jewish traditions.

Why Are These Early Jewish Texts Paradigmatically Important?

This question is crucial, since the documents in central focus were branded as inferior to those in a putative closed canon. Four observations help provide answers to this question.

First, the ante-Mishnaic Jewish texts are extremely important for a perception of life, practice, worship, and thought prior to the composition of the last document in the New Testament (about 150 CE), or fifty years before the first tractate in the Mishnah was completed. The early Jewish documents should not be branded "noncanonical," as almost everyone has done for centuries. That is anachronistic—there was no closed canon of the Hebrew Bible until the second century BCE. It also misrepresents the early Jewish documents; that is, it placards them as inferior to writings eventually defined as "canonical." Many of the documents placed conveniently in the Old Testament Apocrypha and Pseudepigrapha and some of the documents found only at Qumran, especially the *Temple Scroll*, were judged by some early Jews to be superior to documents that were canonized.

Second, these Jewish writings are singularly important because they bridge the gap from the latest book in the Hebrew Scriptures, Daniel (shortly before 164 BCE), and the earliest writing in the New Testament, 1 Thessalonians (ca. 50 CE).

Third, these other Jewish "Scriptures" reflect major historical events. The putative apocryphal documents composed by Jews during the Second Temple period prove that Hellenistic Judaism is not a geographical but a chronological term. Jewish thought was

---

6. See, e.g., J. H. Charlesworth, "The JSHRZ and the OTP: A Celebration," in *Jüdische Schriften in ihrem antik-jüdischen und urchristlichen Kontext* (ed. H. Lichtenberger and G. S. Oegema; *JSHRZ* 1; Gütersloh: Gütersloher Verlagshaus, 2002), 11–34.

shaped by world events. Few references to history are found in the so-called Old Testament Apocrypha; many are in the Old Testament Pseudepigrapha. Most of the writings in the Apocrypha are theological works or fictional histories that cast light on Judaism. In contrast to most of the Apocrypha, 1 Maccabees is not only an example of Jewish interest in history, it reveals how Judaism is being shaped by foreign events.

The most powerful influence on Palestinian Jews in the second century BCE was the shift of power from the Ptolemies in Egypt to the Seleucids in Syria and their intrusion into the religion of the Jews. In 198 BCE Antiochus III pulled Palestinian Jews into the Seleucid Empire and tried to Hellenize them. Thus, Jews in Palestine had been pressured by post-Alexander Greek forces initially from the south and then from the north. Finally, Antiochus IV Epiphanes (175–164), "a sinful root" (1 Macc. 1:10), proscribed Judaism and tried to force all in his kingdom, including Jews, to "give up their particular customs" (1 Macc. 1:42). The resulting revolt was the famous Maccabean rebellion.

The best and most ancient source for this event is 1 Maccabees. During the Maccabean rebellion, Jews made an alliance with Rome, which sets the stage for their future relation: "May all go well with the Romans and with the nation of the Jews at sea and on land forever, and may sword and enemy be far from them" (1 Macc. 8:23 NRSV). What irony; in less than a century Rome will control Judea, and within two centuries Rome will destroy Palestinian Judaism and bring an end to the history of ancient Israel.

In contrast to the Apocrypha, the Pseudepigrapha is replete with references to major events in world history. This point is often missed by most classical historians and even by the specialists on the Pseudepigrapha. Let me now briefly review how the authors of the Pseudepigrapha refer to numerous historical events.

Alexander the Great appears in the Pseudepigrapha as a "faithless man" and one who causes "all Asia" to "imbibe much gore" (*Sibylline Oracles* 3.389–392). The author of the *Book of the Watchers* (*1 Enoch* 1–36) obliquely mentions the successors of Alexander the Great, since the Giants and the Watchers are metaphorical references to the wars among the Diadochi (the Macedonian generals who divided up the civilized world after Alexander's untimely death). The author of the *Psalms of Solomon* mentions the demise of one of the greatest Romans in antiquity, Pompey; this general brought Palestine within the orbit of Roman control in 63 BCE. The author of these psalms refers to Pompey's struggles in Jerusalem and his death in Egypt, calling him "the sinner" who "broke down the strong walls" of Jerusalem (2.1), and the insolent one, the dragon, who was "more despised than the smallest thing on earth and sea" (2.25–26). The Parthian invasion of Palestine in 40 BCE seems mirrored in the *Parables of Enoch* (*1 Enoch* 37–71). Cleopatra appears as "a woman" who will govern "the world" (*Sib. Or.* 3.75).

The greatest non-battle in history, at Actium in 31 BCE, when Octavian (= Augustus) established the age of Roman Imperialism, shapes some pseudepigraphal works. This inexplicable turn of world events is mirrored in one document as "when Rome will also rule over Egypt" (*Sib. Or.* 3.46). Most importantly, the aftershocks of this non-battle caused the author of the *Treatise of Shem* to interpret it through astrology.

Herod the Great (40–4 BCE) appears numerous times in the Jewish apocryphal writings. As expected, he is noted in a very negative way numerous times in the *Sibylline Oracles* and the *Ascension of Isaiah* (4.1). Nero, who died mysteriously in 68 CE, is castigated for his vices in many passages in the Pseudepigrapha, being hailed as "a most piteous king" (*Sib. Or.* 8.690), he who "will flee Italy like a runaway slave" (*Sib. Or.* 4.119; cf. *Sib. Or.* 8.139–159), and the Antichrist (*Ascension of Isaiah* 4.2b–4a).

The destruction of Jerusalem and the burning of the temple in 70 CE by Vespasian's son Titus, who is "a certain insignificant and impious king" (*Sib. Or.* 5.40), are so important it is as if the smoke can be felt when one reads *4 Ezra*. The author of *Sibylline Oracles* claims that Vesuvius's eruption in 79 CE and the ensuing destruction of the cities near Naples, especially Pompeii and Herculaneum (*Sib. Or.* 3.50–54), were God's punishment of the Romans. Why? The Romans were destroyed because they burned the holy city of "a sacred race of pious men" (*Sib. Or.* 3.573)—the Jews.[7]

---

7. Contrast Matthew's redaction of the parable of the marriage feast. He claims that God killed the Jews and burned their city because they were "murderers" (Matt. 22:7). That is, they were responsible for Jesus' death.

Fourth, wise insights later attributed to European savants sometimes appear in these early Jewish texts. For example, the famous
adage, "the mills of God grind slowly" is known from Henry
Wadsworth Longfellow (1807–1864), found in his translation of
"Retribution" by Friedrich von Logau. The often quoted words,
coined by Sextus Empiricus about 1600 years ago, also appear in
the Pseudepigrapha: "The mills of God grind fine flour, though
late" (*Sib. Or.* 8.14).

The Golden Rule is known usually only through Jesus' saying
in Matthew 7:12 and Luke 6:31 (cf. Matt. 19:19; Mark 12:31).
Some may know that it is also attributed to Hillel in the Babylonian Talmud (*b. Shabbat* 31a; also see *Targum Pseudo-Jonathan*
on Lev. 19:18). The maxim is found even earlier in Herodotus
(and later Greek and Latin works) and also in *Ahiqar* (Armenian
recension 8.88), Tobit 4:15, and notably mirrored in the *Letter of
Aristeas* 207; Pseudo-Philo, *Biblical Antiquities* 11.12; and stated
clearly in *Syriac Menander* 250–251. Thus, the Jewish apocryphal
works are mines for maxims familiar from other, usually later,
sources that may have been influenced by the earlier Greek or
Jewish insights.

Why Should One Read These Early Jewish Compositions?

What is the import of these Jewish writings ostensibly outside
the canon? First, students interested in early Judaism and Christian
origins should read these apocryphal works because the compositions were deemed authoritative or scriptural by many religious
Jews during the time of Hillel and Jesus. In fact, many works
described as ancient "revelatory literature" are collected in what
are branded as "noncanonical documents."

Second, the works bridge the chasm between the Old Testament
and New Testament, thereby raising the question of the appropri-
ateness of those adjectives, "Old" and "New." Surely, there is much
new in the so-called old, and many insights old in the "new."

Third, these writings contain the most brilliant work on theodicy
ever written, even deeper and more profound than Job. The author
of *4 Ezra* is so dedicated to honest questioning that even Uriel is
portrayed confessing that no archangel, not even "The Light of

God," has the knowledge that Ezra seeks: "but I do not know (*sed nescio*)" (*4 Ezra* 4:52).[8]

Fourth, and most importantly, the Jewish sacred writings not contained in Torah, New Testament, or Talmud often preserve poetically pellucid perceptions. In these writings you will find the Jew's search for Truth, for God's Word applicable to today. The authors of these writings strive for self-understanding, pursuing questions that seem perennially important: Who are we? Why is meaning so elusive? Is there really a God? Is God still alive, interested in us, and involved in events on earth? Or, are the Scriptures just a chaotic discordant clump of antiquarian myths?

Such Jewish pleas are plaintive, searching for understanding in a brutal and hostile world, which according to Scripture was created by the one-and-only benevolent Creator. How can one trust past revelations? How dare one depend on ancestors for guidance in future paths, when such ways would be not only incomprehensible but also unimaginable to them? If God is powerful, why does God seem so incredibly weak or disinterested in those to whom he has given Torah, God's will? Such questioning is neither archaic nor immoral.

The answers to such questions depended on the informed experiences of groups, sects, or isolated geniuses. The Enoch groups claimed that Enoch alone knew the answers that had been elusive to humans. The Qumranites claimed that all God's secrets found in prophecy had been revealed only to the Righteous Teacher, and then through him to his followers. The apocalyptists had the most enduring answer: the world is characterized by meaninglessness because meaning resides only with the transcendent God, who is apparently beginning to reveal, either from above or from the future, his intention when he began creating. Thus all answers reside in the unfinished drama; God has not ceased creating.

In their penetrating reflections we may find some enduring answers in our own honest search for meaning in this journey called "life." In their inquiry we learn how boldly to confront phenomena and even noumena with questions that are truthful to ourselves and

---

8. Also see J. H. Charlesworth, "Theodicy in Early Jewish Writings: A Selected Overview," in *Theodicy in the World of the Bible* (ed. A. Laato and J. C. de Moor; Leiden: Brill, 2003), 470–508.

those like us. The paradigmatic wandering Jew did not begin in the Middle Ages and continue to the present, and beyond, through the musings of Tevye in *Fiddler on the Roof*. The Jews, wandering for understanding and meaning of "God's chosen," began in the centuries of Second Temple Judaism; that is, in the time of Hillel and Jesus. Hillel asked, "If I am not for myself, who is for me? And when I am for myself, what am I? And if not now, when?" (*m. Avot* 1:14).[9] His contemporary, Jesus, was asked, "Which is the great commandment?" (Matt. 22:36; cf. Mark 12:28) and "Who is my neighbor?" (Luke 10:29). Such questions are uttered by Jews who are encouraged to inquire honestly and from a foundation of integrity grounded in Torah.

How did these Jews provide answers to life's questions? In the books of *Enoch* and *2 Enoch* the antediluvian sage Enoch is depicted as the only one who has seen the secrets to life and eternity. He does not keep the answers in heaven but returns to earth in order to reveal these sacred truths to those on the land. Moreover, the apocalyptists were not primarily exploring time and space when they composed their writings or apocalypses; they were exploring the depths within the human. The genre appears extraterrestrial, but the vision is introspective.

Finally, too often the authors of the apocalypses are portrayed as disinterested in the present world, peering into the distant heavens or putative future age for elusive answers. That perception is misleading. The Jewish apocalyptists were interested in cosmology, but they were not cosmologists. They were excited about the pregnant meaning of time, but they were not chronographers. They were devoted to astronomy and sometimes astrology, but they were neither astronomers nor astrologers. All explorations of time, space, and eternity had one goal: seeking meaning to life's perennial problems through theological reflections on Torah and God.

To claim that these evaluations psychoanalyze the early Jews misses the point, is imperceptive, and overlooks the vast influence of Jewish wisdom traditions in the apocalypses and apocalyptic documents (esp. *1 Enoch, Testaments of the Twelve Patriarchs,*

---

9. Translation by J. Neusner, *The Mishnah* (New Haven and London: Yale University Press, 1988), 674.

2 Enoch, and *4 Ezra*).[10] For early Jews the study of the sciences served not abstract or secular needs; as Rabbi Elazar ben Chisma stated: "Astronomy and geometry are appetizers to wisdom" (*m. Avot* 3:23).[11]

What was revealed to these Jews? First, while we proudly claim that science has disclosed that the moon receives its light from the sun, the ancient Jews were told this fact by Uriel:

> Then Uriel showed me another order (concerning) when light is beamed into the moon, from which (direction) of the bright sun it is beamed. (*1 Enoch* 78:10 [Isaac, *OTP* 1:57])

Second, medical dictionaries and texts, as well as lexicons, inform us of the advances made by scientists such as William Harvey (1578–1657), who discovered the circulation of the blood through the veins and arteries. Now, it appears that Jews knew that long before the time of Jesus, since the idea seems mirrored in the recently published fragments of the *Damascus Document*.[12]

We have seen that the writings not included in the canon are exceptional. What may be the most important lesson they bequeath to us? It is this: they teach us how to be honest with ourselves and God and how to question all inherited answers. In this sense, as T. S. Eliot and other poets clarified, we are all wandering Jews struggling forward on *terra infirma*.

Is There a Lost Bicentennial Library outside the Canon?

The twenty-seven letters, Gospels, apocalypse, and pamphlets collected into the New Testament do not arise out of a graveyard of archaic texts. The Hebrew Bible was alive, since scribes were adding, deleting, and arranging what defines a document. These

---

10. I am grateful to Professor G. Oegema for many pleasant conversations on this topic.

11. My translation. "Geometry" most likely refers to gematria, as indicated in the versions of Danby and Neusner.

12. See Charlesworth and Rietz, eds., *Damascus Document II, Some Works of the Torah, and Related Documents*. See esp. 4Q272 1 I, 6–7 in which we hear about "the blood," "the artery," and "[the spir]it of life" that "moves up and down" (3:174–75).

sacred texts were interpreted lively. And many documents eventually not included in the canon were considered authoritative. This claim to authority is accurate in the sense that God's Word may be found within these documents also, sometimes in a more powerful way, according to Jews who lived during Second Temple Judaism (300 BCE–70 CE). For example, in the *Temple Scroll* God speaks in the first person. In Deuteronomy God's similar speech is known only through third-person discourse. It is clearly paradigmatically different to hear God directly and not only in the words of another.

What are the Seven Misleading Caricatures of Second Temple Judaism?

Before World War II and before the discovery of the Qumran scrolls, scholars—both Christian and Jewish—assumed a worldwide recognition of seven aspects of Second Temple Judaism:

1. The Judaism of the period was clear and was shaped by the cessation of prophecy long before Ezra.
2. Second Temple Judaism was monolithic, orthodox, and normative.
3. It was defined by only four sects: Pharisees, Sadducees, Essenes, Zealots.
4. We possessed compositions by Sadducees, Pharisees, and Essenes.
5. All early Jews recognized a set of customs within official or common Judaism.
6. There was a clear line of development from Ezra to Rabbi Judah the Prince.
7. And, most importantly for us, specialists presupposed that canonization had been completed.

Now, thanks to research by Jews and Christians on the Pseudepigrapha, Apocrypha, Dead Sea Scrolls, Philo, Josephus, the New Testament, the Jewish magical papyri, inscriptions, and rabbinics, we know that the following is correct about Second Temple Judaism:

1. Prophecy did *not* cease long before Ezra.
2. Judaism was *not* monolithic, orthodox, and normative.
3. Judaism was *not* defined by only four sects: Pharisees, Sadducees, Essenes, and Zealots.
4. We do *not* possess writings by pre-70 Sadducees and Pharisees.[13]
5. *No* set customs were recognized by all Jews in a common Judaism.
6. There is *no* clear line of development from Ezra to Judah the Prince.
7. Canonization had *not* been completed before 70 CE.

What Are Ten Misconceptions of Judaism During Jesus' Time?

For centuries, perhaps two millennia, Christian teachers and clergy have emphasized how corrupt were the Jews during the time of Jesus. Focusing only on Matthew, many influential thinkers claimed that the Pharisees are synonymous with hypocrites. These church leaders taught that Jews during Jesus' time were legalistic, very proud of being elected, controlled a promised land, had no concept of sin, felt no need for forgiveness, had no need of salvation, monopolized a polluted temple that was defined by a corrupt liturgy, had no concept of the kingdom of God, believed in a distant God, and rejected any idea of a resurrection. In summation, the impression was that during the time of Jesus, Judaism was a deteriorated and decadent religion.

First, is it representative to placard Judaism as legalistic? Weekly, sermons round the world proclaim the legalism of Judaism during the time of Jesus. Preachers can cite the nineteenth-century authority who wrote the multi-volume *A History of the Jewish People in the Time of Jesus Christ*. This brilliant and influential German, Emil Schürer, claimed that in Judaism "ethic and theology were swallowed up in jurisprudence. The evil results of this external view on practical matters are very evident" (Second Div., II.120).[14] He

13. Except for Paul, who represents not only Pharisaism but also Jesus' teachings.
14. E. Schürer, *A History of the Jewish People in the Time of Jesus Christ* (trans. S. Taylor and P. Christie; Edinburgh: T&T Clark, 1890; repr., Peabody, MA: Hendrickson, 1994).

concluded that "external formalism" of these early Jews was far removed from "true piety" (II.115) and judged that Jewish prayer, the center of spiritual life, "was bound in the fetters of a rigid mechanism" (II.115). In support of Schürer's position, legalism and excessive preoccupation for observing the Sabbath can be found in documents known to him and in many documents discovered since his time, especially in *Some Works of the Torah* (4QMMT) and in the recently published fragments of the *Damascus Document*.

It is fallacious methodology, however, to seek to prove a position by looking only for evidence to prove it. In *Avot* one can find piety that is just as advanced as the moral theology attributed to Jesus by Paul, Mark, John, Matthew, and Luke. The hymnbooks and collections of psalms and odes discovered since Schürer's time disprove his claims. The celebration of Torah, in *Simhat Torah*, reveals that Jews found the Torah a joy. They claimed to be able to know God and to be given a clear teaching regarding God's will.

Second, were Jews proud of being elected? This question is practically impossible to answer. We simply do not have sufficient data to make an erudite response. Surely, many Jews during the time of Jesus felt they were elected. One can also imagine that about the historical Jesus. He seems to be very pro-Jewish and even anti-Gentile (cf. Matt. 10:5–6). There is clear evidence that many Jews claimed to be elected, superior to Gentiles, and even anti-Gentile. It is difficult to assess the statements that suggest this posture; after all, they were written by Palestinian Jews who had seen Gentiles rape their daughters, burn their cities, rob their treasures, and treat them as inferiors. A text is defined by its context, so most anti-Gentile sentiment or proud claims may be conditioned by people forced to live in a subjugated or conquered land.

Third, did Jews control a promised land? Of course, the answer is "no." From the time of Alexander the Great, who died in 323 BCE, Palestine was intermittently controlled successively by Greeks, Romans, and an Idumaean called King Herod the Great. Only for a few decades under the Maccabees and Hasmoneans were Palestinian Jews free to claim that they controlled the land promised to them.

Fourth, is it true that early Jews had no concept of sin and felt no need for forgiveness? Too many historians assume this. One might find some proof for this salacious point, but the evidence is abundantly against it. Since the Psalter was the hymnbook of the Second Temple period, these words were heard repeatedly in the temple:

> Wash me thoroughly of my iniquity,
> and purify me of my sin;
> for I recognize my transgressions,
> and am ever conscious of my sin. (Ps. 51:4–5 JPS *Tanakh*)

During Yom Kippur, the Day of Atonement, the high priest acknowledged his own sins before all those in the temple, following the teaching in Leviticus 16:6. After immersing himself in the *mikveh* (Jewish ritual bath), the high priest would state:

> O God, I have committed iniquity, transgressed, and sinned before thee, I and my house. O God, forgive the iniquities and transgressions and sins which I have committed and transgressed and sinned before thee, I and my house . . . (*m. Yoma* 3:8)[15]

Apparently, too many scholars have not adequately read or understood this tradition. If the high priest knew and confessed his sins publicly, so much more should the Jew of lesser rank.

In the Prayer of Manasseh, composed shortly before or during the time of Jesus, we find a most advanced penitential thought. Note this stirring confession and petition attributed to the wickedest king in Israel:

> And now behold I am bending the knees of my heart before you;
> and I am beseeching your kindness.
> I have sinned, O Lord, I have sinned;
> and I certainly know my sins.
> I beseech you;
> > forgive me, O Lord, forgive me! (Pr. Man. 11–13 [Charlesworth, *OTP* 2:634])

15. Translated by H. Danby, *The Mishnah* (Oxford: Clarendon, 1933).

Studying and reflecting on these compositions helps one comprehend that many Jews during the time of Jesus knew and confessed their sins before God.

Fifth, did Jews express no need of salvation? Often I have heard scholars claim that the concept of "salvation" is not found in early Judaism but was created by Christians who need a "Savior." Here they are either misled by polemics or Christian false claims that Judaism does not have the concept of salvation. Again, let us recall Psalm 51, which would have been chanted by Levites in the temple:

> Save me from bloodguilt,
> O God, God, my deliverer,
> that I may sing forth Your beneficence. (Ps. 51:16 JPS *Tanakh*)

In this Psalm we hear the need to be saved by God, who is portrayed as "deliverer" or savior.

The Jewish author of *4 Ezra*, composed within a few decades of the burning of Jerusalem in 70 CE, is concerned about judgment and salvation. He laments the few that will be "saved" and the many that will be damned. The angel sent to him by God tells Ezra, "for I will rejoice over the few who shall be saved [*qui saluabuntur*]" (*4 Ezra* 7:[60] [Metzger, *OTP* 1:538–39]). The angelic interlocutor informs Ezra that there will be "joy over those to whom salvation [*salus*] is assured" (*4 Ezra* 7:61[131] [Metzger, *OTP* 1:541]). Earlier in the same century, the Jew who composed Pseudo-Philo's *Biblical Antiquities* talks about "the salvation of the souls of the people [*salvatione animarum populi*]" (13.10 [Harrington, *OTP* 2:322]). Clearly, then, the concept of salvation is present in early Judaism and the word appears in numerous documents (though only a few may be shared in this essay).

Sixth, did Jewish ecclesiastics monopolize the temple and corrupt ancient worship and liturgy that was celebrated in it? Twenty years ago, when I was teaching at Duke University, I found it difficult to refer to Jesus' cleansing of the temple. I felt that such a phrase might be a Christian misrepresentation of a historical fact. Then, more and more Jews pointed out to me that some elements of the temple cult had been polluted. Some of the high priests had become corrupt, and the discovery of a weight from the famous Bar Kathros family, in the Upper City of Jerusalem, reminded us that they were not just in their measurements (t. Menaḥot 13:21).[16]

How should we proceed without prejudice? Perhaps we need to consider four distinct concepts: the Holy City, the temple, the cult, and some polluted aspects of the cult. Observing Jesus' claims that some priests were corrupt and that some abuses are evident in the cult does not imply that the temple cult is corrupt. It is evident that Jesus loved the temple, its liturgy, and its cult. The evidence is clearly reliable that Jesus worshiped and taught in the temple. He does clash with some priests, especially the high priests Caiaphas and Annas, but there is no evidence that Jesus considered the temple cult ineffective or corrupt.

Seventh, were Jews ignorant of the phrase "the kingdom of God"? The distinguished New Testament specialist Norman Perrin was famous for his claim that the early followers of Jesus, "the Christians," may have created the concept of the kingdom of God. Perrin claimed that from "the point of view of linguistic usage the form 'Kingdom of God' is comparatively late; it may even be specifically Christian."[17]

The Hebrew, Aramaic, and Greek expression often translated "the kingdom of God" may also be translated "rule of God" or "God's rule." This concept and linguistic expression, "kingdom of God," is found rather frequently in the documents ostensibly outside the canon.

Here are a few examples. The author of Psalm 103:19 celebrates YHWH, "the Lord," who has established his throne in the heavens and "his sovereign rule [malkut] over all the earth." The one who composed Psalm 145:11 praises the Lord's kingdom (malkut). The composer of the Song of the Three Jews, which is an addition to Daniel, blesses God and "your kingdom [basileia]" (v. 33). The Jewish author of Sibylline Oracle 3.46 extols the "immortal king," God, and his "kingdom [basileia]." Tobit 13:2 (1) blesses God and "his kingdom [basileia]." The Wisdom of Solomon 10:10 refers to "the kingdom of God [basileian theou]." The Testaments of the

---

16. For images and discussion, see N. Avigad, Discovering Jerusalem (Nashville and New York: Thomas Nelson, 1983), 129–31.

17. N. Perrin, Jesus and the Language of the Kingdom (Philadelphia: Fortress, 1976), 81.

Twelve Patriarchs mentions the "kingdom of the Lord [*basileia kyriou*]" (*Testament of Benjamin* 9.1). The *War Scroll* mentions "the kingdom" of "the God of Israel" (1QM VI, 6; cf. XII, 7). The poet who created the *Psalms of Solomon* for a synagogue in Jerusalem celebrates "the kingdom of our God [*hē basileia tou theou hēmōn*]" (17.4). The *Testament of Moses*, which most likely reached its final form during the time of Jesus, describes the key features of God's kingdom and refers to "his kingdom [*regnum illius*]" (10.1). In the *Qaddish*, the famous Jewish prayer, the Jew in worship repeatedly chants glory to God and appeals for God to "establish his kingdom [*malkut*]" soon.[18]

It is understandable that New Testament scholars often know the New Testament better than they do early Judaism. This is intolerable, however, if virtually all time is spent studying the New Testament merely in an attempt to comprehend its unique features. The concept of "the kingdom of God," "the rule of God," "God's kingship," or "God's kingdom" appears, as we have seen, in numerous early Jewish texts. This is the context for other Jewish writings, namely all the books in the New Testament.

Eighth, did Jews not believe in a distant God? The study of the Jewish apocalypses have led some experts to conclude that Jews felt God was distant and that angels were imagined to bridge the gap between the heavens and the earth. It is imperative to perceive that angels unite, not separate, the noumenal with the phenomenal. Though early Jews increasingly perceived God to be holy, imperceptible, or ineffable, they did not imagine an absentee deity. Their theological insight reveals the majesty and godliness of God, not his withdrawal from humans. The Lord's Prayer is a good example of a Jewish prayer, and Jesus calls for God to make his kingdom manifest on earth as it is in heaven. Here we do not see a "Christian" Jesus; we see the truly Jewish Jesus. With his Jewish contemporaries, Jesus believed that the one-and-only Creator is now again moving closer and closer to his creations.

Ninth, did Jews reject any idea of a resurrection? Among pre-70 Jews, only the Sadducees reportedly denied belief in res-

18. For more discussion, see J. H. Charlesworth, "The Historical Jesus in Light of Writings Contemporaneous with Him," *ANRW* II 25.1:451–76.

urrection. There is abundant evidence that many Jews during the time of Jesus believed in the resurrection of the dead to immortal life. The belief is found in the *Qaddish* and instilled in many Jews as they recited this prayer in public services. The concept appears among the Qumran scrolls, in a document entitled *On Resurrection*. The belief appears first in the books of *Enoch* and then in Daniel 12. Many of the Jews who wrote works now collected into the Pseudepigrapha developed the concept of resurrection.

Tenth, was Judaism during the time of Jesus a deteriorated and decadent religion? Of course, one can obtain that impression by reading some sections of Matthew and John. But the conclusion cannot be sustained by a careful exegesis of these very Jewish Gospels. Paul warns against any possible supersessionism: "Has God rejected his people? Heavens no" (Rom. 11:1). Suffice it to report that more and more Christian theologians are stressing that the greatest Christian heresy is to denigrate Judaism in an attempt to celebrate Jesus.

The writings ostensibly on the fringes of canon reveal that Second Temple Judaism was one of the most advanced theological worlds in antiquity. It was full of rich symbolic language. The portrayal of a sinful generation just before the destruction of Jerusalem is a Christian polemic that appears first in Matthew, in his editing of the parable of the marriage feast (Matt. 22:1–14; contrast Luke 14:15–24).

What Do We Learn from the Writings on the Edges of the Canon?

Many priceless insights are obtained by reading the full range of Scriptures known to Jews during the time of Hillel and Jesus. Seven seem most important.

First, by reading the so-called Apocrypha and Pseudepigrapha, we learn about the creativity of early Jews, and how they were often significantly influenced by other cultures. It is certain, for example, that the influence from the Greeks antedates Alexander the Great, since the Samaritan papyri, which are self-dated prior to his incursion into the land, contained bullae (seals) that bear figures of Hercules and some of the Homeric myths.[19] The study of the dualism in the *Rule of the Community* indicates, to many scholars, that Persian thought influenced the Jew (or Jews) who have given us this major document. The weighing of souls, as described in the *Testament of Abraham* 12, is influenced by the Egyptian *Book of the Dead*; the scene is distinct from the weighing of deeds (e.g., *1 Enoch* 41, *4 Ezra* 3, and *2 Enoch* 52), which derives most likely from Iranian thought.

Second, these diverse writings—from the conservative nature of *Jubilees* and Sirach to the liberal books of *Enoch* and the Wisdom of Solomon—are not distant from each other. They share commonalities. The authors share a memory of how YHWH has intervened on behalf of his chosen ones, promising the land to Abraham and giving it to his descendants. The Jews who composed the documents in our central focus, mutatis mutandis, felt they belonged to a group, Israel; they were one people. Except for some of the Qumranites and all the Samaritans, they also tended to confess a loyalty to the temple, shared a creed (the Shema), and praised YHWH for his revealed will—Torah.

Third, there was a shared appreciation of Scripture—usually Torah and Prophets. In these Scriptures one finds God's Word. This seems to be true even if Torah was basically defined and Prophets was not so well conceived.

Fourth, many Jews shared a passion for understanding the ineffable One. Our only pre-70 manuscripts are the Qumran scrolls, which include not only works composed at Qumran, like the composite *Rule of the Community*, but also other documents, composed elsewhere and known from the so-called Pseudepigrapha, notably *Jubilees* and most of the books of *Enoch*. In the Qumran scrolls, both the biblical books and others, we find the Tetragram-

---

19. M. Hengel has shown that Jews were aware of and influenced by Greek thought (*Judaism and Hellenism: Studies in Their Encounter During the Early Hellenistic Period* [Philadelphia: Fortress, 1974]), while D. Mendels claims "Greek culture did not have an impressive impact on Jewish historical literature" ("Jewish Historical Writings Between Judaism and Hellenism," in *Jüdische Schriften in ihrem antik-jüdischen und urchristlichen Kontext* [ed. H. Lichtenberger and G. S. Oegema; Gütersloh: Gütersloher Verlagshaus, 2002], 35). Mendels, one of the most erudite scholars of Hellenistic historiography, is correct, depending on the weight given to "impressive" and the fact that he is focusing on "historical literature."

maton written in Paleo-Hebrew script or represented by four dots. This practice for representing God's name placards the fact that the Name must not be pronounced, and that the Creator is not only ineffable but incomprehensible. God will be whatever God will be (Exod. 3:14).

Fifth, many Jews were united by a common pursuit: a search for how one can be faithful to a God who cannot be categorized as "known" and in a land that was promised to the Jews but is periodically and repeatedly possessed or conquered by Persians, Greeks, and Romans—infidels and idolaters.

Sixth, many Jews felt at a loss for truthful and revelatory answers. On the one hand, they were perplexed by reality and secular history. On the other hand, many Jews searched for answers apocalyptically; that is, they knew the present was not pregnant with answers. These were possible only in another world and from another, future, time.

Seventh, Jews—perhaps more and more of them—believed that the present struggle, which was both cosmic and centered in the human heart, was a common search. It was an attempt to find ways to believe in a Creator who is creating anew. The author of the *Rule of the Community* bequeathed to us a major insight: "He is creating the human for dominion of the world" (1QS III, 17–18). That belief was embedded within a conviction that Belial, Satan, now held dominion over history and perhaps creation.

These seven shared perspectives tended to unite the Palestinian Jew, even if the scholar should be leery of any putative "common Judaism." The unifying force of the seven insights may be couched in words shared with us by the author of Sirach:

The sand of the sea, the drops of rain,
And the days of eternity—who can count them? (1:2 NRSV)

It is in shared questions that we sometimes find what is common to Jews in Second Temple Judaism. The answers also led to a common conviction and hope, since Sirach continued with his musings to emphasize that there is only one "who is wise"—it is the Lord (1:8).

These insights make it obvious why not only the scholar but also the student who is interested in understanding and interpreting Scriptures must read and know the so-called apocryphal works. As Professor Craig A. Evans has shown in his many books, knowledge of the writings that were composed during the centuries that separate Hebrew Scriptures from Mishnah (or Old Testament from New Testament) is essential and fundamental.[20] Such knowledge supplies a fuller meaning of words; a comprehension of syntax; an understanding of concepts; a knowledge of history; a grasp of the historical, social, and religious context; a deepened comprehension of exegetical context; a more mature grasp of hermeneutical context; and an awareness of the canonical context.

What Is the Danger and Beauty of the Canon?

The danger of the canon is the tendency to imagine, even think, that God has spoken only in and through a closed book. The beauty of the canon is the guideline, the rule, for how, and in what ways, the One who has spoken in the past may be heard in other writings and persons, whether prophet, priest, or perplexed. The word *canon* should have been, and hopefully will now be, used as the measuring standard by which to discern God's Word in many other words.

Does One Hear God's Voice Only in a Canon?

For many scholars today the canon is what is important and the works not included in it are judged to be both noncanonical and inferior. Most of these scholars are Christians. Their criteria are clearly theological and not historical, even though they will claim that all good theology is informed by historical work. Other scholars will judge the works collected in the Pseudepigrapha as inferior to Torah and Talmud; these are Jewish scholars, and their criteria are likewise theological. With much of the funding in universities, seminaries, and Yeshivas coming from an established institution,

---

20. Notably, see C. A. Evans, *Ancient Texts for New Testament Studies: A Guide to the Background Literature* (Peabody, MA: Hendrickson, 2005), 3–6.

it is unlikely that the curriculum in major research universities will be free from prejudices in favor of the canon. The learned person, however, is free to recognize that God has spoken in documents beyond the writings selected for the canon.

The canon was never intended to be a barrier to the living Spirit or to imply that God had ceased speaking when God's book went to press. The shaping of the canon was more a process than a decision by a Jewish and then a Christian council.

The Bible, the Book of the People, has been bequeathed to Jews and Christians by the People of the Book. The canon (whether the Hebrew Scriptures or the Christian Bible) not only helps distinguish Jew from Christian. It also provides a position from which all may perceive that each can claim to be the People of the Book.

Conclusion

We have learned that the writings branded as "extracanonical" by post-Enlightenment critics were considered sacred by many early Jews—which include Jesus' earliest followers. We have also seen that these works were composed before there was a set or closed canon of Hebrew Scriptures. We have also recognized that the documents putatively outside the canon should not be categorized as inferior to those that were later canonized. Finally, we have learned that the writings ostensibly outside the canon help eradicate many misperceptions of Second Temple Judaism, and that these writings are replete with perspicacious perceptions, references to sin and the need for salvation, and a love and dedication to the one-and-only Creator, who is perceived to be creating anew.

I commend these Jewish masterpieces to you, as you venture out to explore the highways and byways of a canon being shaped by the needs of the People of the Book. For Jews, these writings help connect the Hebrew Scriptures with rabbinics, and ground the earliest Mishnaic tractates in a period long before Judah the Prince. For Christians, these writings generate a love and fondness for Jesus' Jewishness and the life and times of the one they call "Lord."

3

Torah, Torah, Torah

The Emergence of the Tripartite Canon

STEPHEN G. DEMPSTER

Introduction

The debate over the emergence of the Hebrew canon continues, as shown by the flurry of books and articles in scholarly journals. Views that had a virtual "canonical status" in the scholarly community have been decanonized, and a number of significant alternatives compete for canonization. *The Canon Debate* is an apt title for a recent book that examines this situation.[1] The view that held a consensus for over a century used the tripartite structure of the Hebrew Bible as the clue to its evolution. Herbert Ryle,

---

1. L. M. McDonald and J. A. Sanders, eds., *The Canon Debate* (Peabody, MA: Hendrickson, 2002). Regrettably the volume does not contain much debate on the Old Testament canon. It is unfortunate—due to factors outside the editors' control—that the main proponents of one side of the debate are conspicuously missing.

standing on the shoulders of others, argued persuasively that the Torah was canonized about 400 BCE, the Prophets in 200 BCE, and the Writings in 90 CE at a rabbinic council held in Jamnia. This conveniently explained a number of facts, e.g., the reason why Daniel was not placed in the Prophets. It was written too late and thus under the dictum of "once closed always closed" could not be inserted into the already-closed Prophetic division. Many of the underpinnings of this theory have collapsed. The "canonization" of the Writings at a council at Jamnia is but one example. Jack Lewis, in his own words, "an amateur, unpublished in either rabbinics or canon study," had accepted that the evidence for such a council was substantial. But the more he probed beneath the surface he began to discover "a consensus had formed by repetition of what was at first a tentative suggestion."[2] That suggestion, by Heinrich Graetz, was simply accepted by subsequent scholars until it became one of the assured results of modern scholarship and was perpetuated in Ryle's study, which simply asserted that it was common knowledge that a council of rabbis met at Jamnia around 90 CE.[3]

While Ryle's consensus has disappeared, a new one has not yet emerged.[4] Part of the problem is that very little concrete data is available until later times.[5] One scholar has remarked about the problems in reconstructing a history of the formation of the Hebrew Bible: "The gaps in our knowledge are so severe that all of us are driven to speculation and conjecture. Perhaps in our natural and important attempts to say something we all pretend to know more than the available evidence gives us a right to know."[6]

2. J. P. Lewis, "Jamnia Revisited," in McDonald and Sanders, *The Canon Debate*, 146–62, esp. 151.

3. Lewis, "Jamnia Revisited," 146–47.

4. Theoretically this is true, but practically, a slight modification of Ryle's view is held by a majority of scholars. See H. G. L. Peels, "The Blood 'from Abel to Zechariah' and the Canon of the Old Testament," *ZAW* 113 (2001): 583–601, esp. 583–87. The title of the recent volume by McDonald and Sanders (*The Canon Debate*) suggests that a new consensus has not yet emerged.

5. A point also emphasized by Peels ("Blood 'from Abel to Zechariah,'" 386): "The fact that research into the final phase of the formation of the Old Testament canon has led to such divergent insights is somewhat disappointing but not surprising in view of the limited number of external textual witnesses and their nature."

6. E. Kalin, "How Did the Canon Come to Us? A Response to the Leiman Hypothesis," *CTM* 4 (1977): 47–52, esp. 52.

With this warning in mind, the following modest contribution to the origin of the Hebrew Bible specifically considers the emergence of its tripartite structure.[7] This is important for it represents something of a flashpoint for the emergence of the canon. On one side of the debate, many scholars largely accept the main lines of Ryle's thesis for the first two canonical divisions, with some nuances, but push the closing of a third division forward into the second or even third centuries CE.[8] In support of this view, it is sometimes argued that the third division has far more links with Jewish concerns of the first few centuries of the Common Era.[9] On the other side of the debate, a significant minority of scholars argue that the tripartite canon emerged much earlier, during the time of the Maccabees at the latest.[10] To borrow a term from the

7. Consequently this study represents a further development of earlier studies. See S. G. Dempster, "An Extraordinary Fact: Torah and Temple and the Contours of the Hebrew Canon," *Tyndale Bulletin* 48 (1997): 23–53, 191–218; idem, "From Many Texts to One: The Formation of the Hebrew Bible," in *The World of the Arameans: Biblical, Historical and Cultural Studies in Honour of Paul-Eugène Dion* (ed. P. M. Michele Daviau and M. Weigl; Sheffield: Sheffield Academic Press, 2001), 19–56.

8. L. M. McDonald, *The Formation of the Christian Biblical Canon* (rev. ed.; Peabody, MA: Hendrickson, 1995); J. A. Sanders, "Canon: Hebrew Bible," *ABD* 1:837–52; idem, "Spinning the Bible," *BRev* 14 (1998): 23–29, 44–45; E. Ulrich, "The Bible in the Making: The Scriptures at Qumran," in *The Community of the Renewed Covenant* (ed. E. Ulrich and J. VanderKam; Notre Dame, IN: University of Notre Dame Press, 1994), 77–93; J. Barton, *The Oracles of God: Perceptions of Ancient Prophecy in Israel after the Exile* (London: Darton, Longman and Todd, 1986). To be sure there are variations here. Barton, for example, believes that the prophetic collection remained open and included material from the Writings; the one collection was divided later.

9. Sanders, "Spinning the Bible"; see also the tradition-history movement associated with H. Gese and P. Stuhlmacher, who argue for one tradition history that unites the Old Testament with the New. The Masoretic canon, with its conclusion in the Writings, interrupts this historical progression. For an evaluation see C. R. Seitz, "Two Testaments and the Failure of One Tradition-History," in *Biblical Theology: Retrospect and Prospect* (ed. S. Hafemann; Downers Grove, IL: InterVarsity, 2001), 195–211.

10. S. Z. Leiman, *The Canonization of the Hebrew Scripture: The Talmudic and Midrashic Evidence* (Hamden, CT: Archon, 1974); R. Beckwith, *The Old Testament Canon of the New Testament Church* (Grand Rapids: Eerdmans, 1985); E. E. Ellis, *The Old Testament in Early Christianity: Canon and Interpretation in the Light of Modern Research* (Grand Rapids: Baker Academic, 1992); A. van der Kooij, "The Canonization of Ancient Books Kept in the Temple of Jerusalem," in *Canonization and Decanonization: Papers Presented to the International Conference of the Leiden Institute for the Study of Religions Held at Leiden 9–10 January 1997* (ed. A. van der Kooij and K. van der Toorn; Leiden: Brill, 1998), 17–40. See also D. N. Freedman, *The Unity of the Hebrew Bible* (Ann Arbor:

study of the history of Israel, one might call the first group mini-malists and the second group maximalists.[11]

Minimalists claim that their counterparts maximize the later understanding of the rabbinic canon and read it back into the pre-Christian evidence. This is the major criticism of Roger Beckwith's massive study, which has at times been called virtually a funda-mentalist tract.[12] Eugene Ulrich criticizes Elisha Qimron and John Strugnell for a footnote in DJD X that suggests a reference to David in 4QMMT may represent a third canonical division known as the Hagiographa.[13] Such an interpretation, says Ulrich, is nothing but the reflex of "a Kantian category of a tripartite rabbinic canon fixed in our minds and familiar for the past fifteen hundred years," so much so that our "interpretive categories . . . tend to see a tripartite canon in antiquity, whenever any small clue emerges."[14]

On the other hand, maximalists claim that minimalists mini-mize the importance of tradition (for example, Josephus's plain statement about the canon)[15] and the evidence found in such places

---

University of Michigan Press, 1991). F. M. Cross takes more of a mediating position arguing that the canon was fixed toward the end of the first century CE as part of the movement in which the Hillel party ascended among the Pharisees. Consequently the fixation of text and canon "were thus two aspects of a single, complex endeavor" ("The Text behind the Text of the Hebrew Bible," in *Approaches to the Bible: Composition, Transmission and Language* [ed. H. Minkoff; Washington, DC: Biblical Archaeology Society, 1994], 148–61, esp. 160; see also *From Epic to Canon: History and Literature in Ancient Israel* [Baltimore: Johns Hopkins University Press, 1998]).

11. I do not intend any pejorative implications by the use of these terms. For their uti-lization in the historical study of ancient Israel, see I. W. Provan, "Ideologies, Literary and Critical: Reflections on Recent Writing on the History of Israel," *JBL* 114 (1995): 585–606; P. R. Davies, "Method and Madness: Some Remarks on Doing History with the Bible," *JBL* 114 (1995): 699–705.

12. See, e.g., John Barton's review in *Theology* 90 (1987): 63–65.

13. E. Qimron and J. Strugnell, *Qumran Cave 4.V: Miqsat Ma'ase Ha-Torah* (DJD X; Oxford: Clarendon, 1994), 59n10. But it should be noted that Qimron and Strugnell also are much more cautious than they are given credit for (see pp. 111–12).

14. E. Ulrich, "The Non-attestation of a Tripartite Canon in 4QMMT," *CBQ* 65 (2003): 202–14. Note also J. A. Sanders's criticism of those who "try to superimpose the old view on the new evidence" ironically with the new evidence of 4QMMT ("The Issue of Closure in the Canonical Process," in McDonald and Sanders, *Canon Debate*, 252–63, esp. 253).

15. Note Steve Mason's critique of John Barton's claim that Josephus is not limiting the collection of books in the Jewish canon to the books he has mentioned in *Against Apion*: "Barton strains Josephus's words beyond tolerance . . ." ("Josephus and His Twenty-Two

as the prologue to Ben Sira. Earle Ellis writes about the apparent tripartite references in this text,

> The statement . . . mentions each of the three divisions with the same degree of preciseness and, to be meaningful to the reader, it must refer to definite, identifiable books. It could be interpreted otherwise only if one were already convinced that the tripartite canon could not have existed as a subsistent entity at this time. The same applies to the epistle from Qumran (c. 150 BCE).[16]

Apparently Kantian categories can work both ways.[17]

The following study will consider internal evidence within the Bible itself and then external evidence up to the end of the second century CE.

Internal Evidence: Canonical Consciousness in the Biblical Period

James Barr has made the point probably more forcefully than others that

> The men of the Bible were, as we now see it, engaged in the process out of which our Bible in the end would emerge, but they themselves had no Bible: at that time, clearly, the Bible as we know it was not yet there. A scripture in the sense of an already existing defined and delimited, written guide for the religion did not yet exist. In

---

Book Canon," in McDonald and Sanders, *Canon Debate*, 126n55; see Barton, *Oracles of God*, 59).

16. Ellis, *Old Testament in Early Christianity*, 39–40.

17. Another example of how subtly anachronism can influence study is the imposition of a later definition of canon on early evidence. Thus there is a demand for a closed list of books, which of course cannot be found in the early period (except in Josephus). This leads to the predictable conclusion that no such canon existed. Consequently a conceptual wedge is driven between an authoritative collection of books (later definition of canon) and a collection of authoritative books. Note particularly E. Ulrich's use of later definitions of canon: "The Notion and Definition of Canon," in McDonald and Sanders, *Canon Debate*, 21–35. See the pertinent criticisms by A. Steinmann, *The Oracles of God* (St. Louis: Concordia Academic Press, 1999), 184. While not perfect, G. T. Sheppard's distinction between "canon 1" and "canon 2" still provides helpful terminology for describing the differences and similarities between these two types of literature ("Canon," *ER* 3:62–69).

the time of (say) the prophet Isaiah there was as yet no scripture, and he never speaks of there being one.[18]

Barr expands on his statement by claiming that the Protestant heirs of the Reformation with their emphases on Scripture and canon have unconsciously retrojected their beliefs on the people of biblical times.[19] While it is no doubt true that the people of ancient Israel did not have a closed canon of authoritative writings, and that the heirs of the Reformation understood the Bible in a way that distorted some of the evidence, Barr overstates his case. His view would be totally incomprehensible to, say, the author of Psalms 19 and 119. The authors are consumed with the meditation of the Torah so much so that it is the preoccupation of their entire existence, the *'aleph* to *taw* of human life. Similarly much of Isaiah would be inexplicable without assuming a significant body of authoritative literature. While Judaism has often been denigrated as the religion of the People of the Book, it seems that it came by this name honestly.

The idea of revelation as a word from God to communicate with humanity was a fundamental presupposition of Israel's existence. There were essentially three media of revelation: Torah, prophecy, and wisdom.[20] Jeremiah's enemies believed that it would be no great loss to eliminate him since the stream of revelation would not be impaired: "Torah will not perish from the priest, or advice from the wise, or a word from the prophet" (Jer. 18:18). A similar passage appears in a judgment speech in the book of Ezekiel: the people will desperately seek "a vision from a prophet, and torah will perish from a priest and advice from the elders" (Ezek. 7:26).

In the biblical tradition, the Torah and prophets represented essentially words from above—transcendent revelation. Torah came to be associated with Moses, who was regarded as the ultimate

---

18. J. Barr, *Holy Scripture: Canon, Authority, Criticism* (Philadelphia: Westminster, 1983), 1.

19. Barr, *Holy Scripture*, 4.

20. For further development of this idea see M. Margolis, *The Hebrew Scriptures in the Making* (Philadelphia: Jewish Publication Society, 1922). For a heuristic use of this tripartite formulation for the educational field see W. Brueggemann, *The Creative Word: Canon as a Model for Biblical Education* (Philadelphia: Fortress, 1982).

prophet.[21] Priests interpreted the relevance of this Torah for the people. The Word was associated with prophets, and it was regarded as in harmony with the Torah and based upon it. But thirdly, wisdom was more of a human word from below—immanent revelation. For example, the difference between prophecy and wisdom can be seen in the way problems were solved. In trying to determine a new king to replace Saul when David's brothers were paraded before Samuel, the prophet heard a voice in his head saying, "Not this one—but this one."[22] When Solomon sought to determine the correct mother of a child, he asked for a sword.[23] He then heard the voice of God in the cry of the true mother. This type of revelation came to be associated with the sage, who had the powers of observation and insight.

When the Ten Words (or Commandments) were given at Sinai—a fundamental fact of the early Israelite nationhood—they were clearly regarded as sacral and ultimately authoritative.[24] As Lee McDonald remarks, "In a very real sense, Israel had a canon when the tradition of Moses receiving the Torah on Sinai was accepted into the community."[25] In their literary location within the Exodus account, the Ten Words were given hermeneutical prominence as the very words of God and were to be placed in a holy receptacle—none other than the ark of the covenant.[26] These Words merit virtual duplication at the end of the Pentateuch.[27] The sanctity of such a document was clearly underscored. Secondly, the ancient "book of the covenant," a document that regulated Israel's legal

---

21. For some of the complexity of nuance for this term, see J. Jenson, *The Use of Tôrâ by Isaiah: His Debate with the Wisdom Tradition* (Washington, DC: Catholic Biblical Association of America, 1973). I would like to thank my student, H. J. Kim, for bringing this study to my attention.

22. 1 Sam. 16:6–12.

23. 1 Kings 3:16–28.

24. Exod. 20:1–18; Deut. 5:6–22.

25. McDonald, *Formation of the Christian Biblical Canon*, 20. Ulrich criticizes McDonald's confusing terminology here since it seems to collapse authority with canonicity, but to make too sharp a distinction between the two can also cause confusion. The concept of canonicity can become effectively meaningless, simply the result of a rather arbitrary decision. See Ulrich, "Notion and Definition of Canon," in McDonald and Sanders, *Canon Debate*, 34.

26. Exod. 25:16.

27. Deut. 5:6–21.

and moral life, was a text Israel literally bound itself in blood to perform according to the ancient ritual in Exodus 24.[28] Many of the laws of Israel's constitution were undoubtedly ancient and would have had binding authority on the people. In fact the Sinai revelation is the hermeneutical center of the Pentateuch, traversing three books.[29] The figure of Moses as an unparalleled prophet is clearly linked to these traditions.[30]

Many of these written traditions would have been placed in holy sites superintended by priests. When Joshua renewed the covenant, he wrote a record of its regulations in the book of the Torah of God; this record is associated with a holy sanctuary since he erected a stone of witness to the covenant and raised it up near an oak tree by the sanctuary of the Lord.[31] Similarly, Samuel wrote a law about kingship after Saul was installed as a leader; it was placed "before Yahweh"—a reference to a type of sanctuary.[32] When the temple was erected during Solomon's period, it undoubtedly had an archive for these writings, regarded as divine law. In fact after a time of national apostasy, it was no accident that a book of the law was found in the temple by a priest.[33] The reaction to the reading of the book by King Josiah—the tearing of his garments before words of probable judgment for covenant violation—whatever else can be said about this action, it clearly betrays a powerful canon-consciousness.[34]

The binding authority of divine law in large part explains the message of the prophets, preserved in the historical records from Joshua to Kings.[35] It is true that they were regarded as divine messengers, but they did not appear in a vacuum. When Nathan challenged royalty with the words "You are the man!" it was because of the divine authority behind "You shall not kill."[36] Similarly, when

---

28. Exod. 24:1–8.

29. Exod. 19:1–Num. 10:11.

30. Exod. 3–6; 19–24; 32–34; Num. 12:1–8; Deut. 18:15–22; 34:10–12.

31. Josh. 24:25–26.

32. 1 Sam. 10:25.

33. 2 Kings 22:8.

34. 2 Kings 22:11–20.

35. A point observed by many scholars, notably W. Zimmerli, *The Law and the Prophets: A Study of the Meaning of the Old Testament* (New York: Harper & Row, 1965).

36. 2 Sam. 12:1–12, esp. v. 9. See Zimmerli, *Law and the Prophets*, 63.

Elijah slew the prophets of Baal, he was acting on the basis of an early law in Exodus that condemned Israelite idolaters.[37]

When the "written" prophets appeared, those whose words were later preserved in collections, many of their words assume a norm has been violated. Hosea's condemnation of Israel in his first re-corded oracles reads like a litany of violations of the Ten Words.[38] Amos charges the nations with crimes against an unwritten norm of human decency common to humanity,[39] but he charges Judah with rejecting the Torah and statutes of Yahweh,[40] and Israel for specific violations of the same.[41] Although prophets who directed their attention to the southern kingdom worked with somewhat different traditions, certainly Isaiah and Micah focused on Judah's failure to exercise justice and righteousness, which was the heart of the Sinai law.[42] In fact, in 2 Kings, the prophets virtually speak col-lectively in harmony with the Torah: Yahweh bore witness against Israel and Judah through his servants the prophets, "Turn from your evil ways, keep my commandments and my statutes accord-ing to all the Torah which I commanded your fathers and which I sent to you through my servants the prophets."[43]

There is a paucity of knowledge regarding the why and how of the collection, preservation, and textualization of the Latter Prophets' words. It was probably not only because of the success of their ominous predictions, and their poignant descriptions of Israelite identity, but because they were regarded as speaking divine

---

37. 1 Kings 18:40; Exod. 22:19 (22:20 Eng.); cf. Zimmerli, *Law and the Prophets*, 68.

38. Hos. 4:2.

39. Amos 1:3–2:3. There are some scholars who suggest that a "covenant of brother-hood" mentioned in 1:9 referred to a pact between Israel and Tyre made during Solomon's reign which had been recently violated. This may explain the condemnation of Tyre, but it hardly explains the judgment speeches against the rest of the nations.

40. Amos 2:4–5.

41. E.g., Amos 2:8; cf. Exod. 22:25–26 (22:26–27 Eng.). "While scholars have disputed what precise actions were envisaged in the examples of exploitation listed by Amos, it is clear that the prophet was not introducing new ideas but formally indicting Israel for particular actions that fall under the rulings on humaneness and righteousness found in the Book of the Covenant" (A. Phillips, "Prophecy and Law," in *Israel's Prophetic Tradi-tion: Essays in Honour of Peter Ackroyd* [ed. R. Coggins et al.; Cambridge: Cambridge University Press, 1982], 217–32, esp. 220).

42. Isa. 5:1–21; Mic. 6:1–8.

43. 2 Kings 17:13.

words that also offered a future hope. Isaiah urges that his words be preserved as a witness to future generations.[44] Jeremiah's words and their "canonical" authority are vividly captured in the story of a scroll of his oracles being read to Josiah's son. This time the king rips up the prophetic scroll, in direct contrast to his father's response to the book of the Torah.[45] The difference is glaring and does not bode well for the nation. The assumption in this text is that the reading of the prophetic scroll should have made the king rip his garments in repentance, as his father did at the reading of the Torah scroll.[46] Jeremiah then produces another scroll as a replacement to which more oracles are added.[47] This represented an early form of the prophetic book. Such books were probably transmitted and preserved by disciples or followers of the prophets.

In addition to Torah and prophets there is evidence for a third stream of revelation—wisdom. When wisdom makes its first major appearance in the Bible, it is associated with Joseph, who is able to interpret dreams,[48] then with Bezalel, who is responsible for the construction of the tabernacle—the place of worship.[49] David and especially Solomon are conspicuously associated with wisdom, David certainly with music and worship and Solomon with wisdom as a guide to life.[50] Solomon was virtually an apotheosis of wisdom; his superior wisdom became world renowned, and he produced thousands of proverbs and a thousand songs.[51] Musical compositions and prayers addressed to God as well as proverbs and wise sayings were collected and transcribed. These were voices that tried to make sense out of life with a word from below and directed that word not only to humans but back to God. From incidental references, it can be determined that these texts would have been transmitted in the temple and in the royal court. Psalms,

44. Isa. 8:16–21; 30:8.

45. Jer. 36:21–25.

46. A. Dearman has noted the similarities and differences between 2 Kings 22 and Jer. 36 ("My Servants the Scribes: Composition and Context in Jeremiah 36," *JBL* 109 [1990]: 403–21).

47. Jer. 36:32.

48. Gen. 41:39.

49. Exod. 31:3.

50. 2 Sam. 14:20; 1 Kings 3; 5:9–26 (4:29–5:12 Eng.); Prov. 1:1; 10:1; 25:1.

51. 1 Kings 5:9–14 (4:29–34 Eng.).

for example, demanded a liturgical setting, and there is a reference to a section of Solomonic proverbs being transcribed by the scribes of Hezekiah.[52]

It was the crisis of the exile and beyond that probably caused all of these authoritative words to be brought together from the temple, the court, and the prophetic circles.[53] The Pentateuch was beginning to assume a final form, and the so-called Deuteronomistic History was receiving its final redaction. Freedman has argued that both were united to form a record from creation to the exile that served as an explanation of all that went wrong.[54] At the same time, collections of prophetic oracles were redacted and superscriptions were added to them. These editorial additions bore witness to a powerful canonical consciousness. As Gene Tucker remarks,

> The specific intentions of the prophetic superscriptions are reflected above all in the particular vocabulary used to classify the books. The basic concern behind this language is the theological problem of authority and revelation. Thus the fundamental intention of the superscriptions is to identify the prophetic books as the word of God.[55]

The prophetic collections were probably preserved and redacted by the same circles responsible for the books included in the Deuteronomistic History.[56]

Texts representing a third stream needed also to be brought into the picture. The exilic and postexilic communities were faced with

52. Prov. 25:1.

53. For the significance of the exile, see P. R. Ackroyd, *Exile and Restoration: A Study of Hebrew Thought of the Sixth Century* (Philadelphia: Westminster, 1968); D. E. Gowan, *The Theology of the Prophetic Books: The Death and Resurrection of Israel* (Louisville: Westminster/John Knox, 1998); J. M. Scott, ed., *Exile: Old Testament, Jewish and Christian Conceptions* (Leiden: Brill, 1997).

54. D. N. Freedman, "The Earliest Bible," in *Backgrounds for the Bible* (ed. M. P. O'Connor and D. N. Freedman; Winona Lake, IN: Eisenbrauns, 1987), 29–38.

55. G. Tucker, "Prophetic Superscriptions and the Growth of the Canon," in *Canon and Authority: Essays in Old Testament Religion and Theology* (ed. G. W. Coates and B. O. Long; Philadelphia: Fortress, 1977), 56–70, esp. 68.

56. Not only are there similar stylistic features, but there are shared texts: Isa. 36–39 = 2 Kings 18–20; Jer. 40:7–9 = 2 Kings 25:23–26; Jer. 52:1–27 = 2 Kings 24:18–25:21; Jer. 52:31–34 = 2 Kings 25:27–30. For further description and implications, see B. S. Childs, *Introduction to the Old Testament as Scripture* (Philadelphia: Fortress, 1979), 236–37.

a problem. How do we present and preserve the diversity of this material as the unified word from God to us? How do we organize and combine this diverse literature, which explains our present plight, our future hope, and how to live in the meantime?

Clearly there were great collections of material for which sequence was important, and editors worked on individual books. Brevard Childs and James Sanders have called attention to the canonical shape of biblical books, and the tradents responsible for transmitting, updating, and adapting the literature. Childs in particular has written of these individuals who have obscured their tracks, thereby directing attention to the sacred writings themselves.[57] But what of the larger shape of entire collections of Scripture? And was the entire collection simply the result of haphazard growth and arbitrary decisions? My own analysis of the internal evidence indicates that imposed upon the whole was a shape that stressed the ultimate authority of law, the future hope of eschatology, and the practical importance of human response in the present. The material was structured in such a way as to emphasize in particular the Torah as the central fact of life and the importance of developing a Torah mind through meditation on it day and night.

A number of scholars have studied the global shape of the Hebrew Bible and detected substantial evidence for larger canonical redactions, which join these streams of revelation into one channel—an integrated whole.[58] At distinct points in the Hebrew Bible there are remarkable intertextual phenomena. They signal the importance of great collections of Scripture and the splicing together of these collections into an integrated unity, and either function to terminate or initiate these collections. At the beginning of the text, the Word of God is highlighted as the means by which creation comes into being, light shines, and the rhythm of day and

57. Childs, *Introduction to the Old Testament as Scripture*, 59: "The shape of the canon directs the reader's attention to the sacred writings rather than to their editors."

58. J. Blenkinsopp, *Prophecy and Canon: A Contribution to the Study of Jewish Origins* (Notre Dame, IN: University of Notre Dame Press, 1977); O. H. Steck, "Der Kanon des hebraischen Alten Testament," in *Vernunft und Glauben* (ed. J. Rohls; Gottingen: Vandenhoeck & Ruprecht, 1988), 231–52; E. Zenger, *Das Erste Testament: Die Jüdische Bibel und die Christen* (Düsseldorf: Patmos Verlag, 1991); J. Sailhamer, *Introduction to Old Testament Theology: A Canonical Approach* (Grand Rapids: Zondervan, 1995); Dempster, "Extraordinary Fact."

night is established.[59] This word, of course, becomes transcribed into Torah by the great Moses, and becomes the means by which Israelite life is regulated; even in Deuteronomy the king is required to write a copy of the Torah and read it all the days of his life.[60] At the end of the Torah, Moses's death is depicted as bringing to an end an era in the history of Israel.[61] His death is unique in that he died in full possession of his vital powers, and the place of his grave remains unknown "to this day."[62] As for Moses himself, his death is also regarded as the end of an era of prophecy, "for no prophet ever has arisen like him whom God knew face-to-face and through whom such salvation was wrought."[63] This mention of the incomparability of Moses functions not only on a historical level but also on a textual level to distinguish the collection of literature associated with Moses—the five books of the Torah—and thus the importance of ethics, but also it directly alludes to another collection of literature that highlights eschatology. For the mention of a prophet not yet arisen alludes to Deuteronomy 18, which mentions that God would raise up a prophet like Moses to communicate his will to the Israelites.[64] This seems to refer to a succession of prophets. Deuteronomy 34 reflects on a long history of prophets that have come and gone but have not measured up to the Mosaic stature. This points ahead to the next collection of Scripture, in which prophets will be emphasized—prophets who are made in the Mosaic image but do not measure up to his lofty status.

At the beginning of the next major collection of Scriptures, Joshua is told to lead the people into the land and meditate on the Torah day and night, and so make his way prosperous and successful.[65] Here this new collection of Scripture is oriented at the beginning to the Torah and the importance of its guidance for success in the way.[66] Joshua is to be a person of the book. In fact it

59. Gen. 1:1–5.
60. Deut. 17:14–20.
61. Deut. 34:1–12.
62. Deut. 34:6–7.
63. Deut. 34:10–12.
64. Deut. 18:18.
65. Josh. 1:7–9.
66. Read in its immediate context, these texts suggest that the Torah is Deuteronomy (cf. Deut. 29:10 [29:9 Eng.]; 30:10; 31:26) but in the larger context of the canon it

is not to depart from his mouth, which means that it will inform his mind continually. Joshua himself is viewed as the successor to Moses, but his success depends on meditating on the Torah day and night like the ideal Deuteronomic king.[67] He obtains success because he follows the book of Moses—the Torah—and his kingly successors largely fail because the Mosaic law is even lost, to be found only when it is too late to turn back the tide of coming judgment.[68] Josiah, the king without parallel, can only be helped personally by Moses, the prophet without parallel.[69]

Joshua himself is followed not only by political leaders but also by the sporadic and conspicuous appearances of prophets: various anonymous individuals who make predictions,[70] Deborah,[71] Samuel,[72] Nathan,[73] Ahijah,[74] Elijah[75] and Elisha,[76] and Huldah.[77] These are followed by four collections of oracles that thematize the prophetic element: Isaiah, Jeremiah, Ezekiel, and the Twelve. Probably none of these prophets is patterned after Moses more than Jeremiah: the divine word is placed directly in his mouth in accordance with Deuteronomy 18:18.[78] Yet in the historical narrative Elijah probably most represents Moses in that he also appears on Mount Horeb to bear witness to a divine revelation. Elijah, however, does not see the divine form since his head is covered. Consequently God does not know him face to face.[79]

---

is much more than that. Deuteronomy has become more like a theological nucleus and summation of the entire Pentateuch (cf. Ps. 1:1–2; Neh. 8:1). Note in the final redaction of Joshua that "the Mosaic law is everywhere intended. . . . Law as encompassed in the entire Pentateuch is assumed as normative" (Childs, *Introduction to the Old Testament as Scripture*, 246–47).

67. Deut. 17:14–20.
68. 2 Kings 22:8–20.
69. 2 Kings 23:25; cf. Deut. 34:10–12.
70. Judg. 2:1; 6:11; 13:3; 1 Sam. 2:27; 1 Kings 13:1.
71. Judg. 4:4.
72. 1 Sam. 3.
73. 2 Sam. 12.
74. 1 Kings 11:29.
75. 1 Kings 17.
76. 1 Kings 19:19.
77. 2 Kings 22:14.
78. Jer. 1:9.
79. 1 Kings 19:13; cf. Exod. 33:22.

The Prophetic collection concludes with the Twelve, the last prophet of which is Malachi. His series of oracles is concluded with two appendices that differ in style and change his focus:

> Remember the Torah of Moses my servant whom I commanded at Horeb concerning Israel with respect to the statutes and judgements.
> Look I am sending Elijah the prophet before that great and terrible day. He will turn the hearts of the fathers to their sons and the hearts of sons to their fathers before I come and declare a Holy War on the earth.[80]

These two passages join together Moses and Elijah, representing Torah and prophecy, pointing backwards to ethics (Torah) and forward to eschatology (prophecy). Read in combination with the conclusion of Deuteronomy, the uniqueness of Torah is stressed as well as the validity of prophecy and the hope for a prophet like Moses who will finally measure up to the Mosaic stature. As Childs observes, these two texts ensure that "the law and prophets are not rivals but complements" and balance "the memory of the past with the anticipation of the future."[81]

What about the remaining books, the wisdom and worship material? The obvious book to begin with to continue the pattern, with the focus on the Torah, is the Psalter. Not only is it patterned after the Torah in five-fold manner, but it begins with two untitled psalms that connect it explicitly to the Torah in the same way that Joshua was linked to the Torah. The initial two psalms speak of the importance of meditation. A blessing is pronounced over the individual who meditates on the Torah day and night. That person walks in the way of the righteous, and everything he does shall prosper.[82] Likewise the nations are implicitly urged not to meditate on vanity, but to be wise and consider the decree of the Lord, which

---

80. Mal. 3:22–24 (4:4–6 Eng.).

81. B. S. Childs, "The Canonical Shape of the Prophetic Literature," in *Interpreting the Prophets* (ed. J. L. Mays and P. J. Achtemeier; Philadelphia: Fortress, 1987), 41–49, esp. 46. Although Childs sees this appendix as applying primarily to the book of Malachi, this statement could easily be made as a conclusion to the entire prophetic corpus.

82. Ps. 1:2–3.

highlights the Israelite king as God's son.[83] The first psalm connects this new division to the importance of meditation on the Torah, and the second psalm emphasizes the importance of meditation on the Prophets, which often focused on the importance of the Davidic king. Consequently a messianic note is struck here.[84] It is not without interest that this psalm contains the only text in the Hebrew Bible in which the terms *messiah*, *king*, and *son* all coincide, and this at a time when there was no Davidic ruler on the throne.[85]

These two texts then function to introduce the next major collection of Scripture and link it to previous sections by highlighting the importance of Torah study.[86] The remaining writings consist of wisdom literature, some lamentations, apocalyptic and historical narrative—more a potpourri of genres. It is interesting that the three Hebrew books in which the divine name is absent occur in this section (Ecclesiastes, Esther, Song of Solomon). Here is a word from below. But is there any evidence of redaction at the end of this section in the same way that could organize this varied literature into an integrated unity? Freedman argues that the reference to "good" in Nehemiah's concluding prayer makes a link with the resounding emphasis on "good" in Genesis 1.[87] But the word means something quite different in each context. He further argues that the repetition of the last few lines of 2 Chronicles at the beginning of Ezra is evidence of these books having been separated "and thus calling attention to the place at which the narrative was interrupted."[88]

---

83. Ps. 2:2, 7, 10.

84. These texts function to link the next collection of Scripture to the previous two.

85. The lack of a Davidic ruler refers to the time of the final redaction of the Psalter when this psalm was placed as its introduction.

86. J. C. Trebolle Barrera ("Origins of a Tripartite Canon," in McDonald and Sanders, *Canon Debate*, 134) is one of the first scholars working in the area of canonical history of the text who has tried to use this evidence noted by literary scholars in his own study of canon formation. He uses the term "concatenatio" or "concatenation" to describe this editorial phenomenon, and he states that "the final editors of these books were aware that Moses, Elijah and David, or 'the law, the prophets, and psalms' formed an interrelated whole." However, he does not seem persuaded by the literary implications of connecting Ps. 1 with Josh. 1. Just as the latter introduced a larger collection of Scripture, the same would be expected for the former. Moreover why would "David" have to cease with the Psalms? There is much material here that is oriented to David—certainly the wisdom literature, Ruth, and Chronicles.

87. Neh. 13:31. See Freedman, *Unity of the Hebrew Bible*, 93.

88. Freedman, *Unity of the Hebrew Bible*, 83.

This explains the position of Chronicles at the beginning of the Writings in some of the best medieval manuscripts, which according to him probably preserve an original order.[89]

Freedman's explanation for the addition of the initial paragraph of Ezra to the ending of Chronicles is logical. Why would it be necessary to end Chronicles with a partial introduction of the next book in a canonical sequence?[90] There would be no need unless there was an interruption of that order. But Freedman's placement of Chronicles at the beginning of this section would vitiate the verbal repetition that links Joshua 1 and Psalm 1. However, if Chronicles was placed at the end of the third division, it would also explain the "superfluous addition."[91] The partial nature of the addition also becomes more significant. It ends midway through Cyrus's edict ("Who among you from all his people, whose God is Yahweh—let him go up!") with a call for the exiles to go up to Jerusalem to build the temple. If Chronicles is read with the endings of the Torah and the Prophets, perhaps there is a wish for someone in particular—the prophet like Moses—to go up, or the Davidic descendant to build the temple. This would jack up the eschatological temperature since Chronicles now concludes with a reference to Jeremiah's seventy years, the decree of Cyrus, and the focus on the temple. These were all important concerns of the Maccabean period.[92]

By ending the third division with Chronicles, there is a symmetry given to the entire collection as well. Jerome referred to Chronicles

89. See also S. Talmon, "Ezra-Nehemiah," *IDBSup* 317–28, esp. 318. For the hermeneutical significance of such a move, see J. Sanders, "Canon: Hebrew Bible," 846.

90. M. Haran ("Book Size and the Device of 'Catch-Lines' in the Biblical Canon," *JJS* 36 [1985]: 1–11) believes that it is explained by the principle of "catch lines," one book ending with the same words with which the next book begins. But there are no clear examples in the Hebrew Bible.

91. In the following conclusions I largely follow John Sailhamer's insightful analysis: "Biblical Theology and the Composition of the Hebrew Bible," in Hafemann, *Biblical Theology*, 34–36.

92. G. Steins's exhaustive examination of Chronicles concludes that it was specifically written to close the canon during the Maccabean period (*Die Chronik als kanonisches Abschlussphänomen* [BBB 93; Weinheim: Beltz Athenäum Verlag, 1995]). However, there is a significant difference between, on the one hand, some of Chronicles' content concerning the Maccabean period being reflected in an addition to the text that facilitates a change in sequence, and on the other hand, Steins's arguments for the production of the entire book as a conclusion to the canon. Stronger arguments are needed for his position.

as a "chronicle of the whole divine history,"[93] and as such it might have been especially suited to close the canon.

In conclusion, internal evidence suggests the organization of diverse Israelite sacred writings into an integrated unity that indicated the primacy of the Torah, but also the importance of an eschatological impulse and practical concerns. The fact that Torah *study* is important may also indicate the influence of wisdom. When in fact this organization happened is uncertain, but it probably started in the exilic period, when these diverse collections of authoritative writings were brought together and linked literarily. The Torah and Prophets probably received a final redaction in the postexilic period, while the final redaction of the third division happened later. How much later? At least by the time of the addition of the beginning of Ezra to the end of Chronicles.[94]

Now the question of the external evidence needs to be considered. What kind of evidence is there for a tripartite canon?

External Evidence: Canonical Consciousness in the Extra-Biblical Period

Terminology: One-Part and Two-Part Designations

It is clear that throughout intertestamental Judaism and beyond, the Scriptures of Israel could be designated as a totality by a comprehensive title (one-part designation). Such titles[95] are varied and include, for example, the Law,[96] the Holy Writings,[97] the Writings,[98] the Holy Books,[99] and the Book of God.[100]

---

93. Jerome, *Prologus Galeatus.*

94. Zenger (*Das Erste Testament*, 175) points out the relevance of this conclusion in the aftermath of the destruction of the Second Temple in the latter part of the first century CE.

95. For a more comprehensive listing see Beckwith, *Old Testament Canon*, 105–9.

96. 1 Macc. 2:50, 64 (this reference includes material that mostly occurs outside the Torah: Joshua, Caleb, David, Elijah, and Daniel [2:52–60]); Luke 16:16; John 10:34; 12:34; Rom. 3:19; 1 Cor. 14:34.

97. Josephus, *Against Apion* 1.10; cf. Rom. 1:2.

98. Luke 24:45; 1 Cor. 15:3.

99. 1 Macc. 12:9.

100. Philo, *That the Worse Attacks the Better* 139.

In a number of texts dating from the early second century BCE there are scattered references to a bipartite collection of authoritative Scriptures. In two texts, one written toward the beginning of the century (Tobit) and one a little later (Baruch), there are references to two divisions: the Law and the Prophets. Although they are not mentioned together as a name for the Scriptures of Israel,[101] it is clear that they were regarded as divinely authoritative. In Tobit, the Law of Moses is explicitly mentioned,[102] as well as a number of specific prophets.[103] Toward the end of the book, however, there is mention of the prophets collectively. The dying Tobit warns Tobiah of the coming judgment of Nineveh as announced by a prophet.[104] But beyond the judgment, he is reminded that there is eschatological hope as God will restore his people once more and the temple will be rebuilt "just as the prophets of Israel spoke."[105] Tobiah is urged therefore to leave Nineveh because of the coming judgment and wait in hope, being sure to keep "the law and the commandments."[106] Consequently, in Tobit the Torah functions as a guide for ethics and the prophets for eschatology. These are two sources of sacred authority.

Similarly in Baruch, written a little later than Tobit, it is clear that there are two divisions of sacred writings, which the people of Judah have failed to heed. Confession is offered because the people "did not listen to the voice of the Lord our God to walk in the statutes of the Lord"[107] and thereby incurred the curses "written in the law of Moses."[108] Similarly they have not "listened to the voice of the Lord our God according to all the words of the prophets."[109] Later, because of this failure, predictions of judgment

101. See G. Nickelsburg, "Stories of Biblical and Early Post-Biblical Times," in *Jewish Writings of the Second Temple Period* (ed. M. Stone; Philadelphia: Fortress, 1984), 45.

102. For example, Tob. 1:8; 6:12; 7:12, 13.

103. Amos (Tob. 2:6), Nahum (14:4, Sinaiticus), Jonah (14:4, Vaticanus, Alexandrinus).

104. In Sinaiticus the prophet is Nahum, and in Alexandrinus and Vaticanus he is Jonah. This ominous message is regarded as part of the message of "the Prophets of Israel" in Sinaiticus (14:4).

105. Tob. 14:5.

106. Tob. 14:9.

107. Bar. 1:18.

108. Bar. 2:2.

109. Bar. 1:21.

made by Jeremiah are cited as from "thy servants, the prophets,"[110]
which suggests that Jeremiah's words are part of an authoritative
collection.

In other texts the evidence is stronger. In 2 Maccabees Judas
encourages his troops before an important battle by "comforting
them out of the law and the prophets and, by putting them in mind
of the battles they had won previously. . . ."[111] In 4 Maccabees, the
father of the famous martyrs of 2 Maccabees is held up as an example of virtue since he taught his children from "the law and the
prophets."[112] A sampling of biblical heroes follows, which shows
that the law and the prophets include Genesis, Numbers, Daniel,
Isaiah, Psalms, Proverbs, Ezekiel, and Deuteronomy.

At Qumran the Scriptures are referred to, with variations of
"the law and the prophets" denoting the two canonical divisions.
The *Damascus Document* mentions "the books of the Law" and "the
words of the Prophets,"[113] while the *Rule of the Community* exhorts
"to do that which is upright and good just as He commanded by the
hand of Moses and by the hand of all his servants the prophets."[114]
In another passage the judgment of God is perceived coming in the
latter days as a result of "the [pre]cepts which Moses wrote and
your servants the prophets who[m] you [s]ent."[115] Finally, another
text may refer to the fulfillment of prophecies occurring in "the
book of Moses and the words of the Prophets."[116]

In the New Testament there is frequent reference to the two
canonical divisions with varied terminology: "law and prophets"
(7x);[117] "Moses and the prophets" (3x);[118] "the one about whom
Moses wrote in the Law and about whom the Prophets wrote";[119]
"the law of Moses and the prophets";[120] "the prophets and the

110. Bar. 2:20–24.
111. 2 Macc. 15:9.
112. 4 Macc. 18:10.
113. CD VII, 15–17.
114. 1QS I, 2–3.
115. 4Q504 1–2 III, 12–13.
116. 4QMMT C 15. This is a reconstructed text.
117. Matt. 5:17; 7:12; 22:40; Luke 16:16; Acts 13:15; 24:14; Rom. 3:21.
118. Luke 16:29, 31; 24:27.
119. John 1:45.
120. Acts 28:23.

law";[121] and "the prophets and Moses."[122] Books that have been traditionally part of a third division of the Writings are included in this title.

Other evidence comes from the later first century. Josephus, in his description of an authoritative body of religious Jewish literature, limits it to a collection of twenty-two books and refers to it later with the expression: "the laws and the allied documents."[123] Jewish prisoners would rather endure torture and death than to say a word against these texts, which certainly contain literature from what was later known as the Writings.

Finally, near the end of the second century CE, Melito, the bishop of Sardis, visits the Holy Land to determine more accurately the canon of the Hebrew Bible. This suggests that in the West there was a lot of uncertainty about this matter. He calls the Hebrew Bible "the Law and the Prophets," which clearly includes books later known as Hagiographa.[124]

Terminology: Three-Part Designations

So far there is little disagreement among scholars. One-part and two-part designations are common. Just the same it is surprising that there is a variety of labels used. The literature can be referred to as "the holy books," "the holy writings," "the writings," "the law and the prophets," "Moses and the prophets," "the law of Moses and the words of the prophets," "the law and the prophecies," and so on. But what about a three-part designation for these authoritative writings?

(1) The first example of evidence for a tripartite canon comes from Ben Sira. But first it should be stated that his book breathes a canon-consciousness. It is one long implementation of the call to meditate on not only the Torah but the entire corpus of biblical writings.[125] Of course, Ben Sira elevates the law to a supreme status,

---

121. Matt. 11:13.
122. Acts 26:22.
123. Josephus, *Against Apion* 1.43.
124. Eusebius, *Ecclesiastical History* 4.26.12–14.
125. Note S. Schechter and C. Taylor (*The Wisdom of Ben Sira: Portions of the Book of Ecclesiasticus from Hebrew Manuscripts in the Cairo Genizah Collection Presented to the University of Cambridge by the Editors* [Cambridge: Cambridge University Press,

but in his "Praise of the Fathers" of Israel[126] he works with many documents outside the limit of the Torah; this entire section can be loosely described as the Torah and the Prophets since prophecy is repeatedly stressed after the Torah, beginning with Joshua, and the so-called twelve minor prophets can be referred to as a literary collection rather than by naming the individual prophets themselves.[127] "Praise of the Fathers" begins in Genesis with Enoch, stretches to the end of the biblical period with Nehemiah, and then returns to the heroes of Genesis before introducing Simon the high priest. Thus, although Simon is extremely important, he is outside the scope of the biblical boundaries.

The list is as follows, and certain points should be underscored:

Order of Heroes	Canonical Book
Enoch	Genesis
Noah	
Abraham	
Isaac	
Jacob	
Moses	Exodus
Aaron	Exodus, Leviticus, Numbers
Dathan	Numbers

1899], 25–35), who observe that Ben Sira cites virtually every biblical book except Daniel. Steinmann (*Oracles of God*, 40) qualifies this by noting that Ruth and Ezra are not cited and that Schecter may have been influenced by the critical dating of Daniel.

126. Sir. 44–50.

127. Sir. 46:20; 47:1; 48:13 (cf. references to other prophets: 46:13, 15; 49:7, 8, 9 [Hebrew] 10, 13). Note the point by H. Orlinsky ("Some Terms in the Prologue to Ben Sira and the Hebrew Canon," *JBL* 110 [1991]: 483–90), who states that the praise of the fathers is virtually a meditation on the Law and the Prophets. Similarly see the important exhaustive study by A. Goshen-Gottstein, "Ben Sira's Praise of the Fathers: A Canon-conscious Reading," in *Ben Sira's God. Proceedings of the International Ben Sira Conference. Durham-Ushaw College 2001* (ed. R. Egger-Wenzel; BZAW 321; Berlin: de Gruyter, 2002), 235–67. In particular the references to the judges and the Twelve probably indicate the literary works rather than the individuals. Cf. D. M. Carr, who argues that the references to the prophets do not prove the existence of literary collections ("Canonization in the Context of Community: An Outline of the Formation of the Tanakh and the Christian Bible," in *A Gift of God in Due Season: Essays on Scripture and Community in Honor of James A. Sanders* [ed. R. D. Weis and D. M. Carr; JSOTSup 225; Sheffield: Sheffield Academic Press, 1996], 22–64).

Order of Heroes	Canonical Book
Abiram	
Korah	
Phinehas	
Joshua (prophet)	Numbers, Joshua
Caleb	Numbers, Joshua
Judges	Judges
Samuel	Samuel
Nathan	
David	(Chronicles is used as source material for David as musician.)
Solomon	Kings
Rehoboam	
Jeroboam	
Elijah	
Elisha	
Hezekiah	
Isaiah	Isaiah
Josiah	Kings
Jeremiah	Jeremiah
Ezekiel	Ezekiel
Job (Hebrew text)	Ezekiel (possibly Job too but cf. Ezek. 14:14)
The Twelve	The Twelve
Zerubbabel	Ezra–Nehemiah
Joshua (the high priest)	(Haggai, Zechariah)
Nehemiah	Ezra–Nehemiah
Enoch	Genesis
Joseph	
Shem	
Seth	
Adam	
Simon	Outside the boundary of canon

While the canonical issue should not be pressed to the exclusion of the historical factor,[128] since there is a historical thrust to the material and the basic biblical timeline is followed, it is interesting that there is a focus on prophecy in the material from Joshua to the Twelve, and that the biblical material concludes with a reference to Nehemiah, suggesting a biblical trajectory from Genesis to Ezra–Nehemiah.

The fact that an exhortatory blessing marks a transition to Joshua, who is underlined as a prophet, may suggest a canonical division.[129] But no other canonical divisions seem clear other than the conclusion of this long meditation on the Scriptures with Nehemiah.

More evidence of canonical divisions may appear in chapter 39. Throughout Ben Sira's book, there is the frequent correlation of Torah with wisdom:[130]

> Wisdom, knowledge, and understanding of the law, are of the Lord: love, and the way of good works, are from him. (Sir. 11:15)

> The fear of the Lord is all wisdom; and in all wisdom is the performance of the law, and the knowledge of his omnipotence. (19:20)

This receives classic expression in the famous passage about the Torah being the pinnacle of wisdom and its search for a home, which is found in the nation of Israel.[131]

The themes of Torah and wisdom are linked together in a striking way in chapters 38–39. As chapter 38 draws to a close Ben Sira contrasts the scribe with a manual laborer in two poems.[132] The first poem portrays the laborer as not having the time to pursue wisdom and study. In the second composition, the sage does have the time and consequently is able to give himself to the study of

---

128. Cf. Goshen-Gottstein, "Ben Sira's Praise of the Fathers," who tends to downplay the historical factor at times.

129. Sir. 45:26. See P. Guillaume, "New Light on the Nebiim from Alexandria: A Chronography to Replace the Deuteronomistic History," *JHS* 5 (2004), http://www.arts .ualberta.ca/JHS/Articles/article_39.htm.

130. Sir. 11:5; 15:1; 19:20, 24; 33:2, 3; 34:6–8.

131. Sir. 24:1–34.

132. Sir. 38:25–34 vs. 39:1–11. For the analysis see P. Skehan and A. Di Lella, *The Wisdom of Ben Sira* (New York: Doubleday, 1987), 451–53.

literature. But it is not just any literature that will preoccupy his time:

> But he gives his mind to
> and meditates on the law of the Most High;
> he will seek out the wisdom of all the ancients
> and will occupy himself in prophecies.
> He will keep the sayings of the renowned men:
> and he will seek to decipher subtle parables.
> He will seek out the secrets of proverbs,
> and be conversant with enigmatic parables. (Sir. 38:34b–39:3)

The sage will thus be involved primarily in the study of sacred literature. These texts are distinguished in particular as wisdom literature. More specifically they contain: (1) law, (2) wisdom, (3) prophecies, (4) sayings of famous individuals, (5) subtle parables, (6) secrets of proverbs, and (7) enigmatic sayings. There are eight relevant stichoi in this part of the poem, the first pair devoted to the meditation of the law of the Lord, the second to wisdom and prophecies, the third to the discourse of the famous and parables, and the fourth to proverbs and riddles.

The list is obviously governed by a wisdom perspective. The initial four stichoi describe the object of study as the law, wisdom, and prophecy, and the next four lines focus on wisdom. The first couplet of this latter series—the discourse of famous men, whose meaning is found in the parallel line (subtle parables)[133]—and the next one describe this wisdom endeavor further: the deciphering of proverbs and riddles.[134] Consequently there is a movement from the general to the particular with a focus on wisdom. Major collections of Scripture are indicated as the object of study initially, followed by a focus on one of the collections—wisdom. This interpretation would suggest three different canonical divisions in a somewhat different order than are later normally found, with a

---

133. Although the term "famous men" appears at the beginning of the praise of the fathers (44:3), it seems to suggest in this context "the wisdom of the ancients," i.e., Hebrew sages. Cf. Prov. 1:6.

134. Note how Solomon is especially involved in this activity (Sir. 47:15, 17), and cf. Prov. 1:1, 6, where this terminology appears.

unique division called the "wisdom of all the ancients."[135] Perhaps this is evidence of a different canonical arrangement that later coincides with some of the Septuagint evidence.[136] Or perhaps the unique order in which wisdom supplants prophecies is because of the focus of wisdom in the context.[137] But it is interesting that the meditation on the Torah and the study of the Scriptures is of utmost importance for the sage. It is also interesting that the only other close juxtaposition of "law and prophecies" is found in a designation used by Ben Sira's grandson to identify canonical divisions two generations later.[138]

(2) Ben Sira's grandson wrote a Greek prologue to provide a guide to his grandfather's work, which he translated from Hebrew into Greek. The grandson begins by stating that Israel is to be commended for its learning and wisdom since it had received "the law and the prophets and those which followed after them."[139] These three categories of books have been responsible for Israel's wisdom. Then he states that his grandfather, who had received good judgment by giving himself to the regular reading of "the law and the prophets and the other books of our fathers," desired to impart more learning and wisdom to Israel and consequently wrote the present work.[140] The grandson, then, apologizes for his

135. The expression "all the ancients" occurs in the LXX in 1 Kings 2:35ᵇ and 5:10. There it is a more universal picture where it compares Solomon's wisdom as surpassing all the wisdom of the ancient sages of other cultures. More likely here in Ben Sira the term refers not only to Solomon, but also Hezekiah (Prov. 25:1), Agur (30:1), and Lemuel (31:1). A. van der Kooij ("Canonization of Ancient Books," 35) argues that by the use of this expression Ben Sira signifies the more inclusive sense of the Hebrew Bible; however, Ben Sira belies this sense in practice. He limits his description, e.g., in "Praise of the Fathers," to biblical examples. In my judgment, "the wisdom of all the ancients" suggests antiquity and functions as a variant for "the ancestral books" in the Prologue. Van der Kooij insightfully sees this latter expression as an indication of antiquity and thus authority.

136. So Skehan and Di Lella, *Wisdom of Ben Sira*, 452. See also J. C. H. Lebram, "Aspekte der alttestamentlichen Kanonbildung," *VT* 18 (1968): 173–89.

137. Dempster, "From Many Texts to One," 25.

138. Sir. Prologue 24.

139. Sir. Prologue 1–2. This third category more naturally refers to books but need not since the issue of chronological order is not really in focus. What is in view is literary order (e.g., David and Solomon, who are regarded as authors of significant works in a third division, are chronologically prior to many of the prophets). See H. Orlinsky, "Some Terms in the Prologue to Ben Sira."

140. Sir. Prologue 8–10.

translation, noting that there will be a difference between the Greek and the original Hebrew document. But this difference between a translation and the power of the original language can be noted when "the Law itself and the prophecies and the rest of the books" are spoken in their own language.[141]

First, there is a focus on distinctive literature that provides wisdom, and this literature is differentiated from the grandfather's work. That work itself was written with great reliance upon the distinctive literature in order to provide more wisdom, but it is differentiated from it.

Second, this distinctive literature is divided into three categories, repeated three times, and these were said to be known by the grandfather.[142] The fact that two of the categories are used in other works to identify authoritative religious literature does not imply that the third category is excluded from such a designating function. The third category is clearly placed with the other two, on the same level, and distinguished from other literature. It is a clear type of "guilt by association." Scholars who dodge the force of this association by suggesting that the first two divisions refer to authoritative canonical literature—the prophets being not yet closed, and the third division referring to extracanonical literature—have a difficult time explaining the repetition of the three categories without any hint of a distinction.[143] It is true that the third division does not seem to have a specific name. This variability of title does not necessarily indicate a different authoritative category since the material in the third section is clearly linked to the first two— "those [books] which followed," "the other books of the fathers," and "the rest of the books."[144] The recent attempt by E. Ulrich to understand this distinction as similar to a modern bookseller's

141. Sir. Prologue 24–25.

142. A fact not always noted. See A. C. Sundberg Jr., "The Septuagint: The Bible in Hellenistic Judaism," in McDonald and Sanders, *Canon Debate*, 81: ". . . the translator attributes the same Bible to his grandfather as he acknowledges for himself."

143. T. N. Swanson, "The Closing of the Collection of Holy Scripture: A Study of the History of Canonization of the Old Testament" (PhD diss., Vanderbilt University, 1970), 125ff.; Barton, *Oracles of God*, 47–51.

144. A pertinent point made by A. van der Kooij, "Canonization of Ancient Hebrew Books and Hasmonean Politics," in *The Biblical Canons* (ed. J.-M. Auwers and H. J. de Jonge; BETL 163; Leuven: Leuven University Press, 2003), 29–32.

catalogue listing entries of Bible and Theology together, with Bible being replaced by Law and Prophets, does not address the relevant adjectives and seems to be a case of special pleading.[145] It may be that the variant terminology implies the recent closing of a third canonical division, but it also may not. The suggestion that the flexible terminology indicates a flexible form is also a possibility but is not required.[146] Not only is there flexible terminology used for one-part and two-part designations of this literature outside of Ben Sira, but also even in the prologue the second division is twice called "the prophets" and once "the prophecies."

In the discussion of this evidence one can often lose sight of the forest for the trees. The grandson views his grandfather's work as important because it will bring readers into vital touch with the authoritative books, from which so much wisdom has been received, and thereby help them live according to the Torah. Ben Sira's work is important insomuch as it leads to preoccupation with Torah.

(3) A third line of evidence for a tripartite designation for the Hebrew Scriptures is found in a recently published document from Qumran: 4QMMT. This document, which is approximately dated from the early first century BCE to the mid–second century BCE, has been the subject of many studies on the canon. This letter addressed to a leader apparently intends to impress upon him that the Scriptures were being fulfilled. The relevant reference has been partially reconstructed, so there is some doubt about its actual form. The reference states that if the leader believes that the Scriptures are being fulfilled, he will be able to "understand the Book of Moses [and] the Book[s of the P]rophets and Da[vid]." The word "understand" suggests a discerning study much like Daniel's study of authoritative books.[147] Later, in a restored passage, the fulfillment of the prophecies predicted "[in the Book of Moses and the words of the Prophets]" are regarded as coming true. This latter

---

145. E. Ulrich, "Qumran and the Canon of the Old Testament," in Auwers and de Jonge, *Biblical Canons,* 71.

146. E.g., M. Hengel, *The Septuagint as Christian Scripture: Its Prehistory and the Problem of its Canon* (trans. M. E. Biddle; Grand Rapids: Eerdmans, 2002), 97.

147. Dan. 9:2. "The expression בִּינֹתִי denotes here careful study of a written text or the like" (Qimron and Strugnell, *Qumran Cave 4.V,* 59n10).

reference of course should not be counted, but the first one is possibly a label for a canonical division after the prophets. Together they designate a body of sacred, authoritative literature.

The editors of 4QMMT were quick to identify the significance of this and observed that here was evidence for a third division of the Scriptures, with "David" referring to the Scriptures later known as the Hagiographa.[148] Ulrich contributed to the discussion by suggesting that an original two-part canon had been hyperextended "so the Book of Psalms . . . began to establish a new category which eventually would be called the Ketubim or the Hagiographa."[149] He has recently changed his mind, arguing that the reconstructions are problematic.[150] Others have suggested that since David was regarded as a great prophet, his book of Psalms is added to the Prophetic collection[151] or the term "David" was regarded as "the biblical accounts of the Davidic monarchy."[152] If the reconstruction "David" is correct, a more economical explanation, however, is that the canon is already tripartite and two designations can be used to describe it, a short form ("Moses and the words of the prophets") and a long form ("Moses, the words of the prophets and David"). In short, a bipartite designation does not imply a smaller collection of literature, but is simply a more convenient "shorthand" term for a tripartite one. Both designations are interchangeable for the same body of literature.[153]

Again, important as these designations are, the community at Qumran had as its raison d'être the study of such books. As mentioned above, the leader to whom the halachic letter has been sent was to study these books. In another text the community is

148. See note 13 above.

149. Ulrich, "Bible in the Making," 82.

150. Ulrich, "Qumran and the Canon of the Old Testament," 67–68; idem, "Non-attestation of a Tripartite Canon."

151. J. J. Collins, *The Sceptre and the Star: The Messiahs of the Dead Sea Scrolls and Other Ancient Literature* (New York: Doubleday, 1995), 21.

152. L. H. Schiffman, *Reclaiming the Dead Sea Scrolls* (Philadelphia: Jewish Publication Society, 1994), 84. T. Lim ("The Alleged Reference to the Tripartite Division of the Hebrew Bible," *RQ* 77 [2001]: 23–37) argues that David's works are in view, but as van der Kooij ("Canonization of Ancient Books, 32–33") points out this does not seem to be the proper object for the verb "to understand."

153. This is also an insight shared by van der Kooij, "Canonization of Ancient Books," 33.

mandated to take literally the canonical imperatives to meditate on the Torah day and night: "There should not be missing a man to interpret the Torah day and night always, one relieving another. The Many shall be on watch together for a third of each night of the year in order to read the book, to seek the meaning of the ordinance and to bless the community."[154]

(4) The fourth instance of evidence for a tripartite designation is found in 2 Maccabees as an introduction by the so-called epitomist. It includes two short letters that have been prefaced to the document to encourage the celebration of the purification of the temple (1:1–9; 1:10–2:18). In the second, particularly in 2:1–15, there is mention of texts that recount two events in the nation and two similar responses to these events, which resulted in the preservation of sacred texts. In the first case it is stated from a text found among literary records that after the destruction of the temple, Jeremiah the prophet gave to the departing exiles a copy of the law and urged them not to let it depart from their hearts (2:1–3). In the second case, it is stated in a group of records as well as in the memoirs of Nehemiah, who had returned to Judah after the return of the exiles, that he had founded a library consisting of "the acts of the kings and prophets, and the things of David and the letters of the kings concerning holy gifts" (2:13). The writer then brings the reader up to date by continuing with the information that Judas Maccabeus has had to gather the writings that have been lost as a result of the recent war and has made them available for use if any require them (2:14).

These few verses may provide evidence for two further divisions of Scripture during Nehemiah's time in addition to the law: "the acts of kings and prophets," and "the things of David and letters of kings regarding holy gifts." The first division is self-evident, and

154. 1QS VI, 6–8. It is largely clear that books later understood to be canonical had special authority for the Qumran community. They have a unique status in that when books are cited authoritatively they almost always belong to this class. See, e.g., J. A. Fitzmyer, "The Use of Explicit Old Testament Quotations in Qumran Literature and in the New Testament," in *Essays on the Semitic Background of the New Testament* (London: Geoffrey Chapman, 1971), 3–58; J. Lust, "Quotation Formulae and Canon in Qumran," in van der Kooij and van der Toorn, *Canonization and Decanonization*, 67–78; see also the appendix provided by F. Ulrich, "Qumran and Canon," in Auwers and de Jonge, *Biblical Canons*, 80.

the second division could correspond to the prophets (the former prophets—Joshua, Judges, Samuel, Kings—mainly concerned with the rise of kingship and the exploits of kings, and the latter prophets—Jeremiah, Ezekiel, Isaiah, the Twelve—the actual collections of prophetic oracles). Finally, a third division may be indicated by the things regarding David—the Psalter, which is by far the largest book of the third division and also stands at the beginning or near the beginning of many orders of the Writings, and books viewed as written by David's son, Solomon (Proverbs, Ecclesiastes, Songs). The "letters regarding holy gifts" could be another way of describing the content of a significant work at the end of this division, Ezra–Nehemiah, which contains many references to letters and written edicts between Judah and the Persian empire regarding the rebuilding of the temple and the walls of Jerusalem and the bringing of gifts and sacrifices for the temple.[155] This is paralleled in the writer's own day by a similar collection of literature because of the recent crisis. Both historical examples show the importance of the collections of this literature for the people. In studying and meditating upon this literature, the people will find their very life.

While Julio Trebolle Barrera concedes that this information could refer to a tripartite canon, he then states that in another part of 2 Maccabees there is a clear reference to a bipartite designation.[156] But a question arises: Why do the two have to be mutually exclusive?[157] Here then could be a significant parallel to a possible third division entitled "David" at Qumran.

(5) A fifth example of evidence comes from Philo (first century CE). In one text he discusses an ascetic sect, the Therapeutae, who practice their faith by entering closet sanctuaries without food, drink, or anything for the body. What they do bring with them is literature described as "laws and oracles delivered through the mouths of prophets, as well as hymns and anything else that

---

155. See Ezra 4–6, esp. 6:1–12.

156. J. Trebolle Barrera, "Origins of a Tripartite Old Testament Canon," in McDonald and Sanders, *Canon Debate,* 130.

157. Similarly, J. Campbell considers two titles for the same material as logically inconsistent: "4QMMTd and the Tripartite Canon," *JJS* 51 (2000): 181–90. Again, why do the two expressions have to be mutually exclusive?

fosters perfection, knowledge and piety."[158] A natural way of understanding this text is to see it as a description of laws (Torah),
oracles (Prophets), and psalms, representing a third division. The
"anything else" could also be further description of a third division, a possible fourth division, or simply other literature that
the sect used.[159] The fact that all of the units are connected by a
similar conjunction complicates matters, but allows for each of
these possibilities.[160]

Once more the importance of this literature for study, reflection,
and life is emphasized through this casual example. The study of
these special texts functions virtually as a substitute for food and
drink for the members of this sect.

(6) Josephus furnishes a sixth case in point. He makes a statement in his work *Against Apion* in which he contrasts the writings
of the Greeks—which are myriad and contradict one another—
with those of the Jews—which are divinely inspired, having been
received from prophets and numbering only twenty-two volumes.[161]
Josephus then enumerates them in three groupings: five books of
Moses, thirteen books of Prophets, and "the rest of the books
which are hymns to God and precepts for human life." Unfortunately Josephus does not identify the content of the books, but
based on later lists, an educated guess can be made.[162]

158. Philo, *On the Contemplative Life* 25.

159. Such as the writings of the sect itself. See Swanson, *Closing of the Collection of
Holy Scripture*, 248–50.

160. See A. Sundberg, review of R. Beckwith, *The Old Testament Canon in the New
Testament Church*, Int 42 (1988): 82. McDonald (*Formation of the Christian Biblical
Canon*, 39) observes that "the law and oracles delivered by the prophets" suggest one unit
and not two. C. A. Evans ("Scripture of Jesus and His Earliest Followers," in McDonald
and Sanders, *Canon Debate*, 188), however, points out that Moses—the giver of the law—
was regarded as a prophet and thus this text could be understood as a reference at least to
two collections by this designation.

161. Josephus, *Against Apion* 1.37–43. There may be an earlier reference to the number
twenty-two in *Jubilees* (2:23–24), but there is some doubt about whether this occurred in
the original text. See McDonald, *Formation of the Christian Biblical Canon*, 61–62.

162. See, e.g., the lists in which the number twenty-two or twenty-four plays a factor:
Origen (Eusebius, *Ecclesiastical History* 6.25) (he says there are twenty-two but omits
one book, probably the Twelve); *b. Bava Batra* 14b; Jerome (*Prologus Galeatus* for the
Vulgate of Samuel and Kings); Epiphanius (*Panarion* 1.1.8.6; *De Mensuris et Ponderibus*
3–5, 22–23). For convenient summaries of the lists, see Beckwith, *Old Testament Canon*,
119–21, 185–89; McDonald, *Formation of the Christian Biblical Canon*, 268–69.

Recently Steve Mason has argued that there is no reference here to a bipartite or tripartite canon,[163] but it is apparent that Josephus himself divides the material into two broad divisions—Moses and the rest of the prophets—and the second one is subdivided—thirteen prophets and the remainder. These three sections can be conveniently described a few sentences later with a two-part description: "the laws and the allied documents."[164] Consequently this division in Josephus is similar to the tripartite reference in the prologue to Ben Sira: the law, the prophets, and the rest of the books.

As stated at the beginning of this essay, many claims about the formation of canon are largely inferential since there is a paucity of explicit evidence. But in this text, Josephus supplies explicit evidence that is largely ignored in the debate.[165] Mason has made the telling point that without this explicit statement of canon from Josephus, one could easily deduce from Josephus's use of religious literature in his works that he worked with a much broader and more open understanding of canon.[166] But Josephus states that this collection is monolithic—for all brands of Judaism—and it has been closed for quite a while because of "the failure of the exact succession of the prophets."[167]

Moreover, the importance of this authoritative collection of literature cannot be overestimated. Since it is divinely inspired and ancient, it is vastly superior to Greek collections, and it is laden with so much significance that Jews will not just study it—they will die for it if required.[168]

163. S. Mason, "Josephus and His Twenty-Two Book Canon," in McDonald and Sanders, *Canon Debate*, 110–27.

164. Despite Mason's strictures the language of the text suggests division. Most scholars are agreed on this point, whether they argue for a tripartite or bipartite canon. See also S. Z. Leiman, "Josephus and the Canon of the Bible," in *Josephus, the Bible and History* (ed. L. Feldman and G. Hata; Detroit: Wayne State University Press, 1989), 50–58.

165. Here is a text that even meets the criteria of E. Ulrich: a list that has been closed for a long time.

166. "If we lacked the *Against Apion*, Josephus himself would offer a clear case for an open canon. But we do have the *Against Apion*, in which the same Josephus emphatically, but also matter-of-factly, insists that the Judean records have long since been completed in twenty-two volumes" (Mason, "Josephus and His Twenty-Two Book Canon," 126).

167. Mason, "Josephus and His Twenty-Two Book Canon," 125–27.

168. Josephus, *Against Apion* 1.43.

(7) The New Testament provides additional evidence to be adduced for a tripartite canon. Luke 24 describes the resurrected Jesus' appearance to two of his disciples on the Emmaus road. Here there are at least three basic designations for the totality of the Old Testament Scriptures: a one-part title, a bipartite designation, and a tripartite label.

In this account, the resurrected Lord is described as helping his bewildered disciples understand the significance of the recent events leading up to his death. First of all, he rebukes them for not realizing that all these events were predicted by "all that the prophets spoke" (24:25). Luke then writes: "Beginning from Moses and from all the prophets he explained to them in all the scriptures the things concerning himself" (24:27). "Moses and the prophets" designates the Scriptures, as this is where Jesus began to expound "the things concerning himself," but it seems to suggest that this functioned as a beginning point for explanation in "all the scriptures." Later in the same pericope, when Jesus is instructing the rest of his disciples, another expression is used to designate the Scriptures: "These are my words which I spoke to you while I was yet with you, that it is necessary that all things be fulfilled which have been written in the law of Moses and in the prophets and in the psalms concerning me" (24:44). Luke then describes Jesus in the following manner: "Then he opened their mind to understand the scriptures" (24:45). Here it is clear that a three-fold designation for the canon stands alongside a shorter two-fold designation, and an even shorter one-fold designation to refer to exactly the same documents.

Some scholars understand the reference to the Psalter to indicate that it simply functioned as the beginning of a newly developing tripartite canon or that it was tacked onto the end of a bipartite canon concluding the Prophets since David was viewed as a prophet (the Law and the Prophets—including the Psalms).[169] This was because the Psalms in particular contain many explicit references used by early Christians to show that the death and resurrection of Jesus were predicted in their Bible.[170] While this

---

169. So, e.g., Evans, "Scripture of Jesus and His Earliest Followers," 185–95.

170. Hengel, *Septuagint as Christian Scripture*, 105–8; and C. A. Evans, "The Dead Sea Scrolls and the Canon of Scripture in the Time of Jesus," in *The Bible at Qumran: Text, Shape and Interpretation* (ed. P. W. Flint; Grand Rapids: Eerdmans, 2001), 67–79.

is a definite possibility, it is clear that other books outside the Law and the Prophets had messianic significance: one only has to think of Daniel and Chronicles. Moreover, the text does not say "including the psalms": rather this three-part designation refers to "all the Scriptures."[171]

A text like this also shows the importance of not only Jesus as the hermeneutical key to Israel's Scriptures but also the study of these Scriptures for the early Christian community. The repeated reference to the importance of the Scriptures for understanding the stupendous significance of the events surrounding the death and resurrection of Jesus shows the inextricable relationship between early Christians and these texts.

(8) There are a number of lists dating roughly before the end of the second century CE that are relevant to the study. One is a *baraita*, or ancient saying, that is not found in the Mishnah but has been preserved in the Talmud. It enumerates Israel's Scriptures as twenty-four and divides them into three broad divisions: the Torah, the Prophets, and the Writings (beginning with Ruth and Psalms and ending with Chronicles). In Eusebius's *Ecclesiastical History* there are two lists from the early church fathers, one dating to the late part of the second century CE and the other to the early part of the third century CE: the lists of Melito of Sardis[172] and Origen of Alexandria.[173] Melito wished to obtain a more accurate understanding of "the Law and the Prophets," so he traveled to the East seeking such knowledge. His canon numbered twenty-five books.[174] Origen also provided knowledge of the Hebrew canon with a list numbering twenty-two.[175] Both lists differ considerably from the order found in the *baraita* but in each the Latter Prophets

---

171. For a discussion of Jesus' use of the Old Testament, see R. T. France, *Jesus and the Old Testament* (London: Tyndale, 1971). Jesus cites three other books from a division later known as the Writings: Proverbs, Daniel, and Chronicles.

172. Eusebius, *Ecclesiastical History* 4.26.12–14.

173. Eusebius, *Ecclesiastical History* 6.25.

174. He numbers Samuel and Kings as four books, Chronicles as two, and he omits Lamentations and Esther. Some argue that there are twenty-six books and understand "Wisdom" as referring to the Wisdom of Solomon. Others understand it to be a further description of Proverbs. See Beckwith, *Old Testament Canon*, 183–85.

175. He actually only cites twenty-one books. Probably Eusebius (or Origen, his source) has omitted by accident the Twelve.

have been moved to the end, historical books are grouped after the Torah, and the poetic and wisdom literature have been generally kept together. The situation is a bit more complex when the Bryennios text (another list from the early period) is introduced, as the Psalms are placed before Samuel, Kings, and Chronicles to indicate a Davidic emphasis for these books. Aside from this it is similar to the other lists with some minor differences.[176] The fact that these lists all come from Christian sources may explain the eschatological emphasis of the sequence.

The possible external evidence for titles for the Hebrew Bible can be observed below:

Reference	Titles Used for the Hebrew Bible		
Tob. 7:13; 14:5	the law	the prophets	
Bar. 1:17, 21	the statutes of the Lord	the words of the prophets	
Ben Sira 39:1	the law of the Most High	wisdom of all the ancients	prophecies
Prologue of Ben Sira			
a. 1	the law	and the prophets	and the other (books) which followed them
b. 8–10	the law	and the prophets	and the other ancestral books
c. 24–25	the law	and prophecies	and the remainder of the books
2 Macc.			
a. 2:1, 13	(the law) [assumed]	The books concerning kings and prophets	The things of David and the letters of kings regarding votive offerings
b. 15:9	the law	and the prophets	

176. J. P. Audet, "A Hebrew-Aramaic List of Books of the Old Testament in Greek Transcription," *JTS* 1 (1950): 135–54. For a careful comparison of these lists see E. Zenger, "Der Psalter im Horizont von Tora und Prophetie," in Auwers and de Jonge, *Biblical Canons*, 119–21.

Reference	Titles Used for the Hebrew Bible		
Qumran			
1QS I, 3	by the hand of Moses	By the hand of all his servants the prophets	
1QS VIII, 15–16	by the hand of Moses	the prophets	
CD VII, 15–17	the books of the Torah	the books of the prophets	
4QMMT C 10	in the book of Moses	[and in the words of the pro]phets	and in Da[vid]
C 16	[in the book of] Moses	and in [the words of the prophet]s	
4Q504 1–2 III, 13	your [pre]cepts which Moses wrote	your servants the prophets who[m] you [s]ent	
4 Macc. 18:10	the law	and the prophets	
Philo, *On the Contemplative Life* 25	laws	and oracles divinely inspired through prophets	and hymns and other books in which knowledge and piety are fostered and perfected
Jubilees 2:23–24 Number = 22 Josephus, *Against Apion* Number = 22			
a. 1.39–40	the books of Moses (five)	the prophets after Moses (thirteen)	
b. 1.43	the laws	and the allied documents	the remaining four books consist of hymns to God and precepts for human life
New Testament			
Matt. 5:17	the law	and the prophets	
Luke 16:29	Moses	and the prophets	
Luke 16:16	the law	and the prophets	
Acts 26:22	the prophets	and Moses	

Reference	Titles Used for the Hebrew Bible		
Luke 24:44	the law of Moses	and the prophets	and the psalms
2 Esd. Number = 24			
Talmudic Baraita	[the Torah] [assumed]	the prophets	Writings
b. Bava Batra 14b Number = 24		Joshua, Judges, Samuel (1–2), Kings (1–2), Jeremiah, Ezekiel, Isaiah, the Twelve	Ruth, Psalms, Job, Proverbs, Ecclesiastes, Songs, Lamentations, Daniel, Esther, Ezra–Nehemiah, Chronicles (1–2)
Melito Number = 25	the law of Moses: Genesis, Exodus, Numbers, Leviticus, Deuteronomy	and the prophets Jesus Nave, Judges, Ruth, 1–4 Reigns, 1–2 Chronicles, Psalms, Proverbs, Ecclesiastes, Songs, Job; of Prophets: Isaiah, Jeremiah, the Twelve, Daniel, Ezekiel, Esdras	
Origen Number = 22	Genesis, Exodus, Leviticus, Numbers, Deuteronomy	Jesus son of Nave, Judges-Ruth, 1 Reigns (1–2), 2 Reigns (3–4), Chronicles (1–2), Esdras (1–2), Psalms, Proverbs, Ecclesiastes, Songs, Isaiah, Jeremiah-Lamentations-Epistle, Daniel, Ezekiel, Job, Esther [The Twelve?]	
Bryennios Text Number = 23	Genesis, Exodus, Leviticus, Joshua, Deuteronomy	Numbers, Ruth, Job, Judges, Psalms, Samuel (1–2), Kings (1–2), Chronicles (1–2), Proverbs, Ecclesiastes, Songs, Jeremiah, the Twelve, Isaiah, Ezekiel, Daniel, Esdras (1–2), Esther	

The evidence speaks for itself. There is a strong presumption of a third division of canonical literature that begins with David, hymns, psalms, or "remaining" books. This evidence concurs with the internal evidence, which indicates that the sacred literature was organized in such a way so as to emphasize the centrality of Torah for human life.

Different orderings of the canon emerged for various reasons, probably among various groups. Some may have stressed generic consistency, others increased the eschatological temperature, and still others facilitated liturgical usage. From these lists and others it is clear that there were a variety of orders; however, by the second century CE, a text was needed to delineate one particular order. This was because of competing alternatives for sequences and the rise of the use of the codex in which groups of scrolls could be transcribed into one book. In my judgment this particular order remarkably coheres with both the internal and external evidence, and the internal evidence suggests that this order, or one very similar, goes back to the end of the biblical period itself.

Brevard Childs has stated that "the formation of the canon was not a late extrinsic validation of a corpus of writings, but involved a series of decisions deeply affecting the shape of books. . . . Israel did not testify to its own self-understanding, but by means of a canon bore witness to the divine source of its life."[177] The shape of the Hebrew Bible with its tripartite structure emphasizes this life and is one long call to return to Torah, Torah, Torah and thus to develop a Torah-centered mind. The word that gave life in the beginning, by creating light and breathing into Adam's nostrils, is now available in the Torah; by meditating on it day and night one can experience this life in all its fullness.[178]

---

177. Childs, *Introduction to the Old Testament as Scripture*, 59.

178. Cf. Deut. 8:3 and Ps. 119. I think this certainly explains the preoccupation with the study of holy books by the various streams within Judaism, and probably sheds light on that enigmatic book at Qumran called "the book of meditation" (1QS I, 7; CD X, 6; XIII, 2). This could well be a designation for a collection of these holy writings, anchored in the Torah (cf. Josh. 1; Ps. 1).

Excursus: A Note on Canon and Text

How does this view align with the textual evidence, in which there are a variety of text forms for the books of the Hebrew Bible in the pre-Christian period? There seems to be a pluriform text in a pluriform Judaism. Text types probably included the proto-Masoretic, the proto-Samaritan, the Hebrew *Vorlage* of the Septuagint, non-aligned Qumran texts, and texts that may be the basis for Old Testament citations in the New Testament. How does this evidence cohere with the idea of a canon? Some would multiply these texts and not stress text types or families but independent texts themselves, whereas others would organize the many manuscripts on the basis of distinct families.[179] Does this textual situation imply that there is no direct link between text and canon?[180] It is clear that there was at a later date, as one text tradition—probably a central tradition linked to the temple—was adopted and the text was stabilized. In my judgment the very idea of canon would give rise to multiformity. If certain texts were seen to have ultimate importance because they were the Word of God, their use in liturgy and study would imply the importance of transmission. This would result in the production of many copies

179. See the different perspectives in: Cross, "Text behind the Text"; idem, *From Epic to Canon*; E. Tov, "The Contribution of the Qumran Scrolls to the Understanding of the LXX," in *Septuagint, Scrolls and Cognate Writing* (G. J. Brooke and B. Lindars; Atlanta: Scholars Press, 1990), 11–47; idem, "The Status of the Masoretic Text in Modern Text Editions of the Hebrew Bible," in McDonald and Sanders, *Canon Debate*, 234–51. E. Ulrich has a convenient summary of the various perspectives: "The Scrolls and the Study of the Hebrew Bible," in *The Dead Sea Scrolls at Fifty* (R. A. Kugler and E. A. Schuller; Atlanta: Scholars Press, 1999), 31–42. This debate is not unlike the debate between P. Kahle and P. de Lagarde regarding the history of the Septuagint. One stressed multiformity leading to uniformity in the various texts and the other argued that uniformity led to multiformity.

180. Tov ("Status of the Masoretic Text," 247–50) questions this and points out that canon is linked to a presumed archetype text. Giving up the notion of such an archetype cuts the link between canon and text. Note the debate between those who wish to create an eclectic text of the Hebrew Bible and those who seem to have given up on this task, claiming that the various types have equal canonical status among the various early communities: J. A. Sanders, "The Most Original Bible Text, How to Get There? Keep Each Tradition Separate," *BRev* 16 (2000): 40–49, 58; R. S. Hendel, "The Most Original Bible Text, How to Get There? Combine the Best from Each Tradition," *BRev* 16 (2000): 27–39; See also J. A. Sanders, "Text and Canon: Concepts and Methods," *JBL* 98 (1979): 5–29; B. K. Waltke, "How We Got the Hebrew Bible: The Text and Canon of the Old Testament," in Flint, *Bible at Qumran*, 27–50.

localized in many communities, and these would give rise to the production of more localized texts. Scribal errors would become the identity marks of these texts. Consequently various families of manuscripts would emerge. As night follows day—because of canon—there would arise a concern to control the transmission of the text amidst this textual variety. While one could describe this as a move from a dynamic, spontaneous understanding of text to a more fixed, frozen type of verbal inspiration, where a certain form of the text is important, that is only one possibility. One could also understand this as the concept of canon birthing both pluriformity at an early stage and uniformity at a later stage.

At any rate, the earliest Greek recensions attest to revisions of the Septuagint towards the Hebrew of the proto-Masoretic text type, beginning in the late first century BCE.[181] By the late first century CE a rabbinic recension had taken place. This stabilization of the Hebrew text is clearly an implication of a fixed canon, and provides a terminus ad quem for the Hebrew canon.[182]

181. E.g., E. Tov, *The Greek Minor Prophets Scroll from Naḥal Ḥever (8ḤevXII gr)* (DJD VIII; Oxford: Clarendon, 1990), 9–10, 99–158; see also Cross, "Text behind the Text"; and R. Hanhart, "Problems in the History of the LXX Text from its Beginning to Origen," in Hengel, *Septuagint*, 1–17. Clearly early Greek "translations" were revisions of the LXX towards the Hebrew of the proto-Masoretic text type. That this recensional activity extended to Baruch and the additions to Daniel has been used as an argument for dating the fixing of the Hebrew canon later, since this material would have been excluded if the canon had already been decided. While this is a possibility, it should be noted that these works alone of the Apocrypha were revised. See E. Tov, *The Septuagint Translation of Jeremiah and Baruch: A Discussion of an Early Revision of the LXX of Jeremiah 29–52 and Baruch 1:1–3:8* (HSM 8; Missoula: Scholars Press, 1976), 169. Thus canonization may not have affected at first the exact form of the books, simply the books themselves. Daniel is not in question, and Baruch was closely associated with Jeremiah, sometimes being viewed as an appendix (see, e.g., Origen's list).

182. Childs, *Introduction to the Old Testament as Scripture*, 97.

4

The Role of "the Septuagint" in the Formation of the Biblical Canons

R. GLENN WOODEN

The Septuagint version of the Hebrew Scriptures[1] has been influencing the church since the time of the apostles. Even today its influence is felt in congregations the world over, both because it continues to be the Old Testament of one branch of the church, and because it is used by translators and scholars from various branches and traditions of the church when they attempt to make

1. The term "Scriptures" will be used to indicate writings that were considered religiously authoritative, without reference to a canon. "Canon," for brevity's sake, is a list of books sanctioned for reading. The biblical canon consists of the books considered to make up the Bible, for example. On the issues related to this word, see L. M. McDonald, *The Biblical Canon: Its Origin, Transmission, and Authority* (Peabody, MA: Hendrickson, 2007).

sense of the diverse witnesses to the text of the Old Testament/ Hebrew Bible.[2] But, the title of this essay is intended to signal to the reader that we are not considering the Septuagint as a witness merely to the original words of the biblical text; we will not reflect much on how it provides knowledge of what words were in the books of our Old Testament/Hebrew Bible from three hundred to two hundred years before the time of Jesus and Hillel. Rather, we will explore how the Septuagint version has played a role in the development of the canons of Scripture that have been used by both the Jews and Christians up until today.

Reference to the notion of "canon" provides us with an entrance into this topic. When studying the question of the canon of the Christian Bible, we need to ask: Which canon of the church?[3] Those denominations that have roots in the Reformation—the Protestant and Free Church traditions—have the same canon of Old Testament books as Judaism has in its Hebrew Bible, although they are arranged differently. The Roman Catholic Church, the Eastern Orthodox Church, and the Ethiopic Church, although they have the same books as the previous two groups, also have others: Roman Catholics have forty-six books in their Old Testament;[4] Orthodox Christians have forty-nine;[5] and Ethiopian Christians have from

---

2. Generally in scholarship it is not just Christians who talk about the Bible. Obviously, Jewish scholars are deeply involved in the scholarly study of the books in the Hebrew Bible. If Christians say "Old Testament" when we are talking about a Jewish person's "Hebrew Bible," then it is not an "old" testament, because they have no "New Testament." On the other hand, if we are referring to the complete Christian Bible, with its New Testament, then the first testament is to us Christians the "Old Testament." Throughout this article we will use both these phrases: "Hebrew Bible" will be used when I refer only to the Bible of Judaism in its Hebrew-Aramaic form. When I specifically refer to the first section of the Bible of the church, I will use "Old Testament."

3. For a convenient comparative chart, see H. P. Rüger, "The Extent of the Old Testament Canon," in *The Apocrypha in Ecumenical Perspective: The Place of the Late Writings of the Old Testament among the Biblical Writings and Their Significance in the Eastern and Western Church Traditions* (ed. S. Meurer; Reading, UK; New York: United Bible Societies, 1991), 160.

4. F. J. Stendebach, "The Old Testament Canon in the Roman Catholic Church," in Meurer, *Apocrypha in Ecumenical Perspective*, 33–45.

5. M. Konstantinou, "Old Testament Canon and Text in the Greek-Speaking Orthodox Church," in *Text, Theology and Translation: Essays in Honour of Jan De Waard* (ed. S. Crisp and M. M. Jinbachian; [London?]: United Bible Societies, 2004), 89–107.

forty-six to fifty-four books.[6] These different canons of the Hebrew Bible/Old Testament have long traditions and are unlikely to change. The differences raise a variety of historical and theological questions. How did we get the different canons? Did the latter three groups add to the Scriptures? Does the Jewish canon represent a pared down set of books? Should some or all of the "extra" books have the same status as the thirty-nine on which we all agree? Whatever the answers that individual readers give, any exploration of the evidence for the different canons should begin with the development of the Septuagint translation and its reception within the church.[7]

Before we consider that issue, however, it is necessary to clarify what we mean by "the Septuagint."[8] Sometime between three to two hundred years before Jesus and Hillel, Greek-speaking Jews began producing translations of books that we now find in the Hebrew Bible: they started with the Pentateuch, the first five books

6. R. W. Cowley, "The Biblical Canon of the Ethiopian Orthodox Church Today," *Ostkirchliche Studien* 23 (1974): 318–23; G. A. Mikre-Sellassie, "The Bible and Its Canon in the Ethiopian Orthodox Church," *BT* 44 (1993): 111–23.

7. See the following two recent books that cover the topic of canon: L. M. McDonald and J. A. Sanders, eds., *The Canon Debate* (Peabody, MA: Hendrickson, 2002); McDonald, *Biblical Canon* (the earlier editions were *The Formation of the Christian Biblical Canon* [Nashville: Abingdon, 1988; rev. ed.: Peabody, MA: Hendrickson, 1995]). For works specifically devoted to the Septuagint and canon-related issues, see: M. Müller, *The First Bible of the Church: A Plea for the Septuagint* (Sheffield: Sheffield Academic Press, 1996); M. Hengel, *The Septuagint as Christian Scripture: Its Prehistory, and the Problem of Its Canon* (Edinburgh: T&T Clark, 2002); A. Wasserstein and D. Wasserstein, *The Legend of the Septuagint: From Classical Antiquity to Today* (New York: Cambridge University Press, 2006).

8. See L. Greenspoon, "The Use and Abuse of the Term 'LXX' and Related Terminology in Recent Scholarship," *BIOSCS* 20 (1987): 21–29 for a full treatment of this problem. In recent introductions to Septuagint studies see N. Fernández Marcos, *The Septuagint in Context: Introduction to the Greek Version of the Bible* (Leiden: Brill, 2000); K. H. Jobes and M. Silva, *Invitation to the Septuagint* (Grand Rapids: Baker Academic, 2000); J. M. Dines, *The Septuagint* (London and New York: T&T Clark, 2004). And for the use of the Septuagint in biblical studies see E. Tov, *The Text-Critical Use of the Septuagint in Biblical Research* (Jerusalem: Simor, 1997); and R. T. McLay, *The Use of the Septuagint in New Testament Research* (Grand Rapids: Eerdmans, 2003). There are various translation projects that will make the books of the Septuagint available to modern audiences. The three main projects are: the English project NETS (A. Pietersma and B. G. Wright III, eds., *A New English Translation of the Septuagint and the Other Greek Translations Traditionally Included under That Title* [New York: Oxford University Press, 2007]); the French project *La Bible d'Alexandrie* (ed. M. Alexandre and M. Harl; Paris: Cerf, 1986–); and the German project LXX.D (M. Karrer and W. Kraus, eds., *Septuaginta Deutsch: Das griechische Alte Testament in Übersetzung* [Stuttgart: Deutsche Bibelgesellschaft, 2008]).

of the Bible, but eventually translated them all. There is a legend that comes to us in a fictional work called the *Letter of Aristeas*.[9] It tells how seventy-two Jewish men were gathered to the island of Pharos in Alexandria by an Egyptian ruler in the mid-third century BCE to translate the first five books of the Bible. Over time, the number seventy-two became remembered as seventy for some reason, and in Latin seventy is *septuaginta*; that name stuck with the earliest Greek translation of various books, and not only the first five books, but all the books classed together as authoritative Jewish Scriptures.

Today Septuagint is a fuzzy term. Some people think of a particular collection as being "The Septuagint." Due to its widespread use today, students, pastors, and scholars think of the German textual expert Alfred Rahlfs's *Septuaginta*. It is available in a handy one-volume print edition, and since at least the 1980s its text has been available in electronic format.[10] Most scholars do not actually believe that there was a book (codex) form of the Septuagint at the turn of the millennia, but they still talk about "*the* Septuagint," as if Paul, for example, had gone to the local Alexandrian Bible Society bookstore in Tarsus and purchased his own bound copy of *The Septuagint*, from which he preached.[11] In more thoughtful moments, we realize that Paul would not have done that, but rather he cited the Septuagint probably from a combination of memory, some form of crib sheet with important texts written out, and by finding and quoting from locally available scrolls or copies of particular biblical books that belonged to the translation-tradition that we refer to as "the Septuagint." Some scholars will use the term Septuagint more loosely to refer to any Greek version of the Scriptures that were available to the early church. Still others reserve "Septuagint" for the earliest translation of the first five books of the Bible, and they use "Old Greek" for the first translations of the other books. In this discussion

---

9. For a recent translation see R. J. H. Shutt, "Letter of Aristeas," *OTP* 2:831–42.

10. A. Rahlfs and R. Hanhart, *Septuaginta: Id Est Vetus Testamentum Graece Iuxta LXX Interpretes* (Editio altera; Stuttgart: Deutsche Bibelgesellschaft, 2006). The best modern critical edition of the Septuagint is the series *Septuaginta: Vetus Testamentum Graecum* (Göttingen: Vandenhoeck & Ruprecht, 1931–). For a brief overview of modern critical editions see Jobes and Silva, *Invitation to the Septuagint*, 69–75.

11. On this issue, see R. A. Kraft, "The Codex and Canon Consciousness," in McDonald and Sanders, *Canon Debate*, 229–33.

we will use "the Septuagint" as a convenient reference to all the first authoritative Greek translations of the Jewish Scriptures. In the remainder of this article, I want to consider three questions.

1. How have the Greek translations of the Hebrew Scriptures influenced the development of the biblical canons?
2. What influences led to the development of the different Old Testament canons?
3. What can we learn from this complex situation?

We will not be focusing on what should or what should not be the case—who is right and who is wrong. Nor will we concern ourselves with whether some influence should or should not have had an effect. We are considering only how things came to be as they are now.

How Have the Greek Translations of the Hebrew Scriptures Influenced the Development of the Biblical Canons?

To answer this question I want to begin at the most basic level, in the present day, and work backwards. Ask moderately knowledgeable Christians what the "Old Testament" is, and eventually we get around to something like: it is the thirty-nine books of the Hebrew Old Testament. That, of course, would be the answer of those who are the users of the Jewish and Protestant canons, as my reference above to the different church canons makes clear. The different numbers of works included in canons are one problem to which we will soon return briefly. For now, I want to consider another problem. Knowledgeable Christians know that the Old Testament was composed in Hebrew and Aramaic. However, almost every new translation is based not only on the Hebrew Bible, but upon manuscripts from the caves of the Dead Sea, the Septuagint, the Syriac Old Testament (a later Aramaic translation used by Christians), the Latin Old Testament (the Old Latin and Vulgate), and other lesser known ancient translations. In all of this, the Septuagint plays a significant role, and it is striking that in some places it is significantly different from the Hebrew-Aramaic version.[12]

---

12. For a complete introduction to the text of the Septuagint and its role in textual reconstruction, see Tov, *Text-Critical Use of the Septuagint.*

Consider the following two examples, which, as biblical scholars
will know, are from a book whose text is notoriously problematic.
In the first example from 2 Samuel 6:3–5, we find three modern
translations together with their notes: the New International Version (NIV), the New King James Version (NKJV), and the Jewish
Publication Society's *Tanakh* (JPS).

2 Samuel 6:3–5
Material removed based upon the LXX

NIV	NKJV	JPS
3 They set the ark of God on a new cart and brought it from the house of Abinadab, which was on the hill. Uzzah and Ahio, sons of Abinadab, were guiding the new cart	3 So they set the ark of God on a new cart, and brought it out of the house of Abinadab, which was on the hill; and Uzzah and Ahio, the sons of Abinadab, drove the new cart.ᶜ	3 They loaded the Ark of God onto a new cart and conveyed it from the house of Abinadab, which was on the hill; and Abinadab's sons, Uzza[h] and Ahio, guided the ᵈ⁻new cart.
4 with the ark of God on it,ᵃ and Ahio was walking in front of it.	4 And they brought it out of the house of Abinadab, which was on the hill, accompanying the ark of God; and Ahio went before the ark.	4 They conveyed it from Abinadab's house on the hill, [Uzzah walking]ᵉ alongside⁻ᵈ the Ark of God and Ahio walking in front of the Ark.
5 David and the whole house of Israel were celebrating with all their might before the LORD, with songsᵇ and with harps, lyres, tambourines, sistrums and cymbals.	5 Then David and all the house of Israel played music before the LORD on all kinds of instruments of fir wood, on harps, on stringed instruments, on tambourines, on sistrums, and on cymbals.	5 Meanwhile, David and all the House of Israel danced before the LORD to ᶠ⁻[the sound of] all kinds of cypress wood [instruments],⁻ᶠ with lyres, harps, timbrels, sistrums, and cymbals.

ᵃ Dead Sea Scrolls and some Septuagint manuscripts; Masoretic Text *cart 4 and they brought it with
the ark of God from the house of Abinadab, which was on the hill*.

ᵇ See Dead Sea Scrolls, Septuagint and 1 Chron. 13:8; Masoretic Text *celebrating before the LORD with
all kinds of instruments made of pine*.

ᶜ Septuagint adds *with the ark*.

ᵈ⁻ᵈ Septuagint and 4QSamᵃ read *cart alongside*.

ᵉ Cf. vv. 6–7.

ᶠ⁻ᶠ Cf. Kimhi; the parallel passage 1 Chron. 13:8 reads *with all their might and with songs*.

Comparing the NIV against the NKJV and JPS versions, the NIV is different in verses 4 and 5. Consideration of the footnotes to each reveals that the translators of the NIV chose to follow a manuscript tradition that does not have the Hebrew for the underlined material in verse 4, but rather the shorter manuscript tradition, to which the Septuagint is one witness. At verse 5, again, the NIV follows a version of the Hebrew text that is not represented in the Masoretic Text tradition.

2 Samuel 13:34
Material added based upon the LXX

NIV	NKJV	JPS
34 Meanwhile, Absalom had fled. Now the man standing watch looked up and saw many people on the road west of him, coming down the side of the hill. The watchman went and told the king, "I see men in the direction of Horonaim, on the side of the hill."[a]	34 Then Absalom fled. And the young man who was keeping watch lifted his eyes and looked, and there, many people were coming from the road on the hillside behind him.[b]	34 Meanwhile Absalom had fled. The watchman on duty looked up and saw a large crowd coming [c]from the road to his rear,[c] from the side of the hill.

[a] Septuagint; Hebrew does not have this sentence.

[b] Septuagint adds *And the watchman went and told the king, and said, "I see men from the way of Horonaim, from the regions of the mountains."*

[c c] Emendation yields *down the slope of the Horonaim road. The watchman came and told the king "I see men coming from the Horonaim road."* Cf. Septuagint.

Again, as the notes tell readers, the translators of the NIV have deemed that the best witness to what was original is to be found in the Septuagint. Significantly, no other ancient manuscripts or versions are used as support for this change. Thus, when reading 2 Samuel 13:34b in the NIV, it is the Septuagint that is translated, not any existing Hebrew manuscript.

It is commonplace for the text upon which modern translations are based to be arrived at in conversation with various ancient manuscripts and translations (textual criticism) and not merely with the standard Hebrew Bible, the Masoretic Text. In fact, ever since they began to be made, modern translations of the Old Testament have used the Greek translations, and others, as aids to understanding the Hebrew and Aramaic text.

In practice, then, the present limits of the various biblical canons—the Hebrew, Orthodox, Roman Catholic, and Protestant–Free Church canons—have been fixed since the sixteenth century at the latest. But the actual words within those canons are not fixed, as scholars seek to get back as close as possible to a text that best represents the original texts. Thus, sometimes what we have translated in a version of the Old Testament is not the translation of Hebrew or Aramaic, but Greek, from the Septuagint. So, one of the ways that translation has influenced the present canon of Scripture is by serving as a guide to what might have been the original form of the biblical text.

Now let us move back farther to think about another stage in the development of the present canons of the church. Martin Luther is a significant figure in the shaping of the Christian Old Testament canon. Although he is well known for his anti-Semitic views, he still considered the Jewish Bible to be preferable to that preserved by the church of his day.

> And all of us should also take note of this miracle of the Holy Spirit, namely, that he wanted to give the world all the books of Holy Scripture, of both the Old and the New Testaments, solely through Abraham's people and seed, and that he did not have a single book composed by us Gentiles, just as he did not intend to choose the prophets and apostles from among the Gentiles, as St. Paul says in Romans 3 [:2], the Jews enjoy a great advantage, since they "are entrusted with the oracles of God," and according to Psalm 147 [:19], "He declares his word to Jacob, his statutes and ordinances to Israel." And Christ himself says in John 4 [:22], "We worship what we know, for salvation is from the Jews," and Romans 9 [:4–5] says, "To them belong the covenants, the giving of the law, the patriarchs, and Christ."
>
> Therefore we Gentiles must not value the writings of our fathers as highly as Holy Scripture, but as worth a little less; for they are the children and heirs, while we are the guests and strangers who have come to the children's table by grace and without any promise. We should, indeed, humbly thank God and, like the Gentile woman, have no higher wish than to be the little dogs

that gather the crumbs falling from their masters' table [Matt. 15:27].[13]

Luther's motivation to move away from the Latin Vulgate to the Hebrew Bible and the Greek New Testament was only in part due to his dispute with the church of Rome. He was also influenced by the approach of Erasmus and others who called for a return to the original forms of classical literature rather than translations of them—this was the beginning of modern classical scholarship. Whatever his motivations, when Luther began to translate the Old Testament, he turned to the form of the Hebrew Scriptures that was available to him, the Bible that Jews of his day used, the Masoretic Text. When he did that the number of biblical books that he could translate was reduced when compared to the Latin Vulgate Old Testament, and some of the books were shortened due to the material not found in the Hebrew (Daniel being a well-known example). It was at this point that the Christian Old Testament canon of thirty-nine books came into existence.

The Roman Catholic Church was not interested in the Reformers' paring down of the church's long-held understanding of the canon of Scripture, and so pronounced at the Council of Trent (1546) the canonicity of the forty-six traditional Old Testament books. The mutually accepted thirty-nine books were the first canon of the Old Testament, and the seven disputed ones (Wisdom, Ecclesiasticus [Sirach], Tobit, Judith, Baruch, and 1 and 2 Maccabees) were the second canon of the Old Testament—the deuterocanonical books—also known as the Apocrypha.[14]

What does this have to do with the Septuagint and its part in the development of the biblical canons? We need to go back farther to answer that question. In the late fourth century, 390 to 405 CE, the church father Jerome made a translation of the Hebrew Scriptures into Latin, about which more will be said later. That translation was based upon the Hebrew texts available to Jerome and so lacked the materials found only in the Septuagint. Even in Jerome's day

13. M. Luther, *Church and Ministry III* (ed. E. W. Gritsch; Luther's Works 41; Philadelphia: Fortress, 1966), 51.

14. Cf. D. J. Harrington, "The Old Testament Apocrypha in the Early Church and Today," in McDonald and Sanders, *Canon Debate*, 196n1.

the authority of some of those works was disputed and they were rejected by Jerome, but the Greek version of the Old Testament was so important to the church that over time the extra materials were added to his translation and so have remained part of the Old Testament of the Roman Catholic Church up until today. The Eastern Orthodox Church also has books that the Protestant–Free Church canon does not have: 1 Esdras, Tobit, Judith, Wisdom of Solomon, Ecclesiasticus, Baruch, the Epistle of Jeremiah, 1, 2, and 3 Maccabees, and additional parts of Esther and Daniel. Because it is the Greek branch of the church, the Orthodox Church's tradition is the Septuagint version, which could arguably have more continuity with the early church than either the Latin or Hebrew traditions. So, the composition of the Vulgate is that of the Septuagint, which is the form away from which Luther moved.

Thus, this collection of translations that we call "the Septuagint" has exerted significant influence in the church for many hundreds of years.

- Despite Jerome's attempt to use only the Hebrew-Aramaic Bible from the synagogue in the late fourth century, over time it was the Septuagint collection of books that determined the contents of the Christian Old Testament in Latin.
- That Greek collection has determined the canon of the church into the present day in both the Orthodox Church and the Roman Church, with some variations.
- Even after Luther adopted the Hebrew Bible as the Old Testament of the emerging Protestant Church, the Greek versions of the books still influenced Bibles translated from the Hebrew-Aramaic Bible tradition by helping translators determine both the form and meaning of the text where it is difficult.

What Influences Led to the Development of the Different Old Testament Canons?

Those not familiar with this complex history of the canon's development wonder how the different collections, or canons, came to be, and how their wording can be so different in places. Indeed it is problematic for some views of Scripture, such as those who focus on the inspiration of every word, and those who believe that the number of books has been fixed since the time of Jesus. The evidence of the development of the Septuagint challenges such views. The facts of history and existing manuscripts stand as matters with which we must reckon.

Sometime over a three- to two-hundred year period before the fall of Jerusalem in the year 70 CE, the Jews in the Diaspora came to speak Greek better than they could speak or read Hebrew and Aramaic. Whether for their purposes in worship or in schools, as an aid to personal study, or to make their Scriptures known to non-Jews, they translated their Hebrew and Aramaic texts into Greek. And it was very awkward Greek for the most part—not necessarily grammatically incorrect, but more a form of "Hebrew in Greek's clothing" than normal Greek. Someone in Alexandria who heard the Septuagint read might have been reminded of the speech patterns of his neighbor's relative from Jerusalem—someone who was translating his thoughts from Aramaic into Greek as he spoke, rather than speaking Greek fluently. In other words, those Greek versions of the Hebrew Scriptures were obviously translations.

These translations were also made from individual copies of the Hebrew and Aramaic texts that were doubtless locally acquired. Maybe official editions were requested from Judah (Jerusalem), but why would Alexandrian Jews have mistrusted the copies that they had used for worship and teaching? However, even if translators had access to manuscripts that came from the "homeland," we know now, from the discoveries in the caves in the Judean desert, that there were actually different Hebrew versions of some books circulating in Judea at that time. Some copies of books seem to be like what is in the Hebrew-Aramaic texts on which English translations depend. Some, however, are more like what we find reflected in the Greek translations that were passed on to the church (see the notes to the translation of 2 Sam. 6:3–5, above). It is clear to scholars that there were various forms of the same texts circulating at the turn of the millennia. Thus, for example, Jews from Egypt to Mesopotamia could refer to the book that Jeremiah wrote, but one person's book of Jeremiah did not have the same arrangement as another's, or the contents of one's might have had more or less text than another's.[15] In the Septuagint, Jeremiah seems to have been translated from the shorter version, which also has a different arrangement from the Hebrew. Such differences can be seen when comparing the Septuagint with the present Hebrew Bible.[16]

There were other texts that were important to some Greek-speaking Jews, but might not have been as important to those in Judea. A few books that we have in the Septuagint tradition have some significant additions. One of the more famous is the book of Daniel: the Septuagint contains a more lengthy version of the book with the story of Susanna at the beginning, the stories of Bel and the Dragon at the end, and lengthy prayers in chapter three. But, it is also very different in the parallel material in chapters four and five. To read them side by side is to read material that is similar, but not the same.[17] A more drastic difference is found in the translation of material from the books of Ezra and Nehemiah. Known as 1 Esdras in the Apocrypha/deuterocanonical books, this work has four different sources. It begins with the last two chapters of 2 Chronicles (35:1–36:21). Material from the book of Ezra follows that, but it is rearranged and has a unique story added: just after the Chronicles material is the parallel to Ezra 1 and 4 (Ezra 1:1–3 [// 2 Chron. 36:22–23], 4–11; 4:6–24); then in 1 Esdras 3:1–5:6 we find a story about three young men who were serving as bodyguards for King Darius of Persia, one being Zerubbabel (referred to in Ezra, Nehemiah, Haggai, Zechariah, Matthew, and Luke), who wins a contest of wits with the others and is a main figure in the book of 1 Esdras; that story is followed by the remainder of Ezra (2:1–70 [// Neh. 7:7–73]; 3:1–4:5; 5:1–10:44) and then Nehemiah

15. Cf. Y.-M. Min, "The Case for Two Books of Jeremiah," in Crisp and Jinbachian, *Text, Theology and Translation*, 109–23.

16. This will be one of the benefits, for non-specialists, of the translations of the Septuagint. See note 8, above.

17. The existence of other Daniel materials among the Dead Sea Scrolls shows that this biblical character had a rich history and attracted much literary attention. See, for example, E. Eshel, "Possible Sources of the Book of Daniel," in *The Book of Daniel: Composition and Reception* (ed. J. J. Collins and P. W. Flint, with the assistance of C. VanEpps; Leiden and Boston: Brill, 2001), 2:387–94; P. W. Flint, "The Daniel Tradition at Qumran," in Collins and Flint, *Book of Daniel*, 2:329–67; and L. DiTommaso, *The Book of Daniel and the Apocryphal Daniel Literature* (Leiden and Boston: Brill, 2005).

7:73–8:12. The Greek in this book is not the same kind as we find in other books; it is better, fluent Greek.

There are more such differences in the Greek version of the Hebrew Bible/Old Testament. They occur in small and large details, as already noted.[18] Importantly, such translations, with all their differences, were the Scriptures of the early church—of Paul, Luke, and others—and they continued to be for centuries, especially in the Eastern Orthodox Church. Through the daughter translations such as the Syriac and Vulgate, they have continued into the modern era.[19]

At first the nature of the Greek translations might not have been problematic, because they seem to have been part of known manuscript traditions. Soon after the translations were completed, however, dissatisfaction with the quality of the Greek surfaced. Earlier mention was made of the *Letter of Aristeas*; in addition, the famous Alexandrian Jew, Philo, wrote an even more embellished account of the creation of the first translation. Both the *Letter* and Philo seem to be justifying the state of the translation in the face of complaints. They make grand claims about the accuracy of the translations and the quality of the Greek, and we know that neither is true.

After the fall of Jerusalem in 70 CE changes within Judaism led to the ascendancy of one tradition—what has come to be known as rabbinic Judaism. One of the accompanying results was the ascendancy of the form of the Jewish Scriptures used by that group. This meant that there was less diversity among manuscripts, and more authority given to the form within that tradition. This even extended to the Greek versions of those texts. In the second century CE, revisions of the older texts were made by Aquila, Symmachus, Theodotion, and others.[20] Their goal was apparently to bring the

---

18. See the works above in note 8. For a helpful, introductory examination of three different books (Joshua, Esther, 1 Esdras) see K. De Troyer, *Rewriting the Sacred Text: What the Old Greek Texts Tell Us About the Literary Growth of the Bible* (Atlanta: Society of Biblical Literature, 2003).

19. Müller, *First Bible of the Church*.

20. For introductions to these and other revisions see Fernández Marcos, *Septuagint in Context*, 103–87; Jobes and Silva, *Invitation to the Septuagint*, 45–56; P. Lampe, "Aquila's Version," *ABD* 1:319–20; L. J. Greenspoon, "Symmachus, Symmachus's Version," *ABD* 6:251; L. J. Greenspoon, "Theodotion, Theodotion's Version," *ABD* 6:447–48; etc.

translations into line with the authoritative textual stream of their day, the rabbinic text.[21] It would seem that as its influence spread more widely, there was dissatisfaction with those manuscripts and versions that differed from it. This even led to debates between those using the different forms of texts. We know, for example, of arguments between Christians and Jews in which the differences of wording between Christians' versions of a book and the Jews' texts were a point of disagreement.[22]

That dissatisfaction, which was solved in Jewish circles by the revisers just mentioned, also spilled over into the church. After being commissioned to produce a good Latin translation of the Septuagint, Jerome (347/8–420) had moved to Bethlehem and there became familiar with the Hebrew Bible. He understood the importance of it as the original text behind the Septuagint. He had already begun to improve on existing translations of the Septuagint into Latin, but after coming to value the Hebrew Bible he began translating directly from Hebrew.[23] But, Jerome's discontent was not shared by others in the church, such as Augustine, who tried to convince him to produce a Latin translation of the Septuagint.[24] For better or worse, the church

21. On the rabbinic Bible see J. N. Lightstone, "The Rabbis' Bible: The Canon of the Hebrew Bible and the Early Rabbinic Guild," in McDonald and Sanders, *Canon Debate*, 163–84; and Wasserstein and Wasserstein, *Legend of the Septuagint*, 51–83.

22. For a discussion of the changed text as one reason that the Septuagint was to be revised by Jews, see S. Kreuzer, "From 'Old Greek' to the Recensions: Who and What Caused the Change of the Hebrew Reference Text of the Septuagint?" in *Septuagint Research: Issues and Challenges in the Study of the Greek Jewish Scriptures* (ed. W. Kraus and R. G. Wooden; SBLSCS 53; Atlanta: Society of Biblical Literature; Leiden and Boston: Brill, 2006), 225–37. Justin Martyr's *Dialogue with Trypho* 71–73 is an example of such differences, although the particular texts discussed in this dialogue are not currently found in Septuagint manuscripts; some are suspected of being interpolations by Christians. Translations of this work can be found in Justin, *Dialogue with Trypho* (trans. and ed. M. Slusser; Washington, DC: Catholic University of America Press, 2003); as well as online: http://www.bombaxo.com/trypho.html (accessed 10 March 2008); http://www.earlychristianwritings.com/text/justinmartyr-dialoguetrypho.html (accessed 10 March 2008). On Justin Martyr and the apologetic use of the Jewish Greek Scriptures, see Hengel, *Septuagint as Christian Scripture*, 26–47; and Müller, *First Bible of the Church*, 68–78.

23. Insight into the translation of Jerome and his thoughts on both the books and his translation project can be found in his prologues to books and sections of the Vulgate. Translations of these prologues are conveniently collected at http://www.bombaxo.com/prologues.html (accessed 10 March 2008).

24. For a summary of the interaction between Jerome and Augustine, see Müller, *First Bible of the Church*, 83–94.

had cut its theological teeth on the Greek translation, and there was great reluctance to move away from it. Although Jerome translated the Hebrew Bible, the portions of the Septuagint not found in the Hebrew Bible over time found their way into his Vulgate, bringing its contents into line with those of the Septuagint.

To summarize:

- Two hundred years before the birth of Jesus there were various forms of the texts of the Jewish Scriptures.
- Some of those were translated into Greek, forming the Septuagint.
- From early times it was known that the Greek version was different from some Hebrew-Aramaic texts, and that the quality of the Greek was poor.
- When Paul and others preached outside of Israel, they seem to have quoted from the Greek Old Testament, even where it differed from the Hebrew.
- After the destruction of the temple in 70 CE, there was a narrowing of the differences among texts in Judaism. This made the original Greek translations stand out even more.
- Some Greek-speaking Jews and Christians attempted to bring the older translations into line with what was becoming the Hebrew Bible that we have today.
- The church refused to give up its cherished Septuagint translation, which influenced the limits of the canon even when there were new translations from the Hebrew; this remained the case until Martin Luther translated the Old Testament from the Hebrew Bible of his day.

What Can We Learn from This Complex Situation?

We can choose to ignore such a complex situation, or deny it, but it is a fact of history and of the ancient manuscripts that still exist. Rather than argue against this situation, the church might be better served by asking what we can learn from it. There are a few areas that we need to reconsider as Christians, especially those of us with an Old Testament canon of thirty-nine books.

First, the development of the text of the Hebrew Bible/Old Testament was much more complex than most Christians realize. This is disconcerting to some, but the differences among the manuscripts and ancient versions are facts with which scholars must deal. Such matters make us ask hard questions about some of our revered assumptions.

Second, in light of the practice of the church over the last two millennia, we need to reconsider what we mean by inspiration. Protestants have tended to find inspiration in the very words of the text—but the text used by the early church, by Paul, Matthew, Luke, and others, was not the Hebrew-Aramaic text (or text-tradition) that we now have and treasure. It was instead the Greek Jewish Scriptures (or text-tradition), which differed from the Hebrew in not unimportant ways. The church for the most part has been a faith system content to live with translations, not overly concerned with the original texts. I am not sure that is satisfactory, but it is the fact of the matter, even today, when the study of biblical languages and exegetical work seems to be on the decline, even in conservative, evangelical quarters of the church. What this implies is that in practice, for the church, the locus of inspiration is not in the words of the text as originally produced, but in the text as received and used in the church at various times and in various languages. Such inspiration must, therefore, be attributed to the continuing work of God, not to an infusion of power into original texts that are no longer accessible to us and of which we have only faulty copies and uncertain reconstructions.[25]

25. See John Webster's beneficial discussion of revelation, sanctification, and inspiration as they relate to Holy Scripture: J. B. Webster, *Holy Scripture: A Dogmatic Sketch* (Current Issues in Theology 1; Cambridge and New York: Cambridge University Press, 2003). Especially relevant to the problems raised by this essay is his discussion of the sanctification of Scripture (mostly pp. 17–30): "In the context of discussing the relation between divine self-revelation and the nature of Holy Scripture, sanctification functions as a middle term, indicating in a general way God's activity of appointing and ordering the creaturely realities of the biblical texts towards the end of the divine self-manifestation" (9–10); and

> Both terms ["providence" and "mediation"] are readily applicable in the context of discussing the nature of Scripture. God's work of overseeing such processes as tradition-history, redaction, authorship and canonisation could well be described in terms of the divine providential acts of preserving, accompanying and ruling creaturely activities, annexing them to his self-revelation. And the function of these providentially ordered texts in the divine economy could be depicted as mediatorial.

The church's willingness to accept translations over the original text has long been in place. Even when Jews in Alexandria and Christians after 70 CE were refusing to give up their beloved Greek translations, however, they still realized that they were translations; they realized that the Scriptures containing the Law, Prophets, and Writings came from texts in Hebrew and Aramaic. We have lived for centuries with a quasi belief in the importance of the original languages, but have relied almost completely on translations when consulting the Bible in matters of faith and practice. The church is not so much a "People of the Book" as a "People of Translations of the Book." Far from being negative, that very practice has enabled the rapid spread of the gospel far and wide from those early days until now. When people hear about salvation through Jesus Christ, it has not been through sacred texts written in a language foreign to them, but from texts translated into a current language—in the past, Greek, Syriac, Coptic, Latin, and the like; and today, English, French, German, Mi'kmaq, Telugu, and many others.[26]

Third, although Luther's move back to the Hebrew Bible may be questioned in some branches of the Christian family, it was not a wrong move, despite the long practice of the church. Although Christians have been content to use translations and to eschew the original languages from the very beginning of the church, there was still the consciousness that the church's Old Testament really was the *Hebrew* Bible. However, the problem that we face today is the realization that the Hebrew Bible underlying the Septuagint

---

If the term "sanctification" is still to be preferred, it is, as I hope to show, because it covers much of the same ground as both of these terms, whilst also addressing in a direct way the relation of divine activity to creaturely process, without sliding into dualism. (10)

Whereas the Greek translations of the Hebrew Scriptures were employed in the preaching, teaching, and writing of the early church, it might not be without warrant to add "translating" to the list of providential acts, or at the least, the employment of translations, specifically, Greek ones.

26. Cf. Webster, "Reading in the Economy of God's Grace," in *Holy Scripture*, 68–106; and R. Jenson, "The Religious Power of Scripture," *SJT* 52 (1999): 89–105. I am grateful to Ross Wagner for drawing these to my attention in a paper read at St. Mary's College, St. Andrews, Scotland, 14 March 2007. All discussions of the work of God in the reading of Scripture must take into account that, for the most part, the reading is from translations, not from the original languages, unless one is reading in a context where Hebrew, Aramaic, and/or Greek are spoken.

translation was not the Bible of the synagogues in the 1500s or 2000s but the Hebrew Scriptures of the few centuries before Christ, when there was still fluidity in the wording, contents, and arrangement of the books.

Finally, we in the church with an Old Testament canon of thirty-nine books need to question our disdain of the apocryphal/deuterocanonical materials used by our brothers and sisters in the Eastern, Roman, and Ethiopic branches of the church. We may not adopt those extra books and sections of books as part of our Bible, but by not doing so, we stand in opposition to two thousand years of church practice. Might God not be big enough to allow for more than one canon, and even for different versions of the same books, whether the difference is the language or the contents of the books?

In conclusion, it would seem that when Paul and others felt directed by God to take the gospel outside the bounds of their heritage to the Gentiles around them, they decided that the way to proceed was not by asking inquirers to learn Hebrew and Aramaic, but by using a translation of those Scriptures into Greek, and by telling the story of Jesus of Nazareth in Greek. They started a tradition that continues today and that has been part of the spread of Christianity to every continent: people have heard the Scriptures read and the gospel preached in their own language, beginning from the day of Pentecost (Acts 2, especially vv. 7–11). We have not practiced this consistently, but it is inherent in our faith and eventually wins out. That heritage of having the Scriptures in the language of the hearers, and not in their original form, goes back in part to the Septuagint with which apostles and others continued the Pentecost experience. The Septuagint is also part of what the synagogue reacted against when the influence of one of the various traditions of Hebrew texts widened. The Septuagint, then, has had both positive and negative roles in the development of the canons of Scripture among Jews and Christians. It is a collection of translations worthy of the interest it is receiving today among scholars, and worthy of closer attention among students and preachers who want to understand better the roots of our faith.

5

The Apocryphal Jesus

Assessing the Possibilities and Problems

CRAIG A. EVANS

The debate surrounding the usefulness of the extracanonical Gospels for historical Jesus research is a long one, which in one form or another can be traced back to the early church. One thinks especially of second-, third-, and fourth-century fathers who appeal to various Gospels or Gospel recensions in commentaries, treatises, and apologetic works, consciously supplementing, even modifying the tradition of the Gospels that would eventually come to be recognized as canonical. In some ways what these early Christian theologians and apologists were doing was not much different from the objectives and activities of modern research.

The present study undertakes a critical investigation of the status of the question today, advocating an openness to the possibility of early, reliable tradition in these texts, but at the same time urging greater caution in their use. I shall focus on four sources, which in some quarters have been judged as preserving tradition independent of, equal to, and in some cases perhaps even superior to what is preserved in the New Testament Gospels: the *Gospel of Thomas*, Papyrus Egerton 2, the *Secret Gospel of Mark*, and the alleged *Gospel of Peter*. These four sources received prominent attention in John Dominic Crossan's *Four Other Gospels: Shadows on the Contours of Canon*[1] and have continued to generate scholarly dialogue on questions relating to the historical Jesus and the origin of the Jesus tradition and New Testament Gospels. The *Gospel of Thomas* has enjoyed pride of place and is in fact the fifth Gospel in the Jesus Seminar's publication *The Five Gospels*.[2] *Thomas*, with which I begin, will be given more attention here than the other extracanonical Gospel sources.

The *Gospel of Thomas*

The extracanonical Gospel that is the most celebrated is the *Gospel of Thomas*, which survives in complete form in Coptic as the second tractate in Codex II of the Nag Hammadi library (NHC II,2) and partially in three Greek fragments in Oxyrhynchus Papyri 1, 654, and 655.[3] P.Oxy. 654 preserves the *Gospel of Thomas* prologue and sayings §§1–7, and a portion of saying §30. P.Oxy. 1 preserves *Gospel of Thomas* sayings §§26–33. P.Oxy. 655 preserves *Gospel of Thomas* sayings §§24, 36–39, and 77. Although the point has been disputed, it seems that most scholars contend that *Thomas* was originally composed in Greek and that the Oxyrhynchus Papyri

1. J. D. Crossan, *Four Other Gospels: Shadows on the Contours of Canon* (New York: Harper & Row, 1985; repr., Sonoma: Polebridge, 1992).

2. R. W. Funk, R. W. Hoover, and the Jesus Seminar, *The Five Gospels: The Search for the Authentic Words of Jesus* (Sonoma: Polebridge; New York: Macmillan, 1993).

3. For recent studies of the *Gospel of Thomas*, see M. W. Meyer, *The Gospel of Thomas: The Hidden Sayings of Jesus* (San Francisco: HarperCollins, 1992); S. J. Patterson, *The Gospel of Thomas and Jesus* (Sonoma: Polebridge, 1993); R. Valantasis, *The Gospel of Thomas* (New Testament Readings; London and New York: Routledge, 1997); S. J. Patterson, J. M. Robinson, and H. G. Bethge, *The Fifth Gospel: The Gospel of Thomas Comes of Age* (Harrisburg, PA: Trinity Press International, 1998); E. Pagels, *Beyond Belief: The Secret Gospel of Thomas* (New York: Random House, 2003); R. Uro, *Thomas: Seeking the Historical Context of the Gospel of Thomas* (London and New York: T&T Clark, 2003); H.-J. Klauck, *Apocryphal Gospels: An Introduction* (London and New York: T&T Clark, 2003), 107–22.

stand closer to the original form of the tradition.[4] The issue of the original language of *Thomas* will be taken up below.

Church fathers writing in the third and fourth centuries mention a *Gospel of Thomas*. In reference to the Naasenes, a gnostic group, Hippolytus (writing ca. 230) refers to a work "entitled the *Gospel according to Thomas*" (*Refutation of All Heresies* 5.7.20). Soon after, Origen (185–254) also refers to a "*Gospel according to Thomas*" (*Homilies on Luke* 1.5.13–14), a testimony that Jerome (342–420) repeats near the end of the fourth century (*Commentary on Matthew* Prologue). Ambrose (339–397) also mentions the work (*Exposition on the Gospel of Luke* 1.2.10). There is no reason not to identify this document mentioned by the church fathers with the *Gospel of Thomas* found in Egypt. The *Gospel of Thomas* is an esoteric writing, purporting to record the secret (or "hidden") teachings of Jesus.

Most of the codices that make up the Nag Hammadi library have been dated to the second half of the fourth century, though of course many of the writings within these old books date to earlier periods. The codex that contains the *Gospel of Thomas* may date to the first half of the fourth century. In the case of the *Gospel of Thomas* itself (whose *explicit* title reads: *peuaggelion pkata thōmas*, "the Gospel according to Thomas") we have the three Greek fragments from Oxyrhynchus, which date to the beginning and middle of the third century. One of the fragments may date as early as 200. Many scholars allow that *Thomas* was composed as early as the middle of the second century. How much earlier is hotly debated. I will argue that *Thomas* dates no earlier than the end of the second century.

---

4. For critical editions that compare the Coptic and Greek texts of the *Gospel of Thomas*, see J.-E. Ménard, *L'Évangile selon Thomas* (NHS 5; Leiden: Brill, 1975); B. Layton, ed., *Nag Hammadi Codices II, 2–7, Together with XIII, 2*, Brit. Lib. Or. 4926 (1) and P. Oxy. 1, 654, 655* (2 vols.; NHS 20–21; Leiden: Brill, 1989). For an edition with Coptic and English on facing pages, see A. Guillaumont et al., *The Gospel According to Thomas: Coptic Text, Established and Translated* (2nd ed.; Leiden: Brill, 1976). For the Greek texts, plus plates, see B. P. Grenfell and A. S. Hunt, *The Oxyrhynchus Papyri, Edited with Translations and Notes* (London: Egypt Exploration Fund, 1891), 1–3 [= P.Oxy. 1]; idem, *New Sayings of Jesus and a Fragment of a Lost Gospel from Oxyrhynchus* (London: Frowde, 1904) [= P.Oxy. 654]; B. P. Grenfell, *The Oxyrhynchus Papyri*, Vol. 4, *Nos. 654–839* (London: Egypt Exploration Fund, 1904), 1–22 [= P.Oxy. 654], 22–28 [= P.Oxy. 655].

A few scholars still argue that the *Gospel of Thomas* contains primitive, pre-Synoptic tradition.[5] This is possible theoretically, but there are numerous difficulties that attend efforts to cull from this collection of logia (114 in the apparently complete Coptic edition) material that can with confidence be judged primitive, independent of the New Testament Gospels, and even authentic. Quoting or alluding to more than half of the writings of the New Testament (i.e., Matthew, Mark, Luke, John, Acts, Romans, 1–2 Corinthians, Galatians, Ephesians, Colossians, 1 Thessalonians, 1 Timothy, Hebrews, 1 John, Revelation),[6] *Thomas* could very well be a collage of New Testament and apocryphal materials that have been interpreted, often allegorically, in such a way as to advance second- and third-century mystical or gnostic ideas. Moreover, the traditions contained in *Thomas* hardly reflect a setting that predates the writings of the New Testament, which is why Dominic Crossan and others attempt to extract an early version (or versions) of

5. For a selection of studies by scholars who believe that the *Gospel of Thomas* contains primitive, pre-Synoptic tradition, see G. Quispel, "The Gospel of Thomas and the New Testament," *VC* 11 (1957): 189–207; H. Koester, "Q and Its Relatives," in *Gospel Origins & Christian Beginnings: In Honor of J. M. Robinson* (ed. J. E. Goehring et al.; Sonoma: Polebridge, 1990), 49–63, here 61–63; R. D. Cameron, "The Gospel of Thomas: A Forschungsbericht and Analysis," *ANRW* II.25.6:4195–4251. S. L. Davies ("Thomas: The Fourth Synoptic Gospel," *BA* 46 [1983]: 6–9, 12–14) makes the astonishing claim that the *Gospel of Thomas* "may be our best source for Jesus's teachings" (9). See also S. L. Davies, *The Gospel of Thomas and Christian Wisdom* (New York: Seabury, 1983). Davies dismisses too quickly the possible gnostic orientation of many of the sayings; it is surely inaccurate to report that scholars have concluded the *Gospel of Thomas* is gnostic only because it was found among gnostic documents. Most scholars are persuaded that the *Gospel of Thomas* is gnostic in its final form, though to what degree continues to be debated.

6. For a synopsis of parallels between the New Testament writings and the *Gospel of Thomas*, see C. A. Evans, R. L. Webb, and R. A. Wiebe, *Nag Hammadi Texts and the Bible: A Synopsis and Index* (NTTS 18; Leiden: Brill, 1993), 88–144. Scholars who think *Thomas* is dependent on the New Testament writings include C. L. Blomberg, "Tradition and Redaction in the Parables of the Gospel of Thomas," in *The Jesus Tradition outside the Gospels* (ed. D. Wenham; Gospel Perspectives 5; Sheffield: JSOT Press, 1984), 177–205; R. E. Brown, "The Gospel of Thomas and St John's Gospel," *NTS* 9 (1962–63): 155–77; B. Dehandschutter, "L'évangile de Thomas comme collection de paroles de Jésus," in *Logia: Les Paroles de Jésus—The Sayings of Jesus* (ed. J. Delobel; BETL 59; Leuven: Peeters, 1982), 507–15; idem, "Recent Research on the Gospel of Thomas," in *The Four Gospels, 1992: Festschrift Frans Neirynck* (ed. F. Van Segbroeck et al.; 3 vols.; BETL 100; Leuven: Peeters, 1992), 3:2257–62; M. Fieger, *Das Thomasevangelium: Einleitung, Kommentar und Systematik* (NTAbh 22; Münster: Aschendorff, 1991).

Thomas from the extant Coptic and Greek texts. Attempts such as these strike me as special pleading—that is, if the extant evidence does not fit the theory, then appeal to hypothetical evidence. The problem here is that we do not know if there ever was an edition of the *Gospel of Thomas* substantially different from the Greek fragments of Oxyrhynchus or the later Coptic translation from Nag Hammadi. Positing an early form of *Thomas*, stripped of the embarrassing late and secondary features, is a gratuitous move. The presence of so much New Testament material in *Thomas* should give us pause before accepting theories of the antiquity and independence of this writing.

Another major problem with viewing the *Gospel of Thomas* as independent of the canonical Gospels is the presence of a significant amount of material that is distinctive to Matthew (M), Luke (L), and John. This is an important observation, because scholars usually view Mark and Q—not M, L, and the Johannine tradition—as repositories of material most likely to be ancient and authentic. Yet, *Thomas* parallels the later traditions often.

Another telling factor that should give us pause is the presence in *Thomas* of features characteristic of Matthean and Lukan redaction. First, we may consider a few examples involving Matthew. Logia §40 and §57 reflect Matthew 15:13 and 13:24–30, respectively. This Matthean material derives from M and gives evidence of Matthean redaction. Other sayings in *Thomas* that parallel the triple tradition agree with Matthew's wording (cf. Matt. 15:14 = *Gos. Thom.* §34b; Matt. 12:50 = *Gos. Thom.* §99), rather than with Mark's wording. Matthew's unique juxtaposition of alms, prayer, and fasting (Matt. 6:1–18) appears to be echoed in *Gos. Thom.* §6 (= P.Oxy. 654 §6) and §14. In *Thomas* alms, prayer, and fasting are discussed in a negative light, probably reflecting gnostic antipathy toward Jewish piety, which surely argues for viewing *Thomas* as secondary to Matthew. All of this suggests that *Thomas* has drawn upon the Gospel of Matthew.

There is also evidence that the *Gospel of Thomas* was influenced by the Gospel of Luke. The Lukan evangelist alters Mark's "For there is nothing hid except to be made manifest" (Mark 4:22) to "For nothing is hid that shall not be made manifest" (Luke 8:17). It is this redacted version that is found in *Gos. Thom.* §§5–6, with the Greek parallel preserved in P.Oxy. 654 §5 matching Luke's text exactly, which counters any claim that Luke's text only influenced the later Coptic translation.[7] The texts read as follows:

ou gar estin krypton ean mē hina phanerōthē (Mark 4:22)

ou gar estin krypton ho ou phaneron genēsetai (Luke 8:17)

ou gar estin krypton ho ou phaneron genēsetai (P.Oxy. 654 §5)

Elsewhere there are indications that *Thomas* has followed Luke (*Gos. Thom.* §10, see Luke 12:49; *Gos. Thom.* §14, see Luke 10:8–9; *Gos. Thom.* §16, see Luke 12:51–53; cf. Matt. 10:34–36; *Gos. Thom.* §§55, 101, see Luke 14:26–27; cf. Matt. 10:37; *Gos. Thom.* §§73–75, see Luke 10:2). Given the evidence it is not surprising that a number of respected scholars have concluded that *Thomas* has drawn upon the New Testament Gospels.[8]

And finally, not long after the publication of the *Gospel of Thomas* it was noticed that the new Gospel shared several affinities with eastern, or Syrian Christianity, especially as expressed in second-century traditions, including Tatian's harmony of the

---

7. On Luke's influence on the *Gospel of Thomas*, see J. P. Meier, *A Marginal Jew: Rethinking the Historical Jesus*, Vol. 1, *The Roots of the Problem and the Person* (ABRL; New York: Doubleday, 1992), 136; C. M. Tuckett, "Thomas and the Synoptics," *NovT* 30 (1988): 132–57, esp. 146.

8. See R. M. Grant, *The Secret Sayings of Jesus* (Garden City: Doubleday, 1960), 113; B. Gärtner, *The Theology of the Gospel according to Thomas* (New York: Harper, 1961), 26–27, 34, 42–43; E. Haenchen, *Die Botschaft des Thomas-Evangeliums* (Berlin: Töpelmann, 1961), 67–68; R. Kasser, *L'Évangile selon Thomas: Présentation et commentaire théologique* (Neuchâtel: Delachaux et Niestlé, 1961); Ménard, *L'Évangile selon Thomas*; A. Lindemann, "Zur Gleichnis-interpretation im Thomas-Evangelium," *ZNW* 71 (1980): 214–43; W. Schrage, *Das Verhältnis des Thomas-Evangeliums zur synoptischen Tradition und zu den koptischen Evangelienübersetzungen* (BZNW 29; Berlin: Töpelmann, 1964), 1–11. Similar conclusions have been reached by H. K. McArthur, "The Dependence of the Gospel of Thomas on the Synoptics," *ExpTim* 71 (1959–60): 286–87; W. R. Schoedel, "Parables in the Gospel of Thomas," *CTM* 43 (1972): 548–60; K. R. Snodgrass, "The Gospel of Thomas: A Secondary Gospel," *SecCent* 7 (1989–90): 19–38; Tuckett, "Thomas and the Synoptics," 157; Meier, *Marginal Jew*, 1:130–39. According to C. E. Carlston (*The Parables of the Triple Tradition* [Philadelphia: Fortress, 1975], xiii), "many readings of the Gospel of Thomas and a considerable amount of time spent with the secondary literature . . . have not yet convinced me that any of the parabolic material in Thomas is clearly independent of the Synoptic Gospels."

four New Testament Gospels, called the *Diatessaron*. This point is potentially quite significant, for the *Diatessaron* was the only form of New Testament Gospel tradition known to Syrian Christianity in the second century. We must carefully consider the implications of this evidence.

Proponents of the independence and first-century origin of the *Gospel of Thomas* are aware of at least some aspects of this writing's relationship to Syrian Christianity. Crossan and Patterson rightly call attention to Edessa, eastern Syria, as the original provenance of *Thomas*. They point out, among other things, that the name "Judas Thomas" is found in other works of Syrian provenance, such as the *Book of Thomas the Contender* (NHC II,7), which begins in a manner reminiscent of the *Gospel of Thomas*: "The secret words that the Savior spoke to Judas Thomas, which I, even I Mathaias, wrote down" (138.1–3; cf. 142.7: "Judas—the one called Thomas"), and the *Acts of Thomas*, in which the apostle is called "Judas Thomas, who is also (called) Didymus" (§1; cf. §11: "Judas who is also Thomas"). The longer form of the name in the *Acts of Thomas* agrees with the prologue of the *Gospel of Thomas*, where the apostle is identified as "Didymus Judas Thomas." In the Syriac version of John 14:22, "Judas (not Iscariot)" is identified as "Judas Thomas." This nomenclature continues on into later Syrian Christian traditions.[9]

Despite these affinities with Syrian tradition, whose distinctive characteristics, so far as we can trace them, emerged in the second century, Crossan and Patterson (and others) are confident that the *Gospel of Thomas* in fact originated quite early. Patterson thinks *Thomas* must have existed before the end of the first century (though he allows for later editing). Crossan believes that the first edition of *Thomas* emerged in the 50s and the later edition— essentially the extant text—emerged in the 60s or 70s. In other

9. On the apostle Thomas in Syrian Christian tradition, see H.-C. Puech, "Une collection de Paroles de Jésus récemment retrouvée: L'Évangile selon Thomas," in *Comptes Rendus de l'Académie des Inscriptions et Belles-Lettres* (Paris: Institut de France, 1957), 146–67; idem, "The Gospel of Thomas," in *The New Testament Apocrypha*, Vol. 1, *Gospels and Related Writings* (ed. E. Hennecke and W. Schneemelcher; London: SCM; Philadelphia: Westminster, 1963), 278–307; Crossan, *Four Other Gospels*, 9–11; Patterson, *Gospel of Thomas and Jesus*, 118–20; idem, "Understanding the Gospel of Thomas Today," in Patterson, Robinson, and Bethge, *Fifth Gospel*, 37–40.

words, the *Gospel of Thomas* in its first edition is earlier than any of the New Testament Gospels. Indeed, even the later edition of *Thomas* may be earlier than the New Testament Gospels.[10]

Scholars have weighed in on both sides of this question, with many arguing that the *Gospel of Thomas* dates to the second century (e.g., early to mid) and with almost as many (several of whom are members of the Jesus Seminar) arguing that *Thomas* dates to the first century. The latter usually date *Thomas* to the end of the first century, but believe they can identify independent tradition that in some cases should be preferred to its parallel forms in the Synoptic Gospels.

This important question cannot be settled by taking a poll. We need to take a hard look at the *Gospel of Thomas*, especially as it relates to Syrian tradition. This text probably should not be dated before the middle of the second century. Indeed, the evidence suggests that *Thomas* was probably composed in the last quarter of the second century. There is probably nothing in *Thomas* that can be independently traced back to the first century. Let us consider the evidence.

In print and in public lectures Crossan has defended the antiquity and independence of the *Gospel of Thomas* principally on two grounds: (1) He can find "no overall compositional design" in the Gospel, apart from a few clusters of sayings linked by catchwords; and (2) he finds several differences in the parallels with the New Testament Gospels that he believes cannot be explained in terms of Thomasine redaction. Patterson's arguments are similar.[11] As it turns out, the Syrian evidence answers both points.

Almost from the beginning, a few scholars with Syriac expertise recognized the Semitic, especially Syriac, style of the *Gospel of Thomas*. This was, of course, consistent with what has already been said about the form of the name of the apostle. It was further noticed that at points, distinctive readings in *Thomas* agree with

---

10. On the proposal that the *Gospel of Thomas* dates to the first century, see Davies, *Gospel of Thomas*, 146–47; Crossan, *Historical Jesus*, 427–30; Patterson, *Gospel of Thomas and Jesus*, 118–20; idem, "Understanding the Gospel of Thomas," 40–45. The editors of the Greek fragments of the *Gospel of Thomas* (i.e., P.Oxy. 1, 654, and 655) suggested that the original Greek text probably dated to 140 CE, a date that Crossan, Patterson, and others find too late and based on untested and unwarranted assumptions.

11. See Crossan, *Four Other Gospels*, 11–18.

the Syriac version of the New Testament or with the earlier *Diatessaron* by Tatian.[12] It was also wondered if portions of *Thomas* originated in Syriac, instead of Greek, as was widely assumed. In a recent study Nicholas Perrin has put this question to the test. He has analyzed the entire text of *Thomas*, retroverting the Coptic into Syriac and Greek. The results of his investigation are quite impressive. On the assumption that the *Gospel of Thomas* was originally written not in Greek or Coptic but in Syriac, which is not implausible given its Syrian provenance, more than 500 catchwords can be identified linking almost all of the 114 sayings that make up this work. In fact, there were only three couplets (§56 and §57, §88 and §89, and §104 and §105) for which Perrin could find no linking catchwords. These exceptions are hardly fatal to Perrin's analysis, for the original Syriac catchwords could easily have been lost in transmission or in translation into Coptic.[13]

Moreover, Perrin is not only able to explain the order of the whole of *Thomas* in reference to catchwords, he is able to show in places the Gospel's acquaintance with the order and arrangement of Tatian's *Diatessaron*. The mystery of the order of the sayings that make up the *Gospel of Thomas* appears to have been resolved.

12. The *Diatessaron* (from Greek, meaning "through the four [Gospels]") blends together the four New Testament Gospels, plus some material from a fifth Gospel source. See S. Hemphill, *The Diatessaron of Tatian: A Harmony of the Four Holy Gospels Compiled in the Third Quarter of the Second Century* (London: Hodder & Stoughton, 1888); W. L. Petersen, *Tatian's Diatessaron: Its Creation, Dissemination, Significance and History in Scholarship* (VCSup 25; Leiden: Brill, 1994); idem, "Tatian's Diatessaron," in H. Koester, *Ancient Christian Gospels: Their History and Development* (London: SCM; Philadelphia: Trinity Press International, 1990), 403–30. The latter essay provides a very helpful overview. In a comprehensive study Gilles Quispel observed that, in comparison with the Greek New Testament Gospels, the *Gospel of Thomas* and Tatian's *Diatessaron* share a large number of textual variants. Indeed, almost half of the sayings in *Thomas* give evidence of at least one such variant. See G. Quispel, *Tatian and the Gospel of Thomas: Studies in the History of the Western Diatessaron* (Leiden: Brill, 1975). Tatian (ca. 120–185), a disciple of Justin Martyr (ca. 100–165), composed the *Diatessaron*, probably in Syriac and in Syria, sometime between 172 and 185. The *Diatessaron* relies heavily on Matthew and may have been inspired by the earlier harmony of the Synoptic Gospels produced by Justin Martyr.

13. On catchwords in the *Gospel of Thomas* and Syriac as the original language, see N. Perrin, *Thomas and Tatian: The Relationship between the Gospel of Thomas and the Diatessaron* (Academia Biblica 5; Atlanta: Society of Biblical Literature, 2002); idem, "NHC II,2 and the Oxyrhynchus Fragments (P.Oxy 1, 654, 655): Overlooked Evidence for a Syriac *Gospel of Thomas*," VC 58 (2004): 138–51.

Perrin concludes that the *Gospel of Thomas* is indeed dependent
on the New Testament Gospels, but not directly. *Thomas* depends
on the New Testament Gospels as they existed in the *Diatessaron*,
in Syriac.

In my view the principal argument that Crossan and others have
advanced in support of the literary independence of the *Gospel of
Thomas* from the New Testament Gospels has been dealt a crip-
pling blow. It is no longer justified to say that there is no discernible
framework or organizing principle lying behind the composition
of *Thomas*. There clearly is, if this writing of acknowledged Syrian
provenance is studied in the light of the Syriac language.

Just as impressive is the number of specific contacts between the
Gospel of Thomas and Syrian Gospel traditions and other Syrian
religious traditions. What we see is that again and again, where
Thomas differs from the New Testament Gospels, it agrees with
Syrian tradition. This point has not been sufficiently appreciated
by Crossan and others. There are many examples, one of which
we will now consider.

The Syrian tradition sheds light on the Thomasine form of Jesus'
beatitude pronounced on the poor:

Greek Matt. 5:3 "Blessed are the poor in spirit, for theirs is the
kingdom of heaven." (NRSV)

Greek Luke 6:20 "Blessed are you who are poor, for yours is the
kingdom of God." (NRSV)

Gos. Thom. §54 "Blessed are the poor, for yours is the kingdom
of heaven."

Old Syriac Matt. 5:3 "Blessed are the poor in spirit, for yours is the
kingdom of heaven"

Diatessaron "Blessed are the poor in spirit—"

Crossan views *Thomas* §54 as providing strong evidence of the independence of the Thomasine tradition. He notes that the Matthean
gloss "in spirit" is missing in *Thomas* and the forms of the two
clauses are mixed, with the first clause in the third person (as in

Matthew) and the second clause in the second person (as in Luke). Crossan cannot imagine how the author/collector of *Thomas* could have done this: "One would have at least to argue that *Thomas* (a) took the third person 'the poor' from Matthew, then (b) the second person 'yours' from Luke, and (c) returned to Matthew for the final 'kingdom of heaven.' It might be simpler to suggest that *Thomas* was mentally unstable."[14] As it turns out, it is simpler to review the Syrian tradition.

Thomas §54 follows the Syriac form of Matthew (probably from the *Diatessaron*, the only form in which the New Testament Gospel tradition was available for Syriac speakers in the late second century). The omission of the qualifying prepositional phrase "in spirit" should hardly occasion surprise. Not only is it missing from Luke, its non-appearance in *Thomas* is consistent with the Thomasine worldview. Omitting the phrase "in spirit" is not too difficult to explain in light of *Thomas*'s antimaterialistic perspective (cf. *Gos. Thom.* §§27, 63, 64, 65, 95, 110), a perspective consistent with the ascetic views of the Syrian church. No, *Thomas* declares, it is not the poor in spirit who are blessed, it is the poor. So, to return to Crossan's argument, one need only say that *Thomas* (a) took the saying as it existed in Syriac (which accounts for the mix of third and second person, as well as the presence of the phrase "kingdom of heaven") and (b) deleted "in spirit."

Before concluding the discussion of the *Gospel of Thomas*, one other issue needs to be addressed. Stephen Patterson, James Robinson, and others have argued that the genre of the *Gospel of Thomas* supports an early date. Because *Thomas* is like Q, the sayings source on which Matthew and Luke drew, then *Thomas* in its earliest form may approximate the age of Q.[15] This argument

---

14. Crossan, *Four Other Gospels*, 18–19. See also the analysis in Patterson, *Gospel of Thomas and Jesus*, 42–44. The source-critical and exegetical arguments of Crossan and Patterson lose all force in view of the Syrian evidence.

15. On the argument that the sayings genre of the *Gospel of Thomas* is evidence of an early date, see J. M. Robinson, "LOGOI SOPHON: On the Gattung of Q," in J. M. Robinson and H. Koester, *Trajectories through Early Christianity* (Philadelphia: Fortress, 1971), 71–113; idem, "On Bridging the Gulf from Q to the Gospel of Thomas (or *vice versa*)," in *Nag Hammadi, Gnosticism, and Early Christianity* (ed. C. W. Hedrick and R. Hodgson Jr.; Peabody, MA: Hendrickson, 1986), 127–55; Davies, *Gospel of Thomas*, 145; Patterson, *Gospel of Thomas and Jesus*, 113–18.

is wholly specious, not only because it does not take into account the extensive coherence with late-second-century Syrian tradition, which has been reviewed above, or the lack of coherence with pre-70 Jewish Palestine, it fails to take into account that other sayings collections, some in Syria, emerged in the second and third centuries. Among these are the rabbinic collection that became known as the *Pirqe Avot* ("Chapters of the Fathers") and the *Sentences of Sextus*. The latter is particularly significant because it originated in Syria in the second century, the approximate time and place of the emergence of the *Gospel of Thomas*. The evidence suggests that the *Gospel of Thomas* is another second-century collection that emerged in Syria.

The evidence strongly points to a late origin of the *Gospel of Thomas*. The association of the work with Judas Thomas, the arrangement and order of the sayings explained by hundreds of Syriac catchwords that link the sayings, and the coherence of the readings in *Thomas* that differ from the Greek New Testament Gospels with the readings either in the *Diatessaron* or other Christian Syriac works from this period compellingly argue for a late-second-century Syrian origin of the *Gospel of Thomas*. In short, it is the flood of factors that point to the eastern, Syriac-speaking church, a church that knows the New Testament Gospels primarily—perhaps exclusively—through Tatian's *Diatessaron*, a work not composed before 170 CE, that persuades me that the *Gospel of Thomas* does not offer students of the Gospels early, independent material that can be used for critical research into the life and teaching of Jesus.

The Akhmîm Gospel Fragment (the *Gospel of Peter?*)

In a discussion of writings attributed to the apostle Peter, church historian Eusebius of Caesarea (ca. 260–340) mentions a *Gospel of Peter*, which Serapion, bishop of Antioch (in office 199–211), condemned as heretical (*Ecclesiastical History* 6.12.3–6). Serapion quotes no portion of this Gospel, only saying that it was used by docetists. In the winter of 1886–1887, during excavations at Akhmîm in Egypt, a codex was found in the coffin of a Christian monk. The manuscript comprises a fragment of a Gospel, fragments of

Greek *Enoch*, the *Apocalypse of Peter*, and, written on the inside of the back cover of the codex, an account of the martyrdom of St. Julian. The Gospel fragment bears no name or hint of a title, for neither the *incipit* nor the *explicit* has survived. Because the apostle Peter appears in the text, narrating in the first person (v. 60 "But I, Simon Peter"), because it seemed to have a docetic orientation, and because the Gospel fragment was in the company of the *Apocalypse of Peter*, it was widely assumed that the fragment belonged to the *Gospel of Peter* mentioned by Eusebius.[16]

Critical assessments of the newly published Gospel fragment diverged widely, with some scholars claiming that the fragment was independent of the New Testament Gospels, and others that the fragment is dependent on them.[17] Throughout this debate no one seriously asked if the Akhmîm fragment really was part of the second-century *Gospel of Peter*. It was simply assumed that it was.

Then, in the 1970s and 1980s two more Greek fragments from Egypt were published, P.Oxy. 2949 and P.Oxy. 4009, which with varying degrees of confidence were identified as belonging to the *Gospel of Peter*. Indeed, one of the fragments was thought to

16. The ninth-century Akhmîm Gospel fragment was published five years after its discovery, in U. Bouriant, "Fragments du texte grec du livre d'Enoch et de quelques écrits attribués à Saint Pierre," in *Mémoires publiés par les membres de la Mission archéologique française au Caire*, Vol. 9.1 (Paris: Libraire de la Société asiatique, 1892), 137–42. Edited and corrected editions of the text can also be found in J. A. Robinson and M. R. James, *The Gospel according to Peter, and the Revelation of Peter* (London: C. J. Clay, 1892); H. von Schubert, *Das Petrusevangelium* (Berlin: Reuther & Reichard, 1893); idem, *The Gospel of St. Peter* (Edinburgh: T&T Clark, 1893); and more recently in M. G. Mara, *Évangile de Pierre* (SC 201; Paris: Éditions du Cerf, 1973). The Greek text of the *Gospel of Peter* is also found in K. Aland, ed., *Synopsis Quattuor Evangeliorum* (Stuttgart: Deutsche Bibelgesellschaft, 1985), 479–80, 484, 489, 493–94, 498, 500, 507.

17. Those who argue that the newly discovered Akhmîm Gospel fragment depends on the Synoptic Gospels include T. Zahn, *Das Evangelium des Petrus* (Erlangen: Deichert, 1893); H. B. Swete, EUAGGELION KATA PETRON: *The Akhmim Fragment of the Apocryphal Gospel of St. Peter* (London and New York: Macmillan, 1893), xiii–xx. Robinson (*Gospel according to Peter*, 32–33) speaks of "the unmistakeable acquaintance of the author with our Four Evangelists. . . . He uses and misuses each in turn." Those who argue that the fragment is independent of the Synoptic Gospels include A. Harnack, *Bruchstücke des Evangeliums und der Apokalypse des Petrus* (TU 9; Leipzig: Hinrichs, 1893); A. Harnack and H. von Schubert, "Das Petrus-evangelium," *TLZ* 19 (1894): 9–18; P. Gardner-Smith, "The Gospel of Peter," *JTS* 27 (1925–26): 255–71; idem, "The Date of the Gospel of Peter," *JTS* 27 (1925–26): 401–7.

overlap with part of the Akhmîm fragment. The publication of
these fragments renewed interest in the Gospel, because it was felt
that the identity of the Akhmîm fragment as the second-century
Gospel of Peter was confirmed. Indeed, it has also been suggested
that the Fayyum Fragment, or P. Vindob. G 2325, is yet another
early fragment of the *Gospel of Peter*.[18]

In recent years, Koester and a circle of colleagues and students
have given new life to Gardner-Smith's position that the Akhmîm
fragment is independent of the New Testament Gospels. According to Koester, the *Gospel of Peter*'s "basis must be an older text
under the authority of Peter which was independent of the canonical gospels." Koester's student Ron Cameron agrees, concluding
that this Gospel is independent of the canonical Gospels, may
even antedate them, and "may have served as a source for their
respective authors."[19] This position has been worked out in detail
by John Dominic Crossan, who accepts the identification of the
Akhmîm fragment with Serapion's *Gospel of Peter*. In a lengthy
study that appeared in 1985 Crossan argued that the *Gospel
of Peter*, though admittedly in its final stages influenced by the
New Testament Gospel tradition, preserves a very old tradition,
on which all four of the canonical Gospels' Passion accounts

18. For reconstruction of P.Oxy. 2949, see R. A. Coles, "Fragments of an Apocryphal
Gospel (?)," in *The Oxyrhynchus Papyri*, Vol. 41, Nos. 2943–2998 (ed. G. M. Browne et al.;
London: Egypt Exploration Society, 1972), 15–16 (+ pl. II). See also D. Lührmann, "POx
2949: EvPt 3–5 in einer Handschrift des 2./3. Jahrhunderts," *ZNW* 72 (1981): 216–22. P.Oxy.
2949 may date as early as the late second century. The second fragment, P.Oxy. 4009, also
probably dates to the second century. See D. Lührmann and P. J. Parsons, "4009. Gospel of
Peter?" in *The Oxyrhynchus Papyri*, Vol. 60, Nos. 4009–4092 (ed. R. Coles.; London: Egypt
Exploration Society, 1994), 1–5 (+ pl. I); D. Lührmann, "POx 4009: Ein neues Fragment des
Petrusevangeliums?" *NovT* 35 (1993): 390–410. For the proposal that the Fayyum Fragment
also belongs to the *Gospel of Peter*, see D. Lührmann, *Fragmente apokryph gewordener
Evangelien in griechischer und lateinischer Sprache* (with E. Schlarb; MTS 59; Marburg:
N. G. Elwert, 2000), 80–81.

19. On recent scholarly support of the antiquity of the *Gospel of Peter*, see H. Koester,
Introduction to the New Testament (Berlin and New York: de Gruyter, 1982), 2:163; cf.
idem, "Überlieferung und Geschichte der frühchristlichen Evangelienliteratur," *ANRW*
II.25.2:1463–1542, esp. 1487–88, 1525–27; R. D. Cameron, *The Other Gospels: Non-
Canonical Gospel Texts* (Philadelphia: Westminster, 1982), 78. Another Koester student,
B. A. Johnson ("The Empty Tomb Tradition in the Gospel of Peter" [ThD diss., Harvard
University, 1966]), has argued that Peter's empty tomb tradition is not based on the canoni-
cal Gospels, but on an older tradition.

are based.[20] This old tradition is identified as the *Cross Gospel.*
Crossan's provocative conclusion calls for evaluation.

The author of the Akhmîm Gospel fragment apparently possessed little accurate knowledge of Jewish customs and sensitivities. According to 8.31 and 10.38 the Jewish elders and scribes camp out in the cemetery, as part of the guard keeping watch over the tomb of Jesus. Given Jewish views of corpse impurity, not to mention fear of cemeteries at night, the author of our fragment is unbelievably ignorant. Who could write such a story only twenty years after the death of Jesus? And if someone did at such an early time, can we really believe that the Matthean evangelist, who was surely Jewish, would make use of such a poorly informed writing? One can scarcely credit this scenario.

There are worse problems. The Jewish leaders' fear of harm at the hands of the Jewish people (Akhmîm fragment 8.30) smacks of embellishment, if not Christian apologetic. The "seven seals" (8.33) and the "crowd from Jerusalem and the surrounding countryside" that "came in order to see the sealed tomb" (9.34) serve an apologetic interest: the resurrection story is well attested. These details are probably secondary to the canonical tradition. The appearance of the expression, "the Lord's day" (*hē kyriakē*, 9.35), of course, is another indication of lateness (cf. Rev. 1:10; Ignatius, *To the Magnesians* 9:1), not antiquity. The centurion's confession (Akhmîm fragment 11.45) appears to reflect Matthean influence (Matt. 27:54; cf. Mark 15:39; Luke 23:47).[21]

---

20. On the theory that an early form of the *Gospel of Peter* lies behind the Passion narratives of the New Testament Gospels, see J. D. Crossan, *The Cross that Spoke: The Origins of the Passion Narrative* (San Francisco: Harper & Row, 1988), 404: "This book has argued for the existence of a document which I call the *Cross Gospel* as the single known source for the Passion and Resurrection Narrative. It flowed into Mark, flowed along with him into Matthew and Luke, flowed along with the three synoptics into John, and finally flowed along with the intracanonical tradition into the pseudepigraphical *Gospel of Peter.* I cannot find persuasive evidence of anything save redactional modification being added to that stream once it departs its *Cross Gospel* source."

21. On the late and secondary nature of the Akhmîm Gospel fragment (or *Gospel of Peter*), see L. Vaganay, *L'évangile de Pierre* (EBib; Paris: Gabalda, 1930), 83–90; T. W. Manson, "The Life of Jesus: A Study of the Available Materials," *BJRL* 27 (1942–43): 323–37; C. H. Dodd, "A New Gospel," in *New Testament Studies* (Manchester: Manchester University Press, 1953), 12–52; K. Beyschlag, "Das Petrusevangelium," in *Die verborgene Überlieferung von Christus* (Munich and Hamburg: Siebenstern Taschenbuch, 1969), 27–64;

Finally, can it be seriously maintained that the Akhmîm fragment's resurrection account, complete with a talking cross and
angels whose heads reach heaven, constitutes the most primitive
account extant? Is this the account that the canonical evangelists
had before them? Or, is it not more prudent to conclude what we
have here is still more evidence of the secondary, fanciful nature
of this apocryphal writing?[22] Does not the evidence suggest that
the Akhmîm Gospel fragment is little more than a blend of details
from the four canonical Gospels, especially from Matthew, that
has been embellished with pious imagination, apologetic concerns,
and a touch of anti-Semitism?

and É. Massaux, *The Influence of the Gospel of Saint Matthew on Christian Literature
before Saint Irenaeus* (ed. A. J. Bellinzoni; 3 vols.; NGS 5.1–3; Macon, GA: Mercer University Press, 1990–93), 2:202–14. Dodd ("New Gospel," 46) concludes that the Akhmîm
fragment (which he accepts as the *Gospel of Peter*) "depends on all four canonical Gospels,
and probably not on any independent tradition." Beyschlag ("Das Petrusevangelium,"
62, 64) opines that the Akhmîm fragment presupposes all four canonical Gospels. On the
secondary nature of the guard tradition in the Akhmîm fragment, see S. E. Schaeffer, "The
Guard at the Tomb (*Gos. Pet.* 8:28–11:49 and Matt. 27:62–66; 28:2–4, 11–16): A Case of
Intertextuality?" in *Society of Biblical Literature 1991 Seminar Papers* (ed. E. H. Lovering;
SBLSP 30; Atlanta: Scholars Press, 1991), 499–507; and Massaux, *Influence of the Gospel
of Saint Matthew*, 2:202–4.

22. Crossan and others have not sufficiently probed the significance of the fantastic
elements in the Akhmîm Gospel fragment. The fragment describes the risen Jesus as so
tall that his head extended above the heavens and that the cross on which Jesus had been
crucified exited the tomb with him. These are the details of late not early tradition. On the
great height of Jesus, see *Shepherd of Hermas, Parables* 83.1 ("a man so tall that he rose
above the tower"). The *Shepherd of Hermas* was composed sometime between 110 and
140 CE. The mid-second-century addition to *4 Ezra* (i.e., 2 Esd. 1–2) describes the "Son of
God" as possessing "great stature, taller than any of the others" (2:43–47). The Akhmîm
Gospel fragment's description of Jesus' head extending above the heavens probably represents a further and much later embellishment of these traditions. The Akhmîm Gospel
fragment's description of the cross that exits the tomb with the risen Jesus, accompanied
by angels, parallels late Ethiopic tradition, attested in two works, whose original Greek
compositions probably dated no earlier than the middle of the second century. According
to the *Epistle to the Apostles* 16, Jesus assures his disciples: "I will come as the sun which
bursts forth; thus will I, shining seven times brighter than it in glory, while I am carried
on the wings of the clouds in splendor with my cross going on before me, then to earth to
judge the living and the dead" (J. K. Elliott, *The Apocryphal New Testament: A Collection
of Apocryphal Christian Literature in an English Translation* [Oxford: Clarendon; New
York: Oxford University Press, 1993], 566). This tradition, with some variation, is repeated
in the Ethiopic *Apocalypse of Peter* 1: "with my cross going before my face will I come in
my majesty; shining seven times brighter than the sun will I come in my majesty with all
my saints, my angels" (Elliott, *Apocryphal New Testament*, 600).

The evidence strongly suggests that the Akhmîm Gospel fragment is a late work, not an early work, even if we attempt to find an earlier substratum, (gratuitously) shorn of imagined late accretions. But more pressing is the question that asks if the extant ninth-century Akhmîm Gospel fragment really is a fragment of the second-century *Gospel of Peter* condemned by Bishop Serapion in the early third century. The extant Akhmîm fragment does not identify itself, nor do we have a patristic quotation of the *Gospel of Peter* with which we could make comparison and possibly settle the question. Nor is the Akhmîm Gospel fragment docetic, as many asserted shortly after its publication. If the fragment is not docetic, then the putative identification of the fragment with the *Gospel of Peter* is weakened still further. After all, the one thing Serapion emphasized was that the *Gospel of Peter* was used by docetists to advance their doctrines.[23] And finally, as Paul Foster has shown, the connection between the Akhmîm Gospel fragment and the small papyrus fragments that may date as early as 200–250 is quite tenuous.[24] Thus, we have no solid evidence that allows us with any confidence to link the extant Akhmîm Gospel fragment with a second-century text, be that the *Gospel of Peter* mentioned by Bishop Serapion or some other writing from the late second century. Given its fantastic features and coherence with late traditions, it is not advisable to make use of this Gospel fragment for Jesus research.

23. There are serious questions about the alleged docetism in the Akhmîm Gospel fragment. In 4.10 it says that Jesus "himself was silent, as having no pain." This does not say that Jesus in fact felt no pain; it implies that he was silent, even though the experience was indeed painful. Also, the cry from the cross, "My power, [my] power, you have abandoned me!" (5.19), is taken by some to indicate docetism. But what we have here is probably no more than influence from a variant form of Ps. 22:1, where one of the Greek recensions reads "strength" (or "power"), instead of "God." For further discussion on this issue, see J. W. McCant, "The Gospel of Peter: Docetism Reconsidered," *NTS* 30 (1984): 258–73. There really is no compelling basis for seeing docetic tendencies in the Akhmîm Gospel fragment.

24. On the problem of identifying the early Greek fragments with the Akhmîm Gospel fragment, see P. Foster, "Are There Any Early Fragments of the So-Called *Gospel of Peter?*" *NTS* 52 (2006): 1–28. Foster shows it is far from certain that the small Greek fragments P.Oxy. 2949, P.Oxy. 4009, and P.Vindob. G 2325 are from the *Gospel of Peter* mentioned by Bishop Serapion. Foster rightly warns of the circular reasoning in the interpretation of the evidence, where the ninth-century Akhmîm fragment is assumed at the outset to be the *Gospel of Peter* and then the early-third-century papyri are reconstructed on the basis of the Akhmîm fragment, which in turn confirms the assumption that the Akhmîm fragment is indeed the *Gospel of Peter.*

Papyrus Egerton 2

Papyrus Egerton 2 consists of four fragments. The fourth fragment yields nothing more than one illegible letter. The third fragment yields little more than a few scattered words. The first and second fragments offer four (or perhaps five) stories that parallel Johannine and Synoptic materials. Papyrus Köln 255 constitutes a related fragment of the text.[25]

At many points these fragments parallel the New Testament Gospels. The first story is replete with allusions to the Fourth Gospel. Jesus' assertion in lines 7–10 could well be drawn from John 5:39, 45. The lawyers' reply in lines 15–17 appears to be taken from John 9:29, while Jesus' rejoinder in lines 20–23a[26] reflects John 5:46. The attempt to stone Jesus in lines 22–24 parallels John 10:31, while the declaration in lines 25–30 that they were unable to do so because his "hour had not yet come" echoes John 7:30 and 8:20. Reference to Jesus in line 30 as "the Lord" has a secondary ring. The second story is mostly Synoptic. The third story again combines Johannine and Synoptic elements. The opening statement in lines 45–47, "Teacher Jesus, we know that [from God] you have come, for what you are doing tes[tifies] beyond all the prophets," is based upon John 3:2 and 9:29 (cf. also John 1:45;

25. For the Greek text of the London fragments of Papyrus Egerton 2, see H. I. Bell and T. C. Skeat, *Fragments of an Unknown Gospel and Other Early Christian Papyri* (London: British Museum, 1935), 8–15, 26; idem, *The New Gospel Fragments* (London: British Museum, 1951), 29–33. A critical edition has been prepared by G. Mayeda, *Das Leben-Jesu-Fragment Papyrus Egerton 2 und seine Stellung in der urchristlichen Literaturgeschichte* (Bern: Haupt, 1946), 7–11. See also Aland, *Synopsis Quattuor Evangeliorum*, 60, 323, 332, 340, 422.

The superscript numbers in the English translation indicate approximately the line breaks. The text of the more recently discovered Köln fragment has been made available in M. Gronewald, "Unbekanntes Evangelium oder Evangelienharmonie (Fragment aus dem Evangelium Egerton)," in *Kölner Papyri (P. Köln), Bd. 6* (ed. Gronewald et al.; Sonderreihe Papyrologica Coloniensia 7; Cologne: Bibliothèque Bodmer, 1987), 136–45, and in D. Lührmann, "Das neue Fragment des PEgerton 2 (PKöln 255)," in Van Segbroeck et al., *Four Gospels*, 3:2239–55.

26. On enumerating the lines in the Egerton and Köln papyri: Lines 22a and 23a, which are based upon Papyrus Köln 255, are so designated, in order to distinguish them from lines 22 and 23 of Papyrus Egerton 2, fragment 1 recto. The same is done with lines 42a–44a, which also are based upon Papyrus Köln 255, at the end of the same fragment, in order to distinguish them from lines 42–44 of Papyrus Egerton 2, fragment 2 recto.

Acts 3:18). Egerton's use of "teacher" (*didaskale*) is secondary to John's transliteration *rhabbi*, and may be due to its appearance in Mark 12:14a ("Teacher, we know that you are true"). The question put to Jesus in lines 48–50 is taken from Mark 12:14b and parallel, but appears to have missed the original point. Jesus' emotion in line 51 recalls Mark 1:43, while his question in lines 52–54 recalls a form of the question found in Luke 6:46. The remainder of Jesus' saying, which is a paraphrase of Isaiah 29:13, echoes Mark 7:6–7 and parallel.

Crossan's analysis of these fragments leads him to conclude that Papyrus Egerton 2 represents a tradition that predates the canonical Gospels. He thinks that "Mark is dependent on it directly" and that it gives evidence of "a stage before the distinction of Johannine and Synoptic traditions was operative."[27] Helmut Koester agrees with Crossan's second point, saying that in Papyrus Egerton 2 we find "pre-Johannine and pre-synoptic characteristics of language [which] still existed side by side."[28] He thinks it unlikely, contrary to Jeremias, that the author of this papyrus could have been acquainted with the canonical Gospels and "would have deliberately composed [it] by selecting sentences" from them.[29]

Theoretically Crossan and Koester could be correct in this assessment. There are, however, some serious questions that must be raised. First, several times editorial improvements introduced by Matthew and Luke appear in Egerton (e.g., compare Egerton line 32 with Mark 1:40; Matt. 8:2; Luke 5:12; or Egerton lines 39–41 with Mark 1:44; Matt. 8:4; Luke 17:14). There are other indications that the Egerton Papyrus is posterior to the canonical Gospels. The plural "kings" is probably secondary to the singular "Caesar" found in the Synoptics (and in *Gospel of Thomas* §100). The flattery, "what you do bears witness beyond all the prophets," may reflect John 1:34, 45 and is again reminiscent of later pious Christian embellishment that tended to exaggerate the

27. Crossan, *Four Other Gospels*, 183.

28. Koester, *Ancient Christian Gospels*, 207; cf. idem, "Überlieferung und Geschichte," 1488–90, 1522.

29. Jeremias, "Papyrus Egerton 2," in Hennecke and Schneemelcher, *New Testament Apocrypha*, 1:96; Koester, *Ancient Christian Gospels*, 215. Crossan (*Four Other Gospels*, 86) argues that Mark is actually "directly dependent on the [Egerton] papyrus text."

respect that Jesus' contemporaries showed him (see the examples in *Gospel of the Hebrews* 2 and Josephus, *Jewish Antiquities* 18.3.3 §64).

Second, a question arises in response to Koester's statement that it is improbable the author of the Egerton Papyrus "would have deliberately composed [it] by selecting sentences" from the canonical Gospels: Is this not the very thing that Justin Martyr and his disciple Tatian did? Justin Martyr composed a *Harmony* of the Synoptic Gospels and Tatian composed a harmony (i.e., the *Diatessaron*) of all four New Testament Gospels. If Justin Martyr and Tatian, writing in the second century, can compose their respective harmonies through the selection of sentences and phrases from this Gospel and that, why could not the author of the Egerton Papyrus do the same thing?

A third question is prompted by Koester's suggestion that the mixture of Johannine-like and Synoptic elements is primitive, while their bifurcation into the extant canonical forms is secondary. If Koester's suggestion is correct, then the Egerton Gospel does indeed derive from the middle of the first century, as Crossan in fact argues. It would have to be this early, if it were to be used by the Synoptic evangelists. If this is the case, then one must wonder why it is that we have no other fragment, nor any other evidence of the existence of this extraordinarily primitive Gospel. How is it that we do not have other papyri, extracanonical Gospels, or patristic quotations attesting this primitive pre-Synoptic, pre-Johannine unified tradition?

Examples can be found in Justin Martyr's quotations, which sometimes combine materials from two or more Gospels. From *First Apology* 15.9 we read: "If you love those who love you [cf. Matt. 5:46 = Luke 6:32], what new thing do you do [*unparalleled*]? For even the fornicators do this [Matt. 5:46: 'tax collectors'; Luke 6:32, 33: 'sinners']. But I say to you [cf. Matt. 5:44], pray for your enemies [cf. Matt. 5:44: 'love'] and love those who hate you [cf. Luke 6:27: 'do good'] and bless those who curse you and pray for those who mistreat you [cf. Luke 6:28]." In *First Apology* 15.10–12 Justin combines materials from Matthew and Luke to create a lengthy saying that his readers would take as a single utterance. Yet it is a conflation.

In *First Apology* 16.9–13 Justin has assembled, based on memory, a "word" of Jesus that is in reality a pastiche of Synoptic materials, which at one point may also reflect Johannine influence. Although drawn from a variety of contexts, there is nevertheless a general thematic unity that holds these materials together. With respect to composition, the sayings in Papyrus Egerton 2 §1 and §3 are quite similar to Justin's dominical "word."

Another feature that tells against the antiquity and priority of the Egerton Papyrus is the story related in the badly preserved verso of fragment 2. Jesus apparently sows a handful of seed on the Jordan River, from which abundant fruit springs. The story is reminiscent of the kind of stories found in the late and fanciful apocryphal Gospels. For example, in the *Infancy Gospel of Thomas* the boy Jesus sowed a handful of seed that yielded a remarkable harvest (*Infan. Thom.* 10.1–2 [Latin]).[30]

Although the hypothesis of Crossan, Koester, and others remains a theoretical possibility, the evidence available at this time suggests that in all probability Papyrus Egerton 2 represents a second-century conflation of Synoptic and Johannine elements, rather than primitive first-century material on which the canonical Gospels depended. The presence of at least one apocryphal tale akin to those of the least historically viable traditions only strengthens this conviction.

The Secret Gospel of Mark

At the annual Society of Biblical Literature meeting in New York in 1960 Morton Smith announced that during his sabbatical leave in 1958, at the Mar Saba Monastery in the Judean wilderness, he found the first part of a letter of Clement of Alexandria (ca. 150–215) penned in Greek, in what he suggested was an eighteenth-century hand, in the back of a sixteenth-century edition of the letters of Ignatius. In 1973 Smith published two editions of his find, one learned and one popular. From the start, scholars suspected

---

30. The *Infancy Gospel of Thomas* may have originated as early as the late second century; cf. O. Cullmann, "Infancy Gospels," in Hennecke and Schneemelcher, *New Testament Apocrypha*, 1:419. The *Infancy Gospel of Thomas* should not be confused with the *Gospel of Thomas*.

that the text was a forgery and that Smith was himself the forger. Many scholars—including several members of the Jesus Seminar—defended Smith and the authenticity of the Clementine letter. What made the alleged find so controversial were two quotations of a mystical or secret version of the Gospel of Mark, quotations of passages not found in the public Gospel of Mark. In the first, longer passage Jesus raises a dead man and then later, in the nude, instructs the young man in the mysteries of the kingdom of God. The homoerotic orientation of the story is hard to miss.

Despite the facts that no one besides Smith has actually studied the physical document and that the paper and ink have never been subjected to the kinds of tests normally undertaken, many scholars have accepted the Clementine letter as genuine and the validity of its testimony that there really was in circulation, in the second century, a secret version of the Gospel of Mark. Indeed, some scholars have suggested that *Secret Mark* may help us nuance the solution of the Synoptic problem, and, of course, some scholars have suggested that *Secret Mark* is older and more original than public Mark. Learned studies continue to appear, including two recent major monographs.[31]

The sad thing is that all of this labor has been misspent; the Clementine letter and the quotations of *Secret Mark* embedded within it constitute a modern hoax, and Morton Smith almost certainly is the hoaxer. Several scholars have for years suspected this to be the case, but the recently published clear, color photographs of

31. For a sampling of scholarship concerned with the Secret Gospel of Mark, see M. Smith, *Clement of Alexandria and a Secret Gospel of Mark* (Cambridge, MA: Harvard University Press, 1973); idem, *The Secret Gospel: The Discovery and Interpretation of the Secret Gospel according to Mark* (New York: Harper & Row, 1973); F. F. Bruce, *The Secret Gospel of Mark: The Ethel M. Wood Lecture Delivered before the University of London on 11 February 1974* (London: Athlone, 1974); M. W. Meyer, *Secret Gospels: Essays on Thomas and the Secret Gospel of Mark* (Harrisburg, PA: Trinity Press International, 2003). For two recent monographs, see E. Rau, *Das geheime Markusevangelium: Ein Schriftfund voller Rätsel* (Neukirchen: Neukirchener Verlag, 2003); and S. G. Brown, *Mark's Other Gospel: Rethinking Morton Smith's Controversial Discovery* (Waterloo, ON: Canadian Corporation for the Studies in Religion, 2005). An early and outstanding critical review of Smith's books was written by Q. Quesnell, "The Mar Saba Clementine: A Question of Evidence," *CBQ* 37 (1975): 48–67. Quesnell's probing review raised many troubling questions about the authenticity of the Clementine letter.

the document[32] have given experts in the science of forgery detection the opportunity to analyze the document's handwriting and compare it with samples of handwriting from the late Professor Smith. The evidence is compelling and conclusive: Smith wrote the text. Stephen Carlson and Peter Jeffrey have compiled and analyzed the evidence, some of which is as follows:[33]

(1) Magnification of the handwritten text reveals what handwriting experts call the "forger's tremor." That is, the handwriting in question is not really written; it is drawn, in the forger's attempt to imitate a style of writing not his own. Telltale signs of this are everywhere present in the alleged Clementine letter.

(2) Comparison of the style of the Greek of the handwritten text with Morton Smith's style of writing Greek (as seen in his papers and marginal notes in his books) has shown that Smith is the person who wrote (or, "drew") the Clementine letter. For example, Smith had an unusual way of writing the Greek letters tau, theta, and lambda. These unusual forms occasionally intrude in what otherwise is a well-executed imitation of eighteenth-century Greek handwriting.

(3) Some of the distinctive themes in the document are evident in some of Smith's work published before the alleged find in 1958.[34]

32. For good quality color photographs of the Clementine letter, see C. W. Hedrick, "Secret Mark: New Photographs, New Witnesses," *The Fourth R* 13/5 (2000): 3–16. Hedrick thought that his photographs supplied evidence supporting the authenticity of the Clementine letter. As it turns out, they had the opposite effect.

33. For convincing evidence that the Clementine letter is a hoax, see S. C. Carlson, *The Gospel Hoax: Morton Smith's Invention of Secret Mark* (Waco, TX: Baylor University Press, 2005); P. Jeffrey, *The Secret Gospel of Mark Unveiled: Imagined Rituals of Sex, Death, and Madness in a Biblical Forgery* (New Haven: Yale University Press, 2007). In his recent essay, "The Question of Motive in the Case against Morton Smith," *JBL* 125 (2006): 351–83, Scott Brown attempts to cast doubt on Carlson's proposals, particularly with regard to Smith's motives. The question of motive—apart from the discovery of a confession—will remain the most uncertain feature of this strange case. But the handwriting evidence, along with several other pieces of circumstantial evidence, allows much less doubt.

34. Prior to the "discovery" of the letter of Clement and its quotations of *Secret Mark*, Smith linked the idea of a secret Christian doctrine, which he thinks is alluded to in Mark 4:11 ("To you has been given the secret of the kingdom of God," NRSV), to *t. Hagigah* 2.1, which discusses forbidden sexual relationships in Leviticus 18. See M. Smith, *Tannaitic Parallels to the Gospels* (JBLMS 6; Philadelphia: Society of Biblical Literature, 1951), 155–56. Just prior to his visit to the Mar Saba Monastery in 1958, Smith published

(4) The discolored blotch that is plainly visible in the lower left-hand corner of the final page of the printed text of the volume and in the lower left-hand corner of the second page of the handwritten text prove that the handwritten pages were originally part of the printed edition of the letters of Ignatius. These corresponding blotches, as well as many of the other blotches and discolorations that can be seen in the color photographs, are mildew. The presence of this mildew strongly suggests that the book in question was not originally a part of the library of Mar Saba, whose dry climate is not conducive to the production of mold and mildew in books. The mildew in the printed edition of the letters of Ignatius suggests that book spent most of its existence in Europe. We may speculate that in Europe, or perhaps in North America, the book was purchased and the Clementine letter was drawn onto the blank end papers. The book was then taken to the Mar Saba Monastery, where it was subsequently "found" in the library.

(5) One of the Mar Saba documents catalogued by Smith is written in the same hand as the alleged Clementine letter. This document Smith dated to the twentieth century (not to the eighteenth century, as in the case of the Clementine letter). Moreover, the document

---

an article, in which he again makes mention of *t. Hag.* 2.1, only this time linking it to Clement of Alexandria. See M. Smith, "The Image of God: Notes on the Hellenization of Judaism, with Especial Reference to Goodenough's Work on Jewish Symbols," *BJRL* 40 (1958): 473–512, here 507. This distinctive combination—the "secret of the kingdom of God," a rabbinic passage that discusses forbidden sexual relationships, and Clement of Alexandria—is found only in Morton Smith's writings. The combination is also found in the Mar Saba letter, supposedly written by Clement of Alexandria, in which the "secret of the kingdom of God" (a phrase from Mark 4:11) is taught to a young man clothed with only a linen cloth over his "naked" body, followed by mention of "naked [man] with naked [man]," which of course is one form of forbidden sexual relationship.

The anachronism we see in Smith's publications parallels the notorious case of Paul Coleman-Norton, professor of classics at Princeton University. He published an agraphon, in which Jesus humorously remarks that a third set of teeth will be provided to those who are toothless and go into outer darkness, so that they can weep and gnash their teeth. See P. R. Coleman-Norton, "An Amusing Agraphon," *CBQ* 12 (1950): 439–49. We know that this is another case of forgery, for Professor Coleman-Norton used to regale his students with a very similar joke, which ended with a reference to the provision of a third set of teeth. Bruce Metzger was one of Coleman-Norton's students and heard the joke—several years before its "discovery" in North Africa. See B. M. Metzger, "Literary Forgeries and Canonical Pseudepigrapha," *JBL* 91 (1972): 3–24; repr. in Metzger, *New Testament Studies: Philological, Versional, and Patristic* (NTTS 10; Leiden: Brill, 1980), 1–22. The whole matter is succinctly discussed in Carlson, *Gospel Hoax*, 71–72.

Smith dates to the twentieth century is signed "M. Madiotes."
This name is a pseudo-Greek name, whose root means "sphere" or
"globe," or, in reference to a person, "swindler" or "baldy." Carlson
plausibly suggests that here Smith, who was quite bald, is facetiously
alluding to himself (i.e., "M[orton] the baldhead").

(6) The entire story—finding a long-lost document in the Mar
Saba Monastery that is potentially embarrassing to Christianity—
is adumbrated by James Hunter's *The Mystery of Mar Saba*.[35]
Indeed, one of the heroes of the story, who helps to unmask the
perpetrators and expose the fraud, is Scotland Yard Inspector Lord
Moreton. The parallels between Morton Smith's alleged Mar Saba
discovery and Hunter's Mar Saba mystery are fascinating. It should
be added that Smith says in the preface to his publication of the
Clementine letter that his invitation to visit Mar Saba came in 1941
(the year after the publication of Hunter's novel).

(7) Carlson identifies very plausibly the motives behind Smith's
playful deception. We need not go into these details in this context.
They possess a great deal of explanatory power.

The upshot of the whole matter is that Smith's Mar Saba Clementine is almost certainly a hoax and Smith is almost certainly
the hoaxer. No research into the Gospels and the historical Jesus
should take Smith's document seriously.

Concluding Remarks

Many scholarly portraits and reconstructions of the historical
Jesus are badly distorted through the use of documents that are
late and of dubious historical value. The irony is that in trying to
"go behind" the New Testament Gospels and find truth buried
under layers of tradition and theology some scholars depend on
documents that were composed sixty to one hundred years after
the New Testament Gospels. This is a strange way to proceed.

Two of the four extracanonical Gospels reviewed in this essay
originated in the second half of the second century: the *Gospel of
Thomas* and the Egerton Papyrus. A third writing, the Akhmîm

35. J. H. Hunter, *The Mystery of Mar Saba* (New York and Toronto: Evangelical
Publishers, 1940).

Gospel fragment, also cannot date earlier than the middle of the second century, if indeed it is the *Gospel of Peter* mentioned by Bishop Serapion at the beginning of the third century. But there are grave doubts that this document is the *Gospel of Peter*. The Akhmîm Gospel fragment may be part of an unknown writing from an even later period. In any case, scholars are in no position to extract from the Akhmîm fragment a hypothetical mid-first-century Passion and Resurrection Narrative on which the first-century New Testament Gospels relied. Such a theory completely lacks a critical basis.

The remaining document—the quotations of the *Secret Gospel of Mark*, embedded in a long-lost letter by Clement of Alexandria—is a modern hoax and therefore has nothing to offer critical scholarship concerned with Christian origins and the emergence of the Jesus and Gospel tradition. Yet this writing, along with the other texts, has been used in historical Jesus research.

The scholarly track record with respect to the use of these extra-canonical Gospels is, frankly, embarrassing. In marked contrast to the hypercritical approach many scholars take to the New Testament Gospels, several scholars are surprisingly uncritical in their approach to the extracanonical Gospels. It is hard to explain why scholars give such credence to documents that reflect settings entirely foreign to pre–70 CE Jewish Palestine and at the same time reflect traditions and tendencies found in documents known to emerge in later times and in places outside of Palestine.

The Akhmîm Gospel fragment, given its uncertain identity and provenance, is probably of minimal value for Gospel research. The *Gospel of Thomas* and Papyrus Egerton 2, however, are important texts and deserve careful, critical study. Both could be very important witnesses to the development of the Gospel tradition in the second century and possibly to early Gospel harmonies, such as those produced by Justin Martyr and his student Tatian.

But these texts have much less value as sources for the historical Jesus, or as sources for the New Testament Gospels. I urge fellow Gospel scholars and scholars concerned with the historical Jesus to exercise greater caution in the future and proceed with more exacting, evidenced-based criticism and less hypothesis and special pleading.

6

Paul and the Process of Canonization

STANLEY E. PORTER

Introduction

The title of my essay is the heart of the question I wish to address—the relationship of Paul and the process of canonization, or, perhaps even better, Paul *to* the process of canonization.[1] In a recent work, I addressed the five major current theories in some detail, first offering a presentation and then a critique of the reconstructed histories of how Paul's canon of letters came into being.[2] I was admittedly disappointed that in a review of the volume in which this essay appeared—though generally quite favorable toward the

---

1. I am referring here to the process by which Paul's canon of writings was assembled, not formal recognition of the inspiration of these writings by the church.
2. S. E. Porter, "When and How Was the Pauline Canon Compiled? An Assessment of Theories," in *The Pauline Canon* (ed. Porter; Pauline Studies 1; Leiden: Brill, 2004), 95–127. I readily draw upon and incorporate portions of this essay in what follows.

volume as a whole and my essay—it was treated as essentially a (admittedly, valuable) compendium of thought on the issue, rather than a piece of constructive analysis. The reviewer seemed to miss that I had endorsed and developed in significant ways a particular model that had important implications for Paul's involvement in the process of canonization and hence the timeline for some of the incidents involved. In this essay I wish, first, to state some of the important background issues regarding the formation of the Pauline canon, then (drawing on my previous essay) quickly to review the five standard yet inadequate theories regarding Pauline canonical formation, and finally to develop further my own, sixth theory on the formation of Paul's canon.

Background Issues regarding the Formation of the Pauline Canon

There are three inevitably overlapping periods in the development of the Pauline canon—the period during which the letters were written (whether by Paul or by later authors), the period during which the letters were gathered into a corpus, and, finally, the period of transmission during which the texts of these letters were firmly and finally established and used by the church.[3] I will argue below that these three periods overlap far more than most previous research has indicated, and over a shorter period of time. Nevertheless, this entire process remains an underexplored area in Pauline scholarship. One reason for this neglect is that it is a complex area that requires extensive knowledge of biblical studies and church history but lacks important primary evidence, especially for the earliest stages of the Pauline canon's development.[4] What

3. See, similarly, D. Trobisch, *Paul's Letter Collection: Tracing the Origins* (Minneapolis: Augsburg Fortress, 1994), 50, but without forestalling the role of Paul in the collection. E. R. Richards (*Paul and First-Century Letter Writing: Secretaries, Composition and Collection* [Downers Grove, IL: InterVarsity, 2004], 218) makes an important distinction between collecting and publishing the letters, but see below.

4. See H. Y. Gamble, "The New Testament Canon: Recent Research and the Status Quaestionis," in *The Canon Debate* (ed. L. M. McDonald and J. A. Sanders; Peabody, MA: Hendrickson, 2002), 265–94, esp. 267, citing H. Lietzmann, "Wie wurden die Bücher des Neuen Testaments Heilige Schrift?" in *Kleine Schriften* (TU 68; Berlin: Akademie, 1958), 2:15–98.

is certain is that *1 Clement*, written around 96 CE from Rome by the church leader there, seems to have known both Romans and 1 Corinthians.[5] By 140 CE, and the evidence of Marcion's canon, there was some form of consolidated group of Pauline letters. Marcion knew of at least ten Pauline letters; most scholars think he did not know the Pastoral Epistles, because they had not yet been written (if so, an instance of overlap between the first two periods mentioned above). The fact that the Pastoral Epistles are not mentioned, however, does not necessarily mean that they had not been written—he may not have known of them or may have rejected them, as Marcion's canon is one of exclusion from an existing larger corpus.[6] By 200 CE (at the latest), we have tangible documentation in 𝔓[46] of a corpus that is very similar to Marcion's, with ten Pauline letters plus Hebrews[7] (if the traditional dating is accepted—the papyrus may be earlier).[8] However, the compression of letters by the scribe of 𝔓[46] may indicate that he found space to copy the Pastoral Epistles into his codex (he may also have simply

5. Richards, *Paul and First-Century Letter Writing*, 22 and n54. See the results in *The New Testament in the Apostolic Fathers* (ed. Oxford Society of Historical Theology; Oxford: Clarendon, 1905), 37–44 and 137, where citations from Romans and 1 Corinthians are given A ratings (see below).

6. See G. Milligan, *The New Testament Documents: Their Origin and Early History* (London: Macmillan, 1913), 217; K. Lake and S. Lake, *An Introduction to the New Testament* (London: Christophers, 1938), 96; F. F. Bruce, *The Canon of Scripture* (Glasgow: Chapter House, 1988), 144; H. von Campenhausen, *The Formation of the Christian Bible* (trans. J. A. Baker; Philadelphia: Fortress, 1972), 148; J. Barton, "Marcion Revisited," in McDonald and Sanders, *Canon Debate*, 341–54, esp. 342–43; Gamble, "New Testament Canon," 283–84; cf. idem, *The New Testament Canon: Its Making and Meaning* (GBS; Philadelphia: Fortress, 1985), 41; idem, "The Canon of the New Testament," in *The New Testament and its Modern Interpreters* (ed. E. J. Epp and G. W. MacRae; Atlanta: Scholars Press, 1989), 207.

7. E. J. Epp, "Textual Criticism in Exegesis," in *Handbook to Exegesis* (ed. S. E. Porter; Leiden: Brill, 1997), 45–97, esp. 76. Tertullian (*Against Marcion* 5.21), however, states that Marcion knew of two letters to Timothy and one to Titus but rejected them.

8. Y. K. Kim, "Palaeographical Dating of 𝔓[46] to the Later First Century," *Bib* 69 (1988): 248–57, dates 𝔓[46] to as early as the late first century (ca. 80 CE on). See assessments by S. R. Pickering, "The Dating of the Chester Beatty–Michigan Codex of the Pauline Epistles (𝔓[46])," in *Ancient History in a Modern University* (ed. T. W. Hillard et al.; 2 vols.; New South Wales, Australia: Ancient History Documentary Research Centre, Macquarie University; Grand Rapids: Eerdmans, 1998), 2:216–27; P. W. Comfort and D. P. Barrett, *The Text of the Earliest New Testament Greek Manuscripts* (Wheaton: Tyndale, 2001), 204–6.

added extra pages).[9] During the second to fourth centuries, a number of church writers attest to varying degrees of knowledge of the Pauline letters.[10] If the Muratorian canon dates to the second century, a list of thirteen letters is known by then.[11]

Five Theories of Origin of the Pauline Canon

There have been five major theories regarding the gathering together or collection of the Pauline letter corpus. I will look at each of these before proposing a theory that potentially has more to offer in answering how the Pauline canon was formed.

Gradual Collection or Zahn-Harnack Theory

The "snowball" or "gradual collection" theory[12] in modern critical scholarship is first attributed to Theodor Zahn and Adolf Harnack.[13] Zahn and Harnack, though disagreeing on details,

9. J. Duff, "$\mathfrak{P}^{46}$ and the Pastorals: A Misleading Consensus?" *NTS* 44 (1998): 578–90. Contra J. D. Quinn, "$\mathfrak{P}^{46}$—The Pauline Canon?" *CBQ* 36 (1974): 379–85, who claims that the Pastorals were not included because the collection was only of letters to churches.

10. See *New Testament in the Apostolic Fathers*, esp. 137. Note that Vaticanus does not have 1–2 Timothy, Titus, and Philemon of Paul's letters, and that Hebrews and Revelation are written in a fifteenth-century hand apparently to complete the codex.

11. See G. M. Hahneman, *The Muratorian Fragment and the Development of the Canon* (OTM; Oxford: Clarendon, 1992), following A. C. Sundberg Jr., "Canon Muratori: A Fourth-Century List," *HTR* 66 (1973): 1–41, in arguing for a fourth-century date. This has been widely disputed. See, e.g., Bruce, *Canon of Scripture*, 158–69, esp. 166; G. N. Stanton, *Jesus and Gospel* (Cambridge: Cambridge University Press, 2004), 68–71.

12. See Gamble, *New Testament Canon*, 36; A. G. Patzia, *The Making of the New Testament: Origin, Collection, Text & Canon* (Downers Grove, IL: InterVarsity, 1995), 80; Richards, *Paul and First-Century Letter Writing*, 210. C. F. D. Moule (*The Birth of the New Testament* [3rd ed.; San Francisco: Harper & Row, 1982], 263) makes the original reference to "snowball."

13. See T. Zahn, *Geschichte des Neutestamentlichen Kanons* (2 vols.; Erlangen and Leipzig: Deichert, 1888–92), 1:811–39; idem, *Grundriss der Geschichte des Neutestamentlichen Kanons: Eine Ergänzung zu der Einleitung in das Neue Testament* (Leipzig: Deichert, 1904), esp. 35–37; A. Harnack, *Die Briefsammlung des Apostels Paulus und die anderen vorkonstantinischen christlichen Briefsammlungen* (Leipzig: Hinrichs, 1926), 6–27. This encapsulation also draws upon the summaries in B. S. Childs, *The New Testament as Canon: An Introduction* (Valley Forge, PA: Trinity Press International, 1994), 423; C. L. Mitton, *The Formation of the Pauline Corpus of Letters* (London: Epworth, 1955), 15; Gamble, "New Testament Canon," 267–68.

concurred that interest in the Pauline letters existed from the time of their writing. Zahn concluded[14] that the consistent references among various early writers, and reference to the letters in churches separated in distance,[15] indicated that the Pauline letters were collected early on and served a vital liturgical purpose in the church. Zahn's Pauline corpus consisted of ten letters (excluding the Pastoral Epistles) and was completed after the writing of Acts but before the writing of *1 Clement*, around 80 to 85 CE.[16] Harnack, drawing upon Pauline passages referring to the letter-writing process,[17] saw this as evidence of an early collection of Paul's letters, but concluded the process occurred around 100 CE and included the Pastorals.[18] Both Zahn and Harnack recognized a process of selection and limitation in forming the Pauline corpus. However, they differed in the canonical status attributed to this accumulating Pauline material. Zahn bestowed on the letters a canonical status because of their public liturgical use, and thought that Marcion was responding to this canon; Harnack thought that formal canonical status—status equaling that of the Old Testament—did not occur until the second century in response to Marcion's creation of the first Pauline canon.[19] Kirsopp Lake, in contrast to Zahn and Har-

14. Zahn examined the evidence particularly in Marcion, the Apostolic Fathers (e.g., *1 Clement*, Polycarp and Ignatius), and later canonical lists. He was anticipated by B. F. Westcott, *A General Survey of the History of the Canon of the New Testament* (7th ed.; London: Macmillan, 1896), 19ff.

15. E.g., Rome, Smyrna, Antioch, and Corinth, where the actual process of collection may have taken place (see below). See G. Zuntz, *The Text of the Epistles: A Disquisition upon the Corpus Paulinum* (Schweich Lectures 1946; London: British Academy, 1953), 278–79 (who suggests Alexandria); F. F. Bruce, "New Light on the Origins of the New Testament Canon," in *New Dimensions in New Testament Study* (ed. R. N. Longenecker and M. C. Tenney; Grand Rapids: Zondervan, 1974), 3–18, esp. 10; Patzia, *Making of the New Testament*, 81.

16. Zahn, *Geschichte des Neutestamentlichen Kanons*, 1:835.

17. E.g., exalting Paul as a letter writer, or warning against false letters, etc., as in 2 Thess. 2:2; 3:17; 1 Cor. 7:17; 2 Cor. 3:1; 10:9, 10. Harnack, *Die Briefsammlung des Apostels Paulus*, 7–8.

18. Harnack, *Die Briefsammlung des Apostels Paulus*, 6.

19. Following Harnack, J. Knox (*Marcion and the New Testament* [Chicago: University of Chicago Press, 1942], 39–76) proposed that Marcion was responding to an already gathered corpus, noting similarities between Marcion's list and that in the Muratorian canon; cf. W. Bauer, *Orthodoxy and Heresy in Earliest Christianity* (London: SCM, 1971), 221–22. Contra Moule, *Birth of the New Testament*, 260–61. On the response to Marcion,

nack, emphasized the number of letters available. He proposed a more gradual collection process,[20] with each church having its own collection of Pauline letters that differed from the others.[21]

A number of arguments have been raised against this position.[22] There is a discrepancy between positing a short period of time for the collection (e.g., Zahn and Harnack) and positing a much longer period (e.g., Lake)—each by appealing to the same body of evidence. According to Lake, the lists of Marcion, the Muratorian canon, Tertullian, and Origen are all different in length and in order, the earlier with ten and the latter with eight letters.[23] The differing orders, however, probably say nothing about the collection process itself. Lack of mention of a letter does not necessarily mean lack of knowledge,[24] as the later, shorter lists of Tertullian and Origen indicate.[25] Further, if Acts was written by a devoted follower of Paul in the 80s CE or later (an assumption of much contemporary scholarship), it is surprising that it does not make reference to Paul's letters.[26] There is also a lack of evidence regarding how and whether such a compositional process occurred.

see Bruce, *Canon of Scripture*, 144, and von Campenhausen, *Formation of the Christian Bible*, 148.

20. K. Lake, *The Earlier Epistles of St. Paul: Their Motive and Origin* (London: Rivingtons, 1911), 356–59, based on the varied ordering of the Pauline letters among the church fathers and canonical lists. Cf. Lake and Lake, *Introduction*, 96–101.

21. Cf. B. H. Streeter, *The Four Gospels: A Study of Origins* (London: Macmillan, 1930), 526–27; cf. also idem, *The Primitive Church: Studies with Special Reference to the Origins of the Christian Ministry* (London: Macmillan, 1929), 159–62. Streeter traces four distinct stages in the long-term growth of the Pauline corpus: (1) the nucleus of Romans, 1 Corinthians, Ephesians, and perhaps Philippians (known by 96 CE in 1 Clement); (2) the ten letters as evidenced by Marcion (ca. 140 CE); (3) the thirteen letters before 200 CE (as attested by the Muratorian canon); and (4) the fourteen letters with Hebrews ca. 350 CE.

22. For all of the responses to the positions here, more detail can be found in Porter, "Pauline Canon."

23. See Lake, *Earlier Epistles*, 358–59.

24. See D. Guthrie, *New Testament Introduction* (3rd ed.; Downers Grove, IL: InterVarsity, 1970), 646.

25. Lake (*Earlier Epistles*, 357) admits that Tertullian probably knew Colossians and the Pastoral Epistles, even though he did not list them. Streeter's proposal is also potentially thrown off if the Muratorian fragment is a fourth- rather than a second-century document (see above).

26. E.g., W. G. Kümmel, *Introduction to the New Testament* (trans. H. C. Kee; 17th ed.; Nashville: Abingdon, 1975), 186, responded to by W. O. Walker Jr., "Acts and the Pauline Corpus Reconsidered," *JSNT* 24 (1985): 3–23; cf. also Streeter, *Four Gospels*, 555.

Regarding a possible location for the collection of the Corinthian letters, there is much confusion. Even for those who argue that there are portions of all four of Paul's Corinthian letters in canonical 1 and 2 Corinthians, two of the letters would be quite fragmentary, especially if the Corinthians had access to the letters.[27] The basis of the selection process that Zahn and Harnack envision is unclear. It is circular to say that those letters that were useful in the churches were the ones preserved.[28] Finally, whether the Marcionite canon was as instrumental, either as challenge (not very likely)[29] or response, to the formation of the Pauline canon is questionable.[30] The gradual collection theory of the Pauline corpus—as popular as it has been—weaves a narrative around the disparate evidence of the first four centuries, but without a firm foundation established as to how such a process actually occurred.

Lapsed Interest or Goodspeed-Knox Theory

The Goodspeed or Goodspeed-Knox theory of "lapsed interest"[31] has been characterized as one of several "big bang" theories.[32] Opposing the theories of Zahn and Harnack, Edgar J. Goodspeed proposed widespread neglect of Paul's letters:[33] Acts does not

27. On the various letter hypotheses of the Corinthian letters, see, among others, J. C. Hurd Jr., *The Origin of 1 Corinthians* (new ed.; Macon, GA: Mercer University Press, 1983); idem, "Good News and the Integrity of 1 Corinthians," in *Gospel in Paul: Studies on Corinthians, Galatians and Romans for Richard N. Longenecker* (ed. L. A. Jervis and P. Richardson; JSNTSup 108; Sheffield: JSOT Press, 1994), 38–62; M. Thrall, *A Critical and Exegetical Commentary on the Second Epistle to the Corinthians* (2 vols.; ICC; Edinburgh: T&T Clark, 1994, 2000), 1:3–49.

28. See Guthrie, *New Testament Introduction*, 647.

29. Lake and Lake, *Introduction*, 96, who note that it is "rather improbable that [Marcion] made the Corpus, for the Church would hardly have accepted the work of a heretic."

30. Childs, *New Testament as Canon*, 424. Cf. D. Trobisch, *The First Edition of the New Testament* (New York: Oxford University Press, 2000), 5, who notes that the influence of Marcion remains unresolved in scholarly discussion.

31. Guthrie, *New Testament Introduction*, 647.

32. Richards, *Paul and First-Century Letter Writing*, 210.

33. See esp. E. J. Goodspeed, *New Solutions of New Testament Problems* (Chicago: University of Chicago Press, 1927), 1–103; idem, *The Meaning of Ephesians* (Chicago: University of Chicago Press, 1933); idem, *An Introduction to the New Testament* (Chicago: University of Chicago Press, 1937), esp. 210–21 (relied upon below). He was anticipated by J. Weiss, *Earliest Christianity: A History of the Period A.D. 30–150* (completed

know Paul's letters, but much of the literature written after Acts, including Revelation 1–3, and every Christian corpus of letters to follow, seems to know them. This indicates to Goodspeed that there was one collection of letters after which all later ones were patterned. The writing of Acts around 90 CE,[34] with its clear and forceful depiction of Paul, revived interest in Paul as the apostle to the Greeks. The only thing to be added to such an important volume was a collection of Paul's letters, something Paul himself had hinted at (see Col. 4:16). However, Colossians is not mentioned in Acts, so Goodspeed speculates that Colossians and Philemon[35] were the nucleus of the corpus, confirmed by widespread use of Colossians by Ephesians. Ephesians shows familiarity with all nine of the accepted Pauline letters (not counting the Pastorals, which for Goodspeed reflect later knowledge of Paul).[36] Ephesus, by 90 CE the second (to Antioch) most important Christian center, gathered the Pauline letters from surrounding cities and became the center for later letter writing.[37] Ignatius later wrote that Paul mentions the Ephesians in every letter (*To the Ephesians* 12:2), which, Goodspeed contends, makes sense if the collection originated in Ephesus.[38] The Pauline corpus, therefore, was circulated from Ephesus with Ephesians, an encyclical letter that drew upon the entire corpus, as the introduction. John Knox, Goodspeed's pupil, expanded the theory. He proposed that Onesimus was the letter collector,[39] and that, on the basis of Marcion's canon and the

by R. Knopf; trans. and ed. F. C. Grant; 2 vols.; New York: Harper & Row, 1937; repr., Gloucester, MA: Peter Smith, 1970), 2:682–83.

34. See Goodspeed, *New Solutions of New Testament Problems*, 94–103. Cf. J. Knox, "Acts and the Pauline Letter Corpus," in *Studies in Luke–Acts* (ed. L. E. Keck and J. L. Martyn; Philadelphia: Fortress, 1966), 279–87.

35. Goodspeed took Philemon to be the letter to the Laodiceans, thus accounting for its presence in the collection. Goodspeed, *Meaning of Ephesians*, 7.

36. See Goodspeed, *Meaning of Ephesians*, 82–165.

37. Such as Revelation and the letters of Ignatius, as well as the Gospel and letters of John, works that clearly reflect Pauline influence. Ephesus also had Paul's letter of introduction for Phoebe (Rom. 16), according to Goodspeed.

38. Textual difficulties mitigate this interpretation of Ignatius. See B. Weiss, *A Manual of Introduction to the New Testament* (trans. A. J. K. Davidson; 2 vols.; London: Hodder & Stoughton, 1887), 1:43n1.

39. Thus justifying inclusion of the book of Philemon in the corpus. See J. Knox, *Philemon among the Letters of Paul* (rev. ed.; London: Collins, 1959), 10, who refers to how

Marcionite prologues, one could reconstruct a seven-letter Pauline canon, with Ephesians at its head.[40]

The major arguments against Goodspeed's theory are telling.[41] There is no text-critical evidence that Ephesians was ever at the head of a Pauline corpus.[42] Marcion seems to have had Galatians at the head,[43] 𝔓⁴⁶ had Romans, and the Muratorian canon Corinthians. Ephesians is an inappropriate encyclical letter to introduce the Pauline canon, as so much of it reflects Colossians and does not reflect many of the major themes of the Pauline corpus. Zuntz argues that the lack of ascription in Ephesians indicates an early tradition, but that the editor of the collection could not have prefaced the collection of Paul's letters with a blank in the address, as this runs contrary to the notion of an archetypal collection that Goodspeed endorses.[44] If the Pastoral Epistles are authentically Pauline,[45] the relation of these letters to his reconstruction is not clear. Their pseudonymity must be accepted for Goodspeed's theory to succeed. Goodspeed's view of the dating of the compo-

---

his idea (found in the first edition of his work in 1935) was later accepted by Goodspeed (*The Key to Ephesians* [Chicago: University of Chicago Press, 1956]).

40. Knox, *Philemon*, 67–78. The seven-letter corpus consists of the Corinthian letters, Thessalonian letters, and Colossians and Philemon together, along with Romans, Galatians, Philippians, and Colossians. On the seven-letter corpus, see Hahneman, *Muratorian Fragment*, 117–18; H. Y. Gamble, *Books and Readers in the Early Church: A History of Early Christian Texts* (New Haven: Yale University Press, 1995), 59–61.

41. See, e.g., E. Best, *A Critical and Exegetical Commentary on Ephesians* (ICC; Edinburgh: T&T Clark, 1998), 66.

42. Or at the end, where Zuntz thinks a cover letter also could have stood. Zuntz, *Text of the Epistles*, 276.

43. Knox contended that Marcion had transposed Galatians and Ephesians to emphasize the anti-Jewish elements of the canon (*Philemon*, 68).

44. Zuntz, *Text of the Epistles*, 276–77. Goodspeed (*Meaning of Ephesians*, 18) does not take the opening of Ephesians as having the blank, but interprets it as part of the encyclical opening: "to God's people who are steadfast in Christ Jesus." See also his *New Solutions of New Testament Problems*, 11–12, 17. For discussion of the variants (though with doubtful conclusions), see H. W. Hoehner, *Ephesians: An Exegetical Commentary* (Grand Rapids: Baker Academic, 2002), 144–48. F. Blass and A. Debrunner, *A Greek Grammar of the New Testament and Other Early Christian Literature* (trans. R. W. Funk; Chicago: University of Chicago Press, 1961), 213, take the lacuna as "impossible"—perhaps it is just unusual.

45. As some scholars believe, including myself. See G. W. Knight, *The Pastoral Epistles* (NIGTC; Grand Rapids: Eerdmans, 1992), 21–52; L. T. Johnson, *The First and Second Letters to Timothy* (AB 35A; New York: Doubleday, 2001), 55–97.

sition of Acts, while widely held, is not universal, with scholars
opting for a much later date (ca. 125 CE) or a much earlier date
(as early as ca. early 60s CE).[46] If either is correct (and I think the
early date is probably correct), the Goodspeed chronology falls
apart. The evidence that Goodspeed uses to show that Paul's letters
had fallen into neglect can be interpreted in different ways. The
lack of mention of the letters in Acts does not address whether
a collection existed. As noted above, a number of scholars have
recently argued that the letters were indeed used by the author of
Acts. There is also the difficulty of establishing a causal relation
between the writing of Acts and the collecting of the letters. Lastly,
other Pauline cities besides Ephesus have been proposed as the
major places for gathering the Pauline letters, including Corinth
and Alexandria (both noted above). Since a number of cities can
lay claim to evidence for the Pauline collection, there may have
originally been a number of smaller Pauline corpuses, something
that Goodspeed clearly wishes to dispute.[47]

Composite Antignostic or Schmithals Theory

Walter Schmithals is a firm advocate of the Baur hypothesis about
the origins of Christianity,[48] with one decided difference: the mo-
tivating event was opposition to gnosticism.[49] Schmithals's theory,
predicated upon his view of the composite nature of the Pauline
letters, is that the Pauline corpus was formed with a clear antignostic
intent. He identifies the authentic letters of Paul as those written
during the third missionary journey and within only a couple of
years. On the basis of various criteria, he determines that there are

---

46. The major representatives of the late and early dates are (respectively) J. C. O'Neill,
The Theology of Acts in its Historical Setting (London: SPCK, 1970), 21; and A. Harnack,
*Neue Untersuchungen zur Apostelgeschichte und zur Abfassungszeit der Synoptischen
Evangelien* (BENT 4; Leipzig: Hinrichs, 1911), 63–81.

47. See Best, *Ephesians*, 66.

48. See esp. F. C. Baur, *Paul, the Apostle of Jesus Christ, His Life and Work, His Epistles
and His Doctrine* (ed. E. Zeller; trans. A. Menzies; 2 vols.; 2nd ed.; London: Williams &
Norgate, 1873–75); idem, *The Church History of the First Three Centuries* (trans. A. Menzies; 2 vols.; 3rd ed.; London: Williams & Norgate, 1878–79).

49. W. Schmithals, "Zur Abfassung und ältesten Sammlung der paulinischen Haupt-
briefe," *ZNW* 51 (1960): 225–45; repr. in *Paul and the Gnostics* (trans. J. E. Steely; Nashville: Abingdon, 1972), 239–74.

six Corinthian, one Galatian, three Philippian, two Roman, and four Thessalonian letters. On the basis of other lists of Paul's letters,[50] he further determines that there was a seven-letter Pauline corpus in fixed order, with the Corinthian letters at the head, and Romans at the close.[51] Thus, Schmithals concludes that the original Pauline corpus was a construct of the authentic fragments made into a seven-letter canon, with 1 Corinthians 1:2b as the introduction and the doxology of Romans 16:25–27 as the conclusion (a passage long established, so Schmithals believes, as non-Pauline).[52]

One must accept several basic presuppositions to support Schmithals's theory. Even scholars who recognize interpolations in the Pauline canon, or composite letters (e.g., 2 Corinthians or Philippians), do not recognize the fragmentary character of so many Pauline letters. The determination and arrangement of the fragments is closely related to Schmithals's hypothesis of antignosticism driving the creation of this letter collection. Without denying that a form of gnosticism (whether proto- or pre-) was present, one may question whether it colored so many of the original writings and motivated the later situation. Schmithals's defense of the seven-letter canon, to which the other letters were added later, is based upon his estimation of an ancient belief in the sacredness of the number seven; however, he must force the evidence to make this construction fit, including hypothesizing that the later canonical lists (which do not follow his order) are deviants from the original list, which had Corinthians at the head and Romans at the end. If the Muratorian fragment is from the fourth rather than second century (see above), and his other speculations fail, the neatly packaged seven-letter group is compromised. In any case, many would accept more than the seven letters as genuine. Even for those who do not accept a thirteen-letter canon, the evidence seems to be lacking for only a seven-letter canon.[53]

50. E.g., the Muratorian fragment, Tertullian, Marcion (on the basis of Tertullian, *Against Marcion* 4.5; *Prescription against Heretics* 36), 𝔓⁴⁶, D 06 Codex Claromontanus, and Athanasius.

51. The order was 1 and 2 Corinthians, Galatians, Philippians, 1 and 2 Thessalonians, Romans.

52. For important discussion, see H. Y. Gamble Jr., *The Textual History of the Letter to the Romans* (SD 42; Grand Rapids: Eerdmans, 1977), esp. 129–32.

53. Gamble, *New Testament Canon*, 39.

Personal Involvement or Moule and Guthrie Theories

A number of scholars have proposed that a single significant individual was responsible for the gathering and creation of the Pauline corpus. Apart from Knox's implausible proposal that Onesimus gathered the letters, two merit further attention. C. F. D. Moule suggests Luke.[54] Appreciating that Acts does not seem to know of the Pauline letters, Moule posits that Luke gathered the corpus after writing Acts and after Paul's death, when he revisited the major Pauline cities. Moule believes that the similarities in vocabulary, content, and perspective of the Pastoral Epistles and Luke–Acts support this hypothesis.[55] Donald Guthrie proposes that Timothy may have collected Paul's letters. Rejecting any theories based upon neglect of Paul, Guthrie claims that all of the major churches had either direct or indirect Pauline foundations or strong personal connections to him at the time of his death.[56] To support such remembrance of Paul, Guthrie notes factors like the exchange of Pauline letters (Col. 4:16), their public reading (1 Thess. 5:27) and wider distribution (see 1 Corinthians), the circular character of some of the letters (e.g., Romans and Ephesians), and the respect shown for Paul's writings in early church writers, such as Clement (1 Clement 5:5–7). Guthrie attributes the lack of explicit mention of Paul's letters in Acts to its early composition, and the apparent loss of some of Paul's letters (e.g., parts of the Corinthian correspondence) to their lack of edificatory value.

There is much of merit in such personal involvement theories, since any gathering process seems to demand the involvement of

54. Moule, Birth of the New Testament, 264–65.

55. Moule (Birth of the New Testament, 265; "The Problem of the Pastoral Epistles: A Reappraisal," BJRL 47 [1965]: 430–52, corrected in Birth of the New Testament, 281–82) has also proposed Luke as the author of the Pastoral Epistles. This would account for their not being present in the earliest references to the Pauline letters, and is reflected later by Marcion. Cf. S. G. Wilson, Luke and the Pastoral Epistles (London: SPCK, 1979). F. J. Badcock (The Pauline Epistles and the Epistle to the Hebrews in Their Historical Setting [London: SPCK, 1937], 115–33) proposes an unnamed follower of Paul.

56. Guthrie (New Testament Introduction, 653) must mean churches outside of Palestine, since relations near the end of Paul's life with the Jerusalem church were apparently strained at best. See S. E. Porter, The Paul of Acts: Essays in Literary Criticism, Rhetoric, and Theology (WUNT 115; Tübingen: Mohr Siebeck, 1999; repr., Paul in Acts [Peabody, MA: Hendrickson, 2001]), 172–86.

individuals. This undoubtedly accounts for why so many of the theories noted above have included individuals as part of the scenario. The question here is the evidence for Luke or Timothy as the collector. The Lukan hypothesis has more tangible evidence, since there is some substantial means of estimating Luke's literary actions. However, the hypothesis that Luke was the author of the Pastorals has never been widely accepted. Without this link, other questions are raised for the Pauline chronology. The question of why Luke would write Acts but not mention Paul's letters, yet be involved in their collection, is not solved by positing the writing of Acts before the collection, since surely Luke must have known of the letters all along. The hypothesis that Timothy orchestrated the collection is not necessarily aided by criticism of Luke, as the already thin lines of literary connection with Paul are stretched thinner. We have no evidence of Timothy's literary abilities, and the hypothesis seems to be based upon one particular Pauline chronology. Although Guthrie is vigorous in his defense of the authenticity of the Pastoral Epistles,[57] and hence their placement at the end of Paul's life, after the close of Acts, many scholars do not accept this hypothesis.[58]

In the light of the above difficulties, and in line with critical orthodoxy, a Pauline school hypothesis has been posited.[59] This theory recognizes the importance of individuals in collecting the letters—such as Onesimus, Luke, or Timothy, along with other later Pauline followers and coworkers, possibly including Polycarp—but attempts to overcome the chronological difficulties noted. After Paul's death, a number of his followers gathered, possibly edited, and passed on the Pauline tradition, including his letters. They also continued to apply Paul's theology to contemporary church situations, thereby generating the pseudepigraphic deutero-Pauline letters. This significant variation on the personal involvement hypothesis raises its own difficulties, including problems with the concept of pseudepigraphy,

57. See, e.g., D. Guthrie, *The Pastoral Epistles and the Mind of Paul* (London: Tyndale, 1956); idem, *New Testament Introduction*, 584–622, 671–84; idem, *The Pastoral Epistles* (2nd ed.; TNTC; Grand Rapids: Eerdmans, 1990), esp. 224–40.

58. See M. Davies, *The Pastoral Epistles* (NTG; Sheffield: Sheffield Academic Press, 1996), 105–18.

59. Gamble, *New Testament Canon*, 39. Cf. H.-M. Schenke, "Das Weiterwirken des Paulus und die Pflege seines Erbs durch die Paulusschule," *NTS* 21 (1975): 505–18.

recently brought to the fore in scholarly discussion.[60] The question
of deception—in this case, how a devout follower of Paul could have
perpetuated such deception, even if for a noble cause[61]—seems a
high price to pay for accounting for the supposedly deutero-Pauline
letters.

Pauline Involvement or the Trobisch Theory

David Trobisch concentrates upon the first four letters and
Paul's possible personal involvement.[62] If the theory of early personal involvement by a close associate of Paul has merit, as many
scholars recognize (see above), Paul himself could also have been
involved in this process. This is not a new idea.[63] Working at about
the same time as Trobisch, E. R. Richards argues that Paul used a
secretary (much like Cicero had his secretary, Tiro). Hence, Paul
had copies made of his letters, and these letters constituted the
origin of the Pauline letter collection, possibly then assembled by
Paul's secretary, Luke.[64] Trobisch, however, adds significant detail
to justify this position.

60. See Davies, *Pastoral Epistles*, 113–17; E. E. Ellis, "Pseudonymity and Canonicity
of New Testament Documents," in *Worship, Theology and Ministry in the Early Church:
Essays in Honor of Ralph P. Martin* (ed. M. J. Wilkins and T. Paige; JSNTSup 87; Sheffield:
JSOT Press, 1992), 212–24; idem, *The Making of the New Testament Documents* (BIS 39;
Leiden: Brill, 1999), esp. 322–24; S. E. Porter, "Pauline Authorship and the Pastoral Epistles:
Implications for Canon," *BBR* 5 (1995): 105–23.

61. See L. R. Donelson, *Pseudepigraphy and Ethical Argument in the Pastoral Epistles*
(HUT 22; Tübingen: Mohr Siebeck, 1986), 18–22, who notes that the "noble lie" is still a
lie. Why would pseudepigraphic authorship have been necessary if the recipients would
have known that the letters were not written by Paul?

62. See D. Trobisch, *Die Entstehung der Paulusbriefsammlung: Studien zu den Anfängen
christlicher Publizistik* (NTOA 10; Freiburg: Universitätsverlag; Göttingen: Vandenhoeck
& Ruprecht, 1989); idem, *Paul's Letter Collection*; and now *First Edition of the New Testament*. There is significant overlap among these volumes. I draw upon all of them in the
summary below, concentrating on *Paul's Letter Collection*.

63. See Guthrie, *New Testament Introduction*, 657, citing R. L. Archer, "The Epistolary
Form in the New Testament," *ExpTim* 63 (1951–52): 296–98, esp. 297.

64. E. R. Richards, *The Secretary in the Letters of Paul* (WUNT 2.42; Tübingen: Mohr
Siebeck, 1991), esp. 164–65, 187–88; idem, *Paul and First-Century Letter Writing*, 218–23;
idem, "The Codex and the Early Collection of Paul's Letters," *BBR* 8 (1988): 151–66;
followed by E. E. Ellis, "Pastoral Letters," in *Dictionary of Paul and His Letters* (ed. G. F.
Hawthorne, R. P. Martin, and D. G. Reid; Downers Grove, IL: InterVarsity, 1993), 660;
idem, *Making of the New Testament Documents*, 86, 132, 297.

Trobisch[65] notes that many of the early manuscripts, especially the early codices,[66] follow essentially modern canonical order. However, $\mathfrak{P}^{46}$, the oldest Pauline manuscript,[67] arranges the Pauline letters essentially according to length. Hebrews is the one book of the Pauline group that varies regarding ordering, which Trobisch takes to mean that it was added later to the thirteen-letter Pauline collection.[68] Trobisch further believes that the common title of the Pauline letters implies that they were gathered together under Paul's name.[69] He also posits that the overall arrangement of the letters is based upon the addressees, the letters to churches preceding the letters to individuals (ordered by length within these two major groups)[70] and letters to the same place or person kept together.[71] Trobisch also claims that Romans to Galatians is a single literary unit,[72] and that "It is highly probable that this old collection was edited and prepared for publication by Paul himself."[73] This, Trobisch contends, was the first stage in a three-stage process. He believes that Paul edited the four authentic letters[74] so as to unite them together in terms of the thought and amount of personal detail included.[75] The second stage is expansion of the corpus,

65. Trobisch, *Paul's Letter Collection*, 17–26; idem, *Die Entstehung der Paulusbriefsammlung*, 56–62.

66. Such as Sinaiticus (ℵ 01), Alexandrinus (A 02), Vaticanus (B 03), and Ephraem (C 04).

67. Apart from those that are highly fragmentary. The following papyri have only a portion of a single Pauline letter: $\mathfrak{P}^{10, 11, 14, 15, 16, 26, 27, 31, 32, 34, 40, 49, 51, 65, 68, 87, 94}$. A few have only a couple of letters (e.g., $\mathfrak{P}^{30}$ with parts of 1 and 2 Thessalonians, $\mathfrak{P}^{92}$ with Ephesians and 2 Thessalonians).

68. Trobisch, *Paul's Letter Collection*, 20; but cf. idem, *Die Entstehung der Paulusbriefsammlung*, 60. This point was made by Zuntz, *Text of the Epistles*, 15–16. Hebrews appears before 1 and 2 Corinthians but is shorter than 1 and longer than 2 Corinthians. Trobisch thinks that the placement of Hebrews is on account of the scribe not wanting to separate 1 and 2 Corinthians (*Paul's Letter Collection*, 17).

69. Trobisch, *Paul's Letter Collection*, 24.

70. See Trobisch, *Paul's Letter Collection*, 52–54.

71. E.g., 1 and 2 Corinthians, 1 and 2 Thessalonians, and 1 and 2 Timothy. Trobisch, *Paul's Letter Collection*, 25.

72. Trobisch, *Paul's Letter Collection*, 25–47.

73. Trobisch, *Paul's Letter Collection*, 54.

74. See Trobisch, *Paul's Letter Collection*, 55–96; cf. idem, *Die Entstehung der Paulusbriefsammlung*, 100–104, 128–32.

75. See Trobisch, *Paul's Letter Collection*, 62–70. E.g., personal greetings are only important in terms of travel plans, and one of their common ideas is the collection.

and the third comprehensive editions.[76] Accepting Goodspeed's
analysis of Ephesians, Trobisch sees Ephesians (now in its rightful
place, according to the tradition) as the introductory letter for the
appendix to the Pauline corpus.[77] These stages led to the canonical
Pauline collection.[78]

Trobisch's theory of direct Pauline involvement combines a number of contradictory or at least unusual ideas—such as that Paul
may have been instrumental in initiating the collection of his own
letters, while also limiting the authentic Pauline corpus to Baur's
four. One of the major issues is how Trobisch suggests that Paul
instigated the collection of his letters. Trobisch introduces this idea
subtly. Having noted the three purported stages of the development
of letter collections, and working backwards, Trobisch suddenly
concludes that it is "highly [N.B.] probable" Paul was responsible
for stage one, the authorized recensions.[79] This is posited rather
than proved, but, as Murphy-O'Connor has shown, Paul's direct
involvement is not necessary to a theory of staged development
such as Trobisch proposes based upon ancient canonical lists.[80]

76. Trobisch, *Paul's Letter Collection*, 54. Inadvertently, Trobisch claims to provide
support for Goodspeed's hypothesis (see above), in that the thirteen-letter corpus is an
expansion upon the original four letters.

77. Trobisch, *Paul's Letter Collection*, 101n22.

78. J. Murphy-O'Connor adopts a similar three-stage collection process (*Paul the
Letter-Writer: His World, His Options, His Skills* [Collegeville, MN: Liturgical Press,
1995], 120–30), in which collection A consists of Romans, 1 and 2 Corinthians, and Galatians, which originated at Corinth; collection B consists of those letters from neighboring
churches in Asia Minor and Greece; and to which collection C, the personal letters, was
added. Murphy-O'Connor uses violations of the consistent decrease in length (e.g., from
Galatians to Ephesians, and 2 Thessalonians to 1 Timothy), reinforced by the varying
placement of Hebrews, as indicators of section breaks. He also minimizes problems over
the different canonical orderings on the basis that other possible determiners of length
besides number of characters, such as stichoi and Euthalian numbers, indicate very similar
lengths between the books of Galatians and Ephesians, and Colossians and Philippians
(*Paul the Letter-Writer*, 121, 123; on stichometry, see J. R. Harris, *Stichometry* [London:
Clay, 1893]). The result is a very consistent pattern of division of the Pauline corpus that
strengthens Trobisch's analysis. However, Murphy-O'Connor does not require Paul as
the instigator to promote his theory. Instead, he sees possibly Timothy and more likely
Onesimus as involved in this process (*Paul the Letter-Writer*, 130).

79. Trobisch, *Paul's Letter Collection*, 54.

80. Note also that Richards's theory that Paul made copies of his letters does not neces-
sitate Paul as the direct instigator of the collection of his letters, as Richards himself clearly
states in his advocacy of a secretary hypothesis.

There is little to no direct evidence to promote this idea of Pauline involvement except the analogy of Cicero and Tiro. However, as Trobisch notes, Cicero (*Letters to Atticus* 16.5.5) makes an explicit claim regarding the gathering of his letters,[81] which Paul does not make in the letters that Trobisch recognizes as authentic. Furthermore, the analogy of Cicero is instructive. Cicero's known collection, and the one that Trobisch refers to explicitly in his work (*Familiar Letters* bk. 13), consists of letters of recommendation, not the purportedly composite letters of 1 and 2 Corinthians, for example, that Trobisch argues for.[82]

There is a further difficulty in Trobisch's distinction between public and private letters.[83] Trobisch apparently needs to claim that Paul's letters are public to show that such letters were kept in copies, as a private letter—he believes—is one that needed to be sent to fulfill its purpose, and is never a copy but the original. Not only are both of these specific characteristics questionable,[84] but the entire construct of public versus private letter has been criticized.[85] There is also evidence that even private letters regularly

81. Trobisch, *Paul's Letter Collection*, 55; idem, *Die Entstehung der Paulusbriefsammlung*, 100. See also Cicero, *Letters to Atticus* 16.7.1, for an indirect reference.

82. Trobisch, *Paul's Letter Collection*, 56 on Cicero, *Familiar Letters* bk. 13; and 73–86 on the Corinthian letters; cf. Murphy-O'Connor, *Paul the Letter-Writer*, 127. Murphy-O'Connor contends that Richards's theory of a secretary using Paul's copies cannot account for those letters that are composites (*Paul the Letter-Writer*, 118). Murphy-O'Connor clearly assumes that theories of composite letters are proven, a hypothesis that remains unproven to me.

83. Trobisch, *Paul's Letter Collection*, 48–50; idem, *Die Entstehung der Paulusbriefsammlung*, 84–88. The distinction was made by G. A. Deissmann (*Bible Studies* [trans. A. Grieve; Edinburgh: T&T Clark, 1901], 3–59; idem, *Light from the Ancient East* [trans. L. R. M. Strachan; 4th ed.; London: Hodder & Stoughton, 1927], 224–46), but is now seen to be overdrawn. See D. E. Aune, *The New Testament in its Literary Environment* (LEC; Philadelphia: Westminster, 1987), 161; L. T. Johnson, *The Writings of the New Testament: An Interpretation* (Philadelphia: Fortress, 1986), 251.

84. Trobisch himself makes the questionable distinction between a letter being sent and hand delivered by the author, as letters were seen as a substitute for the personal presence of the author. See H. Koskenniemi, *Studien zur Idee und Phraseologie des griechischen Briefes bis 400 n. Chr.* (Suomalaisen Tiedeakatemian Toimituksia B.102.2; Helsinki: Suomalainen Tiedeakatemia, 1956), esp. 88–127.

85. S. K. Stowers, *Letter Writing in Greco-Roman Antiquity* (LEC; Philadelphia: Westminster, 1986), 19: the distinction "does not hold well for either Greco-Roman society in general or for letter writing. Politics, for example, was based on the institutions of friendship and family. . . . Many correspondences in antiquity that were either originally written

had copies made (e.g., Cicero, *Familiar Letters* 9.26.1; 7.18.1; *Letters to Atticus* 13.6.3).[86]

Trobisch accepts a fragmentary hypothesis for the Corinthian letters, and takes Romans 16 as a cover letter sent with a copy of Romans.[87] Much recent scholarship argues for the integrity of the Corinthian letters and Romans.[88] This conclusion jeopardizes Trobisch's analysis since Romans 16 introduces a distinctly personal element that he finds unsuitable for the four public letters of Paul. However, there is also much critical scholarship that sees fragmentary letters in the second part of Trobisch's collection, such as Philippians.[89] Trobisch does not explain this later process of formation in any detail, but it would seem unnecessary to find fragmentary letters in the later pseudepigraphic letters. For Trobisch to admit that there are any authentic letters in the rest of the thirteen threatens his theory, since it alters the symmetry that he sees among the three major parts. However, the critical consensus today is that at least seven of the letters are authentic, including 1 Thessalonians and Philippians in the church letters and Philemon in the personal letters. For any of these letters to be authentic would indicate that, contrary to Trobisch, Paul's involvement with the authentic letters was not necessary for them to be collected, the heart of Trobisch's scheme; or that his rigid principle of decreasing length within each section does not hold as a means of dividing the three sections of the Pauline canon. Few scholars see Ephesians as forming an introductory letter suitable for the Pauline canon—in this case, even a reduced canon of nine letters—nor is it found at the head (or foot) of any Pauline

---

or later edited with an eye toward publication have what we would call a private character: for example, Cicero, Ruricius, Seneca."

86. Murphy-O'Connor, *Paul the Letter-Writer*, 12–13.

87. Trobisch (*Paul's Letter Collection*, 71) seems to assume that Rom. 16 is a cover letter, on the basis of many ancient examples of such letters (the one he cites is from the third century CE). He then gives two characteristics of the cover letter—it is not addressed to the same place as is the original letter, and it most often would mention the enclosed copies of the letter. Thus, he must take Rom. 16:22 as "I [Tertius] copied the letter for you."

88. On the Corinthian letters, see above. On Romans, see Gamble, *Textual History*; J. A. Fitzmyer, *Romans* (AB 33; New York: Doubleday, 1993), 55–68.

89. See J. T. Reed, *A Discourse Analysis of Philippians: Method and Rhetoric in the Debate over Literary Integrity* (JSNTSup 136; Sheffield: Sheffield Academic Press, 1997), esp. 124–52.

letter list.[90] Once all this is admitted, and the possibility of other letters broached, then the unity of Trobisch's group is lost, and with it, his theory.

Pauline/Personal Involvement Theory of the Thirteen Pauline Letters

There is no entirely satisfactory theory as to the origins of the Pauline letter collection. Critical scholarship may never agree on a convincing explanation of how the Pauline letter collection emerged. There is, however, despite the claims of Goodspeed and Knox, no substantive evidence that Paul's letters were ever neglected or had fallen out of use. So, emerge it did, though not without plenty of controversy and confusion from virtually the earliest lists to the present debate over the timing and process of such formation, the limits and ordering of such a collection, what constitutes the authentic letters, and what were the later pseudepigraphic additions. Taking the previous discussion fully into account, in this section I wish to develop my own account of the gathering of Paul's collection of letters.

I wish to begin with a number of assumptions that emerge from the previous discussion. The first assumption is that virtually all theories—including Zahn-Harnack with Marcion, Goodspeed-Knox with Onesimus, Moule with Luke, Guthrie with Timothy, and Trobisch with Paul himself—are agreed that the gathering of the Pauline corpus required personal involvement at a close level. Even the Pauline school theory appears more convincing if one can find recognizable and named people in that school. As a result, the proposals of personal involvement range from Paul himself to early followers,[91] to his opponents,[92] to later followers and supporters. Despite the diversity of possibilities and extent of time that they cover, we should concentrate on establishing reasonable procedures

---

90. Best, *Ephesians*, 66; Zuntz, *Text of the Epistles*, 276. It would be dubious to claim that once the first four letters are removed, then Ephesians stands at the head of a collection. There is still the objection that the content of Ephesians itself is not appropriate as such a letter.

91. E.g., Luke, Timothy, or Onesimus.

92. E.g., Marcion.

to determine who such people might have been and the kinds of actions they could have taken.

A second assumption is that theories requiring the least dissection of the individual letters have a better chance of being accepted as probable—and of being parallel to the situation of other ancient writers and collectors of their letters (e.g., Cicero). The more fragmentary hypotheses, it seems, offer less ground for establishing firm conclusions, whether these are in terms of Schmithals's fragmentary theory with six Corinthian, one Galatian, three Philippian, two Roman, and four Thessalonian letters, or Trobisch's theory with seven Corinthian and two Roman letters (and no other fragmentary letters). This is especially seen in dealing with the Corinthian letters. The fact of two and only two Corinthian letters is a strong argument against extravagant multiple letter hypotheses (this says nothing about how such fragmentary hypotheses are attained).

A third assumption is that—whenever it may have happened—the letters were probably gathered in a particular place. The places proposed include Rome, Smyrna, Antioch, Ephesus, and Corinth, which have been suggested by a range of different theories. This locational assumption coincides with an individual being involved, and points away from there being many Pauline letter collections existing for very long in separate places—an observation supported by the textual evidence.[93] The amount of commonality among the early manuscripts, as both Trobisch and Murphy-O'Connor have shown, clearly supports this assumption.

The facts as we have them make it clear that the Pauline canon emerged fairly early in a form recognizably similar to the New Testament thirteen-letter collection. $\mathfrak{P}^{46}$ is, as Trobisch states, "the oldest manuscript of the letters of Paul."[94] This manuscript, which has been dated from 80 CE to around 200 CE, consists of the following Pauline letters: Romans, (Hebrews), 1 and 2 Corinthians, Ephesians, Galatians, Philippians, and 1 Thessalonians. There

---

93. This is the case even if there were later developments in the size and shape of the Pauline collection, such as addition of Hebrews, alterations in ordering of letters, and even altering the number of letters.

94. Trobisch, *Paul's Letter Collection*, 13, who dates it to around 200 CE. Trobisch appears to have modified his position since *Die Entstehung der Paulusbriefsammlung* (26–27 and n60), where he contends that the 200 date is not so certain and argues instead for the third century.

are a number of important observations to make. Not only does it have Hebrews after Romans and before 1 and 2 Corinthians, but it has Ephesians before Galatians, and, of course, breaks off in 1 Thessalonians. Trobisch claims that the amount and type of variation in placement of Hebrews, along with other internal and external differences, indicates that Hebrews was not part of the original Pauline corpus but was added later to a relatively fixed corpus of Paul's letters.[95] Furthermore, though many scholars, including its original editor, Kenyon, and many since, believe that 𝔓⁴⁶ originally also included only 2 Thessalonians and Philemon,[96] other scholars (as noted above) believe that the Pastorals were included as well.[97] Trobisch also believes that this is the case, as he notes that "There is no manuscript evidence to prove that the letters of Paul ever existed in an edition containing only some of the thirteen letters."[98] This statement helps make sense of the evidence that Paul's letters were probably known earlier than even 𝔓⁴⁶. *First Clement*, it is widely agreed, quotes Romans and 1 Corinthians[99] and also probably quotes Titus,[100] with the possibility of at least alluding to 2 Corinthians, Galatians, Ephesians, Philippians, Colossians, and 1 Timothy.[101] It is likely not accidental that all but 1 and

95. For the sake of argument here, I accept this as the case (Trobisch, *Paul's Letter Collection*, 20). However, the inclusion of Hebrews in the early sources with Paul's letters merits further discussion.

96. See F. G. Kenyon, *The Text of the Greek Bible* (rev. A. W. Adams; 3rd ed.; London: Duckworth, 1975), 70–71.

97. See Duff, "𝔓⁴⁶ and the Pastorals," 578–90.

98. Trobisch, *Paul's Letter Collection*, 22.

99. See *New Testament in the Apostolic Fathers*, 37–55. The examples include (from the a and b passages in the A category): *1 Clem.* 35.5, 6 citing Rom. 1:29–32; *1 Clem.* 33.1 citing Rom. 6:1; *1 Clem.* 37.5 and 38.1 citing 1 Cor. 12:21–26; *1 Clem.* 47.1 citing 1 Cor. 1:11–13; *1 Clem.* 49.5 citing 1 Cor. 13:4–7; *1 Clem.* 24.1 citing 1 Cor. 15:20, 23; *1 Clem.* 24.4, 5 citing 1 Cor. 15:36, 37 (there are c and d rated passages as well). *First Clement* also quotes Hebrews. Cf. W. K. Lowether Clarke, *The First Epistle of Clement to the Corinthians* (London: SPCK, 1937), 34, 35.

100. *1 Clem.* 1.3 citing Titus 2:4, 5, and possibly *1 Clem.* 2.7 and 24.4 citing Titus 3:1; 2:21; 3:17. On possible echoes of the Pastoral Epistles, see H. E. Lona, *Der erste Clemensbrief* (Göttingen: Vandenhoeck & Ruprecht, 1998), 49–51.

101. *1 Clem.* 36.2 citing 2 Cor. 3:18; *1 Clem.* 2.1 citing Gal. 3:1; *1 Clem.* 5.2 citing Gal. 2:9; *1 Clem.* 36.2 citing Eph. 4:18; *1 Clem.* 46.6 citing Eph. 4:4–6; *1 Clem.* 59.3 citing Eph. 1:18; *1 Clem.* 3.4 and 21.2 citing Phil. 1:27; *1 Clem.* 47.1, 2 citing Phil. 4:15; *1 Clem.* 59.2 citing Col. 1:12, 13; *1 Clem.* 61.2 citing 1 Tim. 1:17. Cf. Streeter, *Four Gospels*, 526–27.

2 Thessalonians and 2 Timothy are possibly quoted or alluded to in *1 Clement*.[102]

The question of who was involved in the collection of Paul's letters is probably more complex than simply deciding between Paul or some other person or persons. The framing of the question often has the person involved collecting the letters after they had been distributed to their various audiences. This is a possibility, as the geographical distribution of the letters of Paul is not very wide. Even if one includes the Pastoral Epistles as letters addressed to individuals located in the Asia Minor Mediterranean area, we have all of the letters confined to a stretch from Galatia in the east (probably Roman provincial Galatia) to Rome in the west, with Colossae, Laodicea/ Ephesus, Philippi, Thessalonica, and Corinth in between (a distance of roughly 1,100 miles). Most of the letters were sent to destinations within a radius of not more than about 150 miles around the Aegean Sea, all of them places where there were some Pauline supporters.[103] In the light of the traveling possible during that time (Paul himself serves as an excellent example), it is not unlikely that someone could have gathered the letter collection that resulted (missing out some letters that were either no longer extant or thought not to be of value, perhaps because of their particularistic nature).[104] Such a process apparently occurred early, resulting in the relative fixity of the contents of the manuscripts that contain Paul's letters and their order (see below). The person involved could have been any of Paul's close companions and followers, including Luke or Timothy.

An alternative to personal involvement in collecting the letters after the fact is personal involvement at the time of writing and

102. I find it interesting that at several points where the Historical Society disputes whether *1 Clement* quotes Paul, an alternative is found in Acts and/or 1 Peter. See *1 Clem.* 59.2 citing Col. 1:12, 13, but also in Acts 26:18 and 1 Pet. 2:9 (*New Testament in the Apostolic Fathers*, 50, 54). It is arguable that much material in Acts, especially that regarding Paul, goes back to Paul, and that Paul and Peter may have shared the same scribe, Silvanus (1 Pet. 5:12).

103. See Murphy-O'Connor, *Paul the Letter-Writer*, 128, who uses such information in terms of his collection B.

104. On the issue of the particularity of the letters and the problems related to collecting the Pauline letters, see N. A. Dahl, "The Particularity of the Pauline Epistles as a Problem in the Ancient Church," in *Neotestamentica et Patristica: Eine Freundesgabe, Herrn Professor Dr. Oscar Cullmann zu seinem 60. Geburtstag überreicht* (NovTSup 6; Leiden: Brill, 1962), 261–71.

sending. Whereas some scholars might welcome the idea that Paul himself was involved in his letter-collecting, as does Trobisch, these same scholars might not wish to limit the number of letters to four.[105] Several factors indicate that we need not choose between Paul or others close to him as being involved in the collection process, or necessarily limiting the collection to four letters. As noted above, scholars for a number of years have suggested that Paul might have made copies of his letters at the time he was writing them with his scribe and missionary companions. This would follow the pattern of many ancient writers—among them, Seneca and Cicero as literary authors (who speak of actual letters, not composites made out of the fragments of earlier letters), and Zenon as a documentary writer—who made copies of their letters before having them dispatched.[106] This allowed the writers not only to refer to their letters in the future—perhaps explaining why 1 and 2 Thessalonians, and Colossians and Ephesians, among others, have verbal material in common—but to have the copies either with them or in the possession of their companions. The only explicit statement that might give the idea Paul had this sort of thing in mind is in 2 Timothy 4:13,[107] a book that Trobisch contends is not authentically Pauline, and can therefore hardly be used as evidence by him in his theory.[108] Some would contend that what we have here is a later pseudepigrapher including such a statement in order to create Paul as collector of his letters, rather than Paul himself making such a claim. This strikes me as unnecessarily deceptive. Instead, this claim provides supporting evidence for the authenticity of the Pastoral Epistles and hence the entire thirteen-letter corpus falling within the purview of Paul's authentic letters.[109]

---

105. Cf. Ellis, *Making of the New Testament Documents*, who apparently wants to maintain a thirteen-letter corpus, with Paul as its originator.

106. See Richards, *Paul and First-Century Letter Writing*, 156–65, 214–15. Paul is widely regarded in classical studies as one of the great letter writers of the ancient world. If that is true—and his corpus of letters argues that it is—then it is logical to think that Paul followed the conventions of ancient letter writing, including producing copies.

107. This passage is subject to other interpretations as well.

108. Other statements by Paul, such as his reference to a scribe (Rom. 16:22) or to taking the pen in hand (Gal. 6:11), also imply that Paul was using the scribal system.

109. See Richards, *Secretary in the Letters of Paul*, 164–65; Ellis, *Making of the New Testament Documents*, 86, 297, who also cites 1 Cor. 5:9–11.

Such a scenario has recently been proposed by Bo Reicke.[110]
Reicke notes that—consistent with the scribal procedures noted
above—Paul worked and traveled with a literary "team" that was
involved in the composition of his letters (note that letters such
as 1 and 2 Corinthians, Galatians, Philippians, Colossians, 1 and
2 Thessalonians, and Philemon all have salutations from Paul and
others).[111] From the period of 51–61 CE, according to Reicke, Paul
wrote all of his letters, with the help of his companions. The letters
fall into two categories: nine letters to churches and four personal
letters. Reicke's order of composition is 2 and 1 Thessalonians
(52–53 CE), Galatians (55 CE), 1 Corinthians (56 CE), 1 Timothy
(56 CE),[112] 2 Corinthians (57 CE), Romans (58 CE), Titus (58 CE),
Philemon (59 CE), Ephesians (59 CE), 2 Timothy (60 CE), and
Philippians (61/62 CE). Reicke believes that Philemon, Ephesians,
and 2 Timothy were written from a Caesarean imprisonment, but
Philippians from a Roman imprisonment.[113] One need not follow
Reicke on every detail of his ordering of the letters, or his theory
of imprisonment, except to note that Paul ends up having written all of his letters and arriving at Rome. Previous scholars have
noted that Rome is one of the possible places where the collection
of Pauline letters was made.[114]

On the basis of this analysis, the Pauline chronology with regard
to his letters could have unfolded something like this. During the
course of his several missionary journeys, Paul composed his mix

110. B. Reicke, *Re-examining Paul's Letters: The History of the Pauline Correspondence* (ed. D. P. Moessner and I. Reicke; Harrisburg, PA: Trinity Press International, 2001),
39–102. The chronology of J. A. T. Robinson (*Redating the New Testament* [Philadelphia:
Westminster, 1976], 31–85) is also compatible with this scenario.

111. Reicke, *Re-examining Paul's Letters*, 30.

112. Reicke, *Re-examining Paul's Letters*, 52–56. Reicke realizes that there are differences between the Pastoral Epistles and the rest of the Pauline corpus, but he attributes this
to a number of possible factors, including the audience or Paul's scribal help. Reicke also
notes that these letters have a lot of similarities in content and historical details with the
rest of Paul's corpus, and fit better within his chronology rather than being later pseudepigraphal writings.

113. Reicke believes that Paul was probably released from his Roman imprisonment
in 63 CE, traveled to Spain, and then was recaptured and killed by Nero in 65 CE (Reicke,
Re-examining Paul's Letters, 38).

114. If "all roads led to Rome," then it is not surprising that a variety of people—Paul
and his companions included—brought their manuscripts with them when they came to
Rome. I appreciate James Charlesworth suggesting this idea to me.

of personal and ecclesial letters (we have noted above that copies of both literary and documentary letters were kept—alleviating the need for various fragmentary hypotheses of letters such as Rom. 16 and Corinthians). For each of them he used scribes, and for most if not all of them copies were kept, according to the custom of the time.[115] These copies were kept in the possession of either Paul or his companions, which often meant the same thing as they traveled together. Whether he wrote his prison letters from Caesarea, or Caesarea and Rome, or just Rome, eventually Paul was imprisoned in Rome. We do not know of any other letters that he wrote, which means that both Paul and his closest companions may have been directly responsible for collecting his letters—not as an afterthought by means of visiting the various cities and gathering the letters (and hence running the risk of certain ones being lost), but by virtue of their having copies of the letters in their possession. In essence, this means that the collection of Paul's letters also implies their publication, as they were made more widely known first perhaps by Paul and then by successive generations of Paul's followers. One might expect on this basis to have all of the letters that Paul is reported to have written, including other letters to the Corinthians and to the Laodiceans (if the letter to the Ephesians is not this letter). It is not certain why these letters are missing, unless they simply were not copied originally (Richards suggests that Paul's "severe letter" was sent off in anger and haste)[116] or were themselves lost in the course of Paul's travels, including his shipwrecks.

A number of other factors may also be explained or integrated by this scenario. One is the close connection between some wording in the book of Acts and the Pauline letters.[117] If Luke was a traveling companion of Paul, and was with him, for example, when

115. I find Richards's hypothesis plausible in the light of practice in the ancient world, the nature of the Pauline correspondence, and the indications from the Pauline corpus as a whole. See also O. Roller, *Das Formular der paulinischen Briefe: Ein Beitrag zur Lehre vom antiken Briefe* (BWANT 4.6; Stuttgart: Kohlhammer, 1933).

116. Richards, *Paul and First-Century Letter Writing*, 220–21. He notes that not all letters were copied. Cicero himself admits that he did not have copies of all of his letters (*Letters to Atticus* 6.5.5).

117. I take an early date for the composition of Acts, on the basis of its ending with Paul alive and in prison. See Harnack, *Neue Untersuchungen*, esp. 81.

Paul was in prison near the end of his life (Col. 4:14; Philem. 24; 2 Tim. 4:11), it explains his access to Paul's writings. The major limitation here is that Luke supposedly gives no direct evidence of Paul's letters in Acts.[118] A useful analogy can be drawn between how Luke handles Jesus tradition in his Gospel and in Acts.[119] In the Gospel, Luke cites the words of Jesus extensively, and there is no question that (as the prologue says, Luke 1:1–4) he has used sources such as Mark and others that contained the words of Jesus. However, in Acts, apart from the ascension and the words of Jesus in 1:4–5, 7–8, there is no other explicit indication of Luke's knowledge of Jesus tradition. In other words, here we have proof that, even though Luke knew important facts, he did not feel compelled to relate them. The same is perhaps true regarding knowledge of Paul's letters. What saves this from being sheer hypothesis are indicators throughout Acts that, although Luke does not depict Paul as a letter writer or quote his letters explicitly, he seems to know what Paul had written in some of his letters. This is shown by numerous verbal, conceptual, and perspectival factors, as Walker has shown.[120] Of course, if the compiler was Timothy, the problem of Acts does not emerge as strongly. Further, the literary connection between Paul and 1 Peter might be better explained if both Paul and Peter were in Rome, with the two of them sharing the same scribe, Silas/Silvanus (1 Pet. 5:12; cf. 2 Cor. 1:19; 1 Thess. 1:1; 2 Thess. 1:1).[121] It may also explain how it is that a statement

118. See Dahl, "Particularity of the Pauline Epistles," 265–66, who recognizes the problem.

119. In Porter, "Pauline Canon," 126n120, I admitted having lost sight of who first originated this analogy and apologized for not making explicit reference to its source. I would still welcome being informed of its originator so that I can include reference in any future reprint or use of it.

120. Walker, "Acts and the Pauline Corpus Reconsidered," 63–70, following especially M. S. Enslin, "'Luke' and Paul," *JAOS* 58 (1938): 81–90; idem, "Once Again, Luke and Paul," *ZNW* 61 (1970): 253–71; and now with further evidence in W. O. Walker Jr., "Acts and the Pauline Corpus Revisited: Peter's Speech at the Jerusalem Conference," in *Literary Studies in Luke–Acts: Essays in Honor of Joseph B. Tyson* (ed. R. P. Thompson and T. E. Phillips; Macon, GA: Mercer University Press, 1998), 77–86. See also S. Walton, *Leadership and Lifestyle: The Portrait of Paul in the Miletus Speech and 1 Thessalonians* (SNTSMS 108; Cambridge: Cambridge University Press, 2000).

121. On the issues involved (though overly skeptical in his conclusions), see P. Achtemeier, *1 Peter* (Hermeneia; Minneapolis: Fortress, 1996), 349–52.

such as is found in 2 Peter 3:16 can be made, in which it is implied that the author had access to a collection of Paul's letters, that is, that the letters were already gathered together in some way.[122] The scenario of Paul's imprisonment in Rome is also consistent with his ability to be involved in such a collection and dissemination process (Acts 28:30–31)—unless Paul's collection and dissemination took place after his release and before his final imprisonment. Lastly, this scenario would also possibly explain the context thirty years later in which quotation of and allusion to a wide range of Paul's letters in *1 Clement*, a letter written to the Corinthian church by Clement from Rome, could occur.[123]

If this scenario is correct, it is not surprising that variation in the Pauline corpus occurs within relatively narrow parameters—the corpus of Paul's letters originated in a particular location at the instigation of a small group of one or more people, including possibly Paul and some of his closest associates. As noted above, the variation in the manuscripts that does exist revolves around the book of Hebrews, the alternating of Ephesians and Galatians (e.g., $\mathfrak{P}^{46}$), some uncertainty over Colossians and Philippians (e.g., D 06 Codex Claromontanus), and whether the Pastorals are included (e.g., $\mathfrak{P}^{46}$).[124] I have already addressed the question of Hebrews. As Murphy-O'Connor has shown, however, if one does not rely only upon counting characters, but uses other evident ancient forms of measurement, such as the indicated stichoi, the fluctuation in placement of Hebrews is the only real variable[125]—there

---

122. See Richards, *Paul and First-Century Letter Writing*, 221–22. I realize that many scholars think that 2 Peter is pseudepigraphic. The point above would still hold, although the time of accessing the letters might be later. However, if 2 Peter is authentic, there is nothing that conflicts with the scenario I have created.

123. On Clement, see J. B. Lightfoot, *The Apostolic Fathers: Part 1. S. Clement of Rome* (2 vols.; London: Macmillan, 1890), 1:14–103.

124. Schmithals, *Paul and the Gnostics*, 256. Schmithals, citing the Muratorian canon (is this evidence for its early date?), Marcion, and Tertullian (*Against Marcion* 4.5; *Prescription against Heretics* 36), claims that Romans was placed elsewhere as well (*Paul and the Gnostics*, 254).

125. Apart from $\mathfrak{P}^{46}$, Hebrews only appears either at the juncture of the church and personal letters (that is, between 2 Thessalonians and 1 Timothy), or at the end of the Pauline corpus (or at the beginning). A possible exception is the numbering of the chapters in B 03 Codex Vaticanus. But, as Trobisch notes (*Paul's Letter Collection*, 21–22), it is only the numbering of the chapters that places Hebrews after Galatians, since the books

is otherwise virtual fixity to the manuscript ordering, at least in the early stages.[126] The placement of Colossians before Philippians is understandable, as they are within 200 characters of each other, and have similar stichoi in some traditions. In any event, this transposition only occurs in D 06 Codex Claromontanus and a fourteenth-century minuscule (5).[127] The placement of Ephesians before Galatians only occurs in 𝔓[46], but this ordering does reflect actual length, with Ephesians 700–900 letters longer, depending upon whose count is followed.[128] This may in fact be the original ordering. In other words, the evidence seems to point towards consistency in the composition and ordering of the entire Pauline corpus (whether one accepts 𝔓[46] or not), not just within three groups of letters. If one removes Hebrews from the Pauline canon,[129] there is a clearly established Pauline corpus that essentially follows the principle of decreasing size[130] from Romans to 2 Thessalonians, what might be called the church letters, and then begins again with an ordering in decreasing size from 1 Timothy to Philemon, what might be called the personal letters.[131]

---

themselves are written with Hebrews after 2 Thessalonians. Contra Murphy-O'Connor, *Paul the Letter-Writer*, 123–25.

126. Murphy-O'Connor, *Paul the Letter-Writer*, 125.

127. Murphy-O'Connor (*Paul the Letter-Writer*, 123) dismisses this as "an error without historical significance."

128. The number of stichoi in some traditions, however, is similar. Murphy-O'Connor (*Paul the Letter-Writer*, 124) again dismisses this transposition as "an insignificant error." Cf. Trobisch, *Paul's Letter Collection*, 17, where he notes that 𝔓[46] in its entirety is arranged according to length, with Hebrews placed before 1 Corinthians so as not to separate the two Corinthian letters.

129. If one accepts that this variation indicates Hebrews was a later addition, it appears to have been added at the end of the corpus to indicate ambivalence over its authorship, or at the end of the church letters (after 2 Thessalonians) because it is not a personal letter, but in this case still reflecting indecision over authorship.

130. This pattern is thus found not only in modern arrangements of the Pauline canon (Bruce, *Canon of Scripture*, 130n50), but in ancient times as well.

131. Philemon is typically considered a personal letter, even if it is more than that (J. A. Fitzmyer, *The Letter to Philemon* [AB 34C; New York: Doubleday, 2000], 23). Much of the dispute over authenticity of the Pastoral Epistles concerns the personal elements found in the letters and the fact that they are addressed to individuals associated with Paul's mission (see E. E. Ellis, *Paul and his Recent Interpreters* [Grand Rapids: Eerdmans, 1961], 49–57, for an older but representative survey of opinion). See now also J. T. Reed, "To Timothy or Not? A Discourse Analysis of 1 Timothy," in *Biblical Greek Language and Linguistics: Open Questions in Current Research* (ed. S. E. Porter and D. A. Carson; JSNTSup 80; Shef-

Conclusion

Viewing the Pauline corpus in this way opens up further insights regarding its actual formation. We do not need to divide the corpus into three groups, reflecting three stages of formation. It is possible to view it as two groups, but two groups each united according to principles of organization and orientation of the letters within it, within a single process of formation. It is even possible that Paul was involved in this organizing process. If the corpus of authentic Pauline letters extends beyond the four that Trobisch posits—as I (and most scholars) think is virtually certain,[132] and as the organization noted above seems to suggest—then Paul's chances of being involved are increased, as he would have perhaps been the only person, apart from his few closest associates, who would consistently have had access to the many copies produced by his scribes and companions. The only other person or persons who would have had such access would probably have been his closest followers, such as Luke, or possibly Timothy.[133] If Paul were not the initiator of the collecting process, and if there were not copies of the letters readily available, then the act of instigating the Pauline collection must have fallen to one of these close companions. As Guthrie says, and as virtually all of the theories noted above (except for that of Goodspeed) acknowledge, there is no evidence that Paul's reputation fell into disrepute. Thus, the collecting process must have involved a close follower or advocate of Paul, who perhaps undertook such action near the end of Paul's life, possibly when he was in prison in Rome, or very soon after his death. Luke is the most likely figure for such a scenario, on the basis of the internal Pauline evidence (Col. 4:14; Philem. 24; 2 Tim. 4:11), church tradition regarding Luke's relation to Paul

___

field: JSOT Press, 1993), 90–118, who notes the clear indications of the personal nature of the correspondence addressed to Timothy.

132. Critical scholarship would, as noted above, endorse seven letters, but the above formulation suggests that there are structural reasons regarding the shape of the Pauline corpus for seeing all thirteen as authentic. Less likely is that nine letters are authentic, since that requires bracketing out an entire category of letters, the personal letters, in which at least one letter, Philemon, is commonly acknowledged to be genuine.

133. See Guthrie, *New Testament Introduction*, 655–57, for defense of Timothy. The relationship of this theory to the issue of the authenticity of the Pastoral Epistles is unavoidable.

(especially in Acts, but also in Irenaeus, *Against Heresies* 1.23.1; 3.10.1; 3.14.1; etc.), and even much critical scholarship regarding the authorship of Acts.[134]

In any case, there is reasonable evidence to see the origin of the Pauline corpus during the latter part of Paul's life or sometime after his death, almost assuredly instigated by Paul and/or a close follower or followers, and close examination of the early manuscripts with Paul's letters and of related documents seems to support this hypothesis.

---

134. See Porter, *Paul of Acts*, 187–206. This close companion could have assembled a number of smaller letters into larger ones, especially if he had been close to Paul and knew his mission strategy—assuming that such a hypothesis is necessary.

7

Wherein Lies Authority?

A Discussion of Books, Texts, and Translations

L EE M ARTIN M C D ONALD

Introduction

For generations now, biblical scholars have foraged the biblical, noncanonical, and rabbinic writings in the first and second centuries and the early church fathers in order to gain an understanding of the origins and development of the Bible. In the Bible there are a number of texts that illustrate some of the growth and development of biblical literature (e.g., Josh. 18:6–8; 24:26; 2 Kings 17:13; 2 Chron. 36:22–23; cf. Ezra 1:1–3; Prov. 25:1; Luke 24:44; John 21:24; 2 Pet. 3:15–16; etc.), and many references elsewhere that offer suggestions about the processes that gave rise to the emergence of our current Bible.[1]

---

1. These are listed in L. M. McDonald, "Appendix A: Primary Sources for the Study of the Old Testament/Hebrew Bible Canon," and "Appendix B: Primary Sources for the

I will focus here especially on three interconnected and highly
significant issues related to the origin of the Bible, namely lists or
catalogues of books, variations in ancient biblical manuscripts,
and the translation of the Scriptures into various ancient languages. These issues clarify best the importance that the early
church placed on its sacred literature, when this took place, and
how that literature was formed into a fixed book that was eventually called the Bible. It is important to know how and when certain
biblical manuscripts were acknowledged as Scripture in the early
church, as well as the texts that they used and the understanding
of the sacredness of the texts in the church. The significant task
of translating these texts into another language also reveals their
sacred status in the communities that translated and received them.
While I will refer briefly and occasionally to both the origins and
transmission of the Hebrew Bible to illustrate or contrast the development of the Scriptures, I will focus my comments on three
canonical questions related to the origins of the New Testament
canon of Scripture. These include the variableness of the traditions in the early church in regard to which books are sacred, as
well as which text and translation(s) of Scripture are authoritative
in the life of the church. These issues raise the more fundamental
question about the authority the early Christians attributed to
these writings.

Books

It is often wrongly assumed that the ancient world was vitally interested in many of the issues that preoccupy us today. For example,
some biblical scholars assume that the question of which books
belong in the Bible was of special concern in the ancient world. If
that is so, however, it is strange that the writers of antiquity left
almost no record of such interest and there is little trace of how and
why some books were recognized and received but others were not.
Even the scanty information that we do have cannot be assumed to
have been widely or generally acknowledged in the early church.

Study of the New Testament Canon," in *The Canon Debate* (ed. L. M. McDonald and
J. A. Sanders; Peabody, MA: Hendrickson, 2002), 580–84.

Some students of the Bible assume that the ancient writers were consciously aware of writing sacred Scripture, but almost without exception, this was not the case. The attention given to preserving the biblical tradition without additions or deletions (Deut. 4:2; Rev. 22:18–19) was simply not observed in the transmission of the biblical manuscripts that have survived antiquity. Long after the recognition of the Law as sacred Scripture, the Qumran community continued to make changes in the various texts in their possession.[2] Those who are familiar with ancient New Testament manuscripts also know of the variableness both in which books are included in those manuscripts as well as the texts of those books. We will discuss that issue below.

When the church began, the development of the book or codex was in its early stages and the technology for producing codices (or books) was not yet sufficiently advanced to contain in one volume all of the books of the current Bible. For this reason, the manuscripts that have survived antiquity often have a different order of books than the current Bibles and are generally incomplete. Only in the fourth century, when the technology for producing books allowed for the production of a single volume containing all of the books that comprised the Christian Bible, do we begin to see complete Bibles containing both the Old and New Testaments.[3] One searches in vain to find in the first thousand years of the church any manuscript or volume that contains all of—and only—the books of the Bible. The manuscripts that survive either have fewer or more books than we currently possess in our Bibles.

Some of the earliest biblical manuscripts that include both the Old and New Testament literature often include along with them several noncanonical writings and frequently omit several of the later acknowledged canonical books. This is the case in some of the best known uncial manuscripts of the fourth century and later. Nothing in the texts themselves suggests why these other books

---

2. These changes are discussed in D. J. Silver, *The Story of Scripture: From Oral Tradition to the Written Word* (New York: Basic, 1990), 134–39, and in L. M. McDonald, *The Formation of the Christian Biblical Canon* (Peabody, MA: Hendrickson, 1995), 73–74.

3. H. Y. Gamble, *Books and Readers in the Early Church: A History of Early Christian Texts* (New Haven and London: Yale University Press, 1995), discusses carefully and at length the development of books, or codices, and the early Christian preference for them over scrolls.

were included or why some canonical ones were excluded. For example, 𝔓⁷² (third to fourth century) is the oldest surviving manuscript of Jude and 1–2 Peter (in that order), but it also contains several other writings in the following order: the *Nativity of Mary* (or the *Apocalypse of James*), the eleventh *Ode of Solomon*, Jude, Melito's *Homily on the Passover*, a hymn fragment, the *Apology of Phileas*, Psalms 33 and 34, and finally 1–2 Peter. This codex is not uniform, and clearly the writings that are bound together in it are not from the same era nor produced by the same hand. The fact that 1–2 Peter are separate from Jude in this codex may suggest that they were not yet accepted as sacred literature, or perhaps there is some other explanation that currently eludes us.

Likewise, 𝔓⁴², a late sixth- or even seventh-century papyrus manuscript, contains portions of Luke 1 and 2 in Greek and Coptic, but the manuscript also forms a part of an extensive collection of odes or hymns taken from the Jewish Bible and apocryphal literature. P^{apr} (or P₂, a palimpsest) includes Acts, the Catholic Epistles, and Revelation, but also fragments of 4 Maccabees. Codex Sinaiticus (א) contains mixed in the Old Testament collection 2 Esdras, Tobit, Judith, 1–4 Maccabees, Wisdom of Solomon, and Sirach, and the New Testament portion of the codex contains also the *Epistle of Barnabas* and the *Shepherd of Hermas*. Codex Alexandrinus (A) contains Baruch, the Letter of Jeremiah, Tobit, Judith, 1–2 Esdras, 1–4 Maccabees, Wisdom of Solomon, Sirach, and Psalm 151 all mixed in with other Old Testament books without distinction, and in the New Testament part *1–2 Clement* and *Psalms of Solomon* are included. Codex Claromontanus (D) contains the *Shepherd of Hermas*, the *Acts of Paul*, and the *Apocalypse of Peter*. I have shown elsewhere that the various lists or catalogues of sacred books that come from the fourth to the sixth centuries do not reflect a uniform view of which literature is sacred or canonical.[4]

The famous collection of Oxyrhynchus papyri (ca. late third to fourth century to around the late sixth or early seventh century CE), which continue to be published, contains many Christian canonical writings that were found alongside other religious noncanonical

---

4. These lists are in L. M. McDonald, "Appendix C: Lists and Catalogues of Old Testament Collections" and "D: Lists and Catalogues of New Testament Collections" in McDonald and Sanders, *Canon Debate*, 584–97.

writings but without anything that distinguishes them. This collection contains the largest number of New Testament papyri found in any one location and warrants a closer look. The New Testament writings among these papyri include portions of fifteen New Testament books: Matthew, Luke, John, Acts, Romans, 1 Corinthians, Galatians, Philippians, 1–2 Thessalonians, Hebrews, James, 1 John, Jude, and Revelation. Those New Testament books that are missing from the *earlier* Oxyrhynchus papyri include Mark, 2 Corinthians, Ephesians, Colossians, 1–2 Timothy, Titus, Philemon, 1–2 Peter, and 2–3 John. Mark and 1 Peter are among the later Oxyrhynchus papyri. This, of course, raises questions about why some books were omitted and why others were included. What did all of this mean to the community that preserved these writings in the late third and fourth centuries?

Eldon Epp has suggested that the presence of more than one copy of a manuscript in a collection of ancient documents should attract our attention and that a multiple presence may indicate something more about the special status of the manuscript in the community that preserved them. With that in mind, he lists both the multiple and single copies of noncanonical books at Oxyrhynchus as follows:

- *Shepherd of Hermas* (seven copies)[5]
- *Gospel of Thomas* (three copies)
- *Gospel of Mary* (two copies)
- *Acts of Peter* (one copy)
- *Acts of John* (one copy)
- *Acts of Paul* (one copy)
- *Didache* (one copy)
- *Sophia of Jesus Christ* (one copy)
- *Gospel of Peter* (two copies)
- *Apocalypse of Peter* (possibly one copy)

5. In her commentary on this book, Carolyn Osiek claims: "No other noncanonical writing was as popular before the fourth century as the *Shepherd of Hermas*. It is the most frequently attested post-canonical text in the surviving Christian manuscripts of Egypt well into the fifth century" (*The Shepherd of Hermas* [ed. H. Koester; Hermeneia; Minneapolis: Fortress, 1999], 1).

- Three unknown Gospels or sayings of Jesus
- *Acts of Paul and Thecla*

Epp says that all of these books, except perhaps the *Letter of Abgar* (not listed above), were second-century writings and may have been candidates for inclusion in Christian sacred literature. More importantly for our purposes, he concludes that there is nothing at Oxyrhynchus that suggests that the New Testament literature was somehow different from the rest of the religious literature found there. They were found side by side with the so-called noncanonical literature.[6] Whichever churches produced or received these religious manuscripts also used them as sacred literature.

In the last half of the fourth century, Athanasius of Alexandria was the first to list the twenty-seven Christian books that now comprise the canon, though he also included several of the apocryphal books in his Old Testament canon. It is obvious, however, from the various lists and catalogues of the New Testament writings that survive antiquity from his time and later that he was not speaking for the whole church at large during his generation. Indeed, many of these New Testament catalogues and lists are different from the list that he provides. Eusebius (ca. 320–330 CE) offers the first datable listing of books that belong to the "recognized (*homologoumenoi*) books" and they include the four Gospels, Acts, the letters of Paul (thirteen), 1 John, 1 Peter, and possibly Revelation. Among the doubted or disputed books (*antilegomena*), he lists James, Jude, 2 Peter, 2 and 3 John, and Revelation (*Ecclesiastical History* 3.25.1–3). He himself seems conflicted about the widespread acceptance of Revelation.

Eusebius's analysis of what was widely acknowledged by the fourth century reflects the evidence that we find in other surviving lists or catalogues from the fourth and fifth centuries. A simple comparison of these lists shows that there was a generally acceptable core of writings circulating in the early church of the fourth to the sixth centuries, but that there was considerable flexibility on the fringes of the biblical canon. Some books thought initially by some elements of the church to be inspired by God were later

---

6. E. J. Epp, "The Oxyrhynchus New Testament Papyri: 'Not without Honor Except in their Hometown'?" *JBL* 123 (2004): 5–55, esp. 10–30.

removed from inclusion in the church's sacred Scriptures, namely, the *Shepherd of Hermas,* the *Epistle of Barnabas,* and *1–2 Clement.* Some Christian communities continued to accept and read this literature and several other noncanonical texts in worship for centuries, as we see from the surviving lists and catalogues of sacred books in the early Christian community. There is no debate about their usage, but the implications of what it means for understanding canonical formation is precisely where much of the canonical debate takes place.[7] Also, we can conclude that the current interest in establishing a fixed Christian biblical canon was not of as much concern in the earlier development of the church as it later became. This situation began to change in the fourth century, and it is important for students of canon development to consider the social context in which this issue emerged.[8] Historically, of course, the church has never fully agreed on which books comprise its Bible.

Texts

Those who study ancient biblical manuscripts know that all of these manuscripts differ from one another to greater or lesser degrees. While there are many common characteristics in several families of manuscripts, no two biblical manuscripts are exactly identical. This makes the task assigned to textual critics of establishing the earliest and most authentic text of the Bible a significant challenge, and they know that their task is both highly complex and frequently imprecise. Since all ancient biblical manuscripts were copied by hand from earlier ones until the invention of the printing press, the differences between the various manuscripts multiplied in transmission over many centuries. Ancient manuscripts were therefore subject to human error, even those more meticulously copied by the rabbis. The rabbinic tradition often reflects the importance of transmitting a faithful and accurate biblical text. The following rabbinic text from the Babylonian Talmud illustrates both the care,

7. See L. M. McDonald, *The Biblical Canon: Its Origin, Transmission, and Authority* (Peabody, MA: Hendrickson, 2007).
8. This is discussed in McDonald, *Formation of the Christian Biblical Canon,* 178–90.

but also the concern, to preserve the biblical text. We observe in the Babylonian Talmud that anyone making a copy of the Scriptures must do so with a copy before him and not from memory.

> Rabban b. bar Hanah said in the name of R. Johanan, "It is forbidden to write one letter save from a copy." . . . R. Hisda found R. Hananel writing scrolls without a copy. He said to him: You are quite qualified to write the whole Torah by heart, but thus have the Sages ruled: It is forbidden to write one letter save from a copy. Seeing that he said, "You are qualified to write the whole Torah by heart," we may conclude that he could produce them correctly, and we see that R. Meir actually did write?—In case of emergency it is different—Abaye allowed the members of the household of Bar Habu to write tefillin and mezuzoth without a copy. What authority did he follow? The following Tanna, as it has been taught: R. Jeremiah says in the name of our Teacher: Tefillin and mezuzoth may be written out without a copy, and do not require to be written upon ruled lines. The Law, however, is that tefillin do not require lines, but mezuzoth do require lines, and both may be written without a copy. What is the reason?—They are well known by heart. (*b. Meggilah* 18b)[9]

The trained eye readily finds both deliberate and accidental changes in the surviving New Testament manuscripts, but textual scholars also recognize that these texts were received and circulated as sacred literature in the early churches. There is only limited reference to those differences among a handful of ancient writers, but they are of special concern today, and they make the recovery of the original text of the Bible highly complex.

Transmission of Ancient Texts

Textual critics have various opinions about the level of care that was involved in the transmission of ancient biblical manuscripts, and generally speaking most have preferred the oldest textual sources to help them construct the most likely original text of the church's Scriptures. There are important qualifications to this statement, of course, since some of the earliest manuscripts

---

9. Translation by I. Epstein, *The Babylonian Talmud* (London: Soncino, 1948–49).

in the so-called Western family did not receive as careful attention in the detail of transmission as did those in the later Alexandrian text family.

There is no textual family of manuscripts that receives a perfect score in preserving the earliest and best text of the New Testament. Many textual scholars appear to have given up dependence upon a single family of texts and have instead opted for a more eclectic text that allows them to appeal to a variety of textual traditions to determine the most reliable texts of the Scriptures.[10] Textual critics also appeal for greater understanding of the variety of differences between the surviving manuscripts and the social context that accounts for them. Metzger and Ehrman discuss the difficulty of locating an original text and cite as a prime example the letters of Paul.[11] For example, most scholars acknowledge the likelihood that 2 Corinthians originally existed in two or three and possibly even more letters. Most biblical scholars agree that Paul wrote 2 Corinthians 10–13, but not at the same time as he wrote 2 Corinthians 1–9. Is the current shape of Paul's letter to the Philippians the original form? Does Philippians 3:1 begin a new letter from Paul or was it written significantly later or earlier? Likewise, 2 Corinthians 6:14–7:1 is likely an interpolation into the text, even if it was written by Paul. Which original text is the goal of textual critics, the canonical form or the earliest form of the biblical text? Metzger and Ehrman rightly ask about Paul's use of an amanuensis and how we can get back to what Paul actually dictated orally to his writers.[12] They ask more importantly, "what does it mean to establish an 'original' text?"[13]

---

10. E. J. Epp, "Issues in New Testament Textual Criticism: Moving from the Nineteenth Century to the Twenty-First Century," in *Rethinking New Testament Textual Criticism* (ed. D. A. Black; Grand Rapids: Baker Academic, 2002), 17–76, esp. 71–75. In the same volume, see also J. K. Elliott, "The Case for Thoroughgoing Eclecticism," 101–24, who states: "It may well be that modern textual criticism is less confident about the need to, or its ability to, establish the original text and that its best contribution to biblical studies is to show how variation arose, ideally in what directions, and to explain the significance of all variants" (124).

11. B. M. Metzger and B. D. Ehrman, *The Text of the New Testament: Its Transmission, Corruption, and Restoration* (New York and Oxford: Oxford University Press, 2005), 272–73.

12. Metzger and Ehrman, *Text of the New Testament*, 273.

13. Metzger and Ehrman, *Text of the New Testament*, 274.

Emanuel Tov has shown considerable interest in other texts of the Hebrew Bible along with the MT of the First Testament or Old Testament. He has discovered that the Old Greek, the Dead Sea Scrolls, and other ancient texts sometimes depend on a more ancient and reliable Hebrew text than does the MT.[14] He suggests that we may be able to discover an earlier form of the biblical text through a careful investigation not only of the MT, but also the Old Latin, the Greek Bible, the Samaritan Pentateuch, and the Dead Sea Scrolls. He argues that in some cases, these texts may provide an earlier witness than what we find in the MT, the standard biblical text for most Jews as well as for most biblical scholars today. Traditionally, conservative Christian biblical scholars have spoken disparagingly about the Septuagint (LXX) and in favor of the MT, but scholars more recently have begun asking whether in some instances the Old Greek might preserve a more ancient text than does the MT. We should also remember that the Greek Bible was the Bible of early Christianity and, as most seminary students already know, it was used by the New Testament writers in some 94 percent of their citations from the Jewish Scriptures.

The church has not possessed the elusive "original manuscripts" since perhaps the beginning of the circulation of Paul's letters. Textual critics know that their discipline is a combination of art and science, and they have studied thousands of ancient manuscripts identifying families that manifest common characteristics (Western, Alexandrian, and Byzantine texts), and all manuscripts within those families are slightly different from those that preceded or followed them. Accidental and deliberate changes were regularly made in the New Testament manuscripts. In regard to intentional changes, Bart Ehrman observes that "the texts of these books were by no means inviolable; to the contrary, they were altered with relative ease and alarming frequency. Most of the changes were accidental, the result of scribal ineptitude, carelessness, or fatigue.

14. See E. Tov, "Large Scale Differences," in *The Earliest Text of the Hebrew Bible: The Relationship between the Masoretic Text and the Hebrew Base of the Septuagint Reconsidered* (ed. A. Schenker; SBLSCS 52; Atlanta: Society of Biblical Literature, 2003), 143, who states: "My own intuition tells me that more often than not the LXX reflects an earlier stage than MT both in the literary shape of the biblical books and in small details." See also E. Tov, "The Status of the Masoretic Text in Modern Text Editions of the Hebrew Bible," in McDonald and Sanders, *Canon Debate*, 234–51.

Others were intentional, and reflect the controversial milieu within which they were produced."[15] All of the ancient manuscripts, regardless of changes made to them, functioned as Scripture in the ancient churches that preserved and transmitted them and read them in their worship and catechetical instruction.

In antiquity, special care was taken in copying and preserving important classical writings, such as Homer, Pindar, Plato, Xenophon, Cicero, and Plutarch, and the originals from which copies were made were often placed in sacred shrines or museums as in the case of the Library at Alexandria.[16] The same practice took place in Judaism. According to the *Letter of Aristeas*, the high priest, Eleazar, selected those who would translate the Law and gave to them both gifts for the king, who had requested that a copy of the Hebrew Scriptures be translated into the Greek language, and also a copy of the Scriptures themselves. The condition of the scrolls that arrived in Egypt for the translation task also suggests that they were in the possession of the high priest and were in the sanctuary. For example, we read: "So they arrived with the gifts which had been sent at their hands and with the fine skins on which the Law had been written in letters of gold in Jewish characters; the parchment had been excellently worked, and the joining together of the letters was imperceptible" (*Let. Aris.* 176 [Shutt, *OTP* 2:24]). That everything came from the high priest himself also suggests that sacred literature was placed in the temple.

This also fits appropriately with a later time when the city of Jerusalem fell captive to the Romans in 70 CE and lay in ruins. As Josephus reports, Titus told him that he could have anything he wanted from the city. Josephus indicated that he would like to have

15. B. D. Ehrman, *The Orthodox Corruption of Scripture: The Effect of Early Christological Controversies on the Text of the New Testament* (New York and Oxford: Oxford University Press, 1993), 275. He claims that many of the debates over Christology affected the accuracy of the transcription of the New Testament manuscripts (274–80). For a careful discussion of the kinds of errors or mistakes and changes made in the transmission of the ancient manuscripts, see Metzger and Ehrman, *Text of the New Testament*, 250–71.

16. Nina Collins has described the origin of the library and also the Greek translation of the Law that was placed in the famous Alexandrian Library (*The Library in Alexandria and the Bible in Greek* [Leiden and New York: Brill, 2000], 117–37). See also the interesting description of the library and its origins in L. Canfora, *The Vanished Library: A Wonder of the Ancient World* (Berkeley and Los Angeles: University of California Press, 1987).

some of his family and friends freed from captivity, but also said
that he wanted to have some sacred volumes out of the temple.
Being a priest, Josephus was "not ignorant of the prophecies in
the sacred books" (*Jewish War* 3.352 [Thackeray, LCL]), and was
invited to take important biblical scrolls from the Jewish temple
to Rome where he began his career as a historian and defender of
the Jewish people. Josephus tells the story of taking these sacred
volumes:

> Again, when at last Jerusalem was on the point of being carried by
> assault, Titus Caesar repeatedly urged me to take whatever I would
> from the wreck of my country, stating that I had his permission. And
> I, now that my native place had fallen, having nothing more precious
> to take and preserve as a solace for my personal misfortunes, made
> request to Titus for the freedom of some of my countrymen; I also
> received by his gracious favour a gift of sacred books. Not long after
> I made petition for my brother and fifty friends, and my request
> was granted." (*The Life* 417–418, [Thackeray, LCL])

Like those who took care of the library at Alexandria and in
other places where libraries were kept, the Jews took special care
to produce accurate copies of their sacred literature. This tradition continued for centuries, and there are numerous Jewish texts
that reflect this care taken in the copying and preservation of their
sacred literature. The process of copying manuscripts sometimes
included deliberate and accidental alterations of the original documents, so the Jews took special measures to preserve the accuracy
of the manuscripts of sacred writings. For example, according to
the Tosefta,

> A verse which is written in the singular they do not present in the
> plural, and one which is written in the plural they do not present
> in the singular. R. Judah says, "He who translates a verse just as
> it is presented in Scripture—lo, such a one is a deceiver, but the
> one who adds to what is written, lo, this person is a blasphemer."
> A translator who stands before a sage is not permitted either to
> leave anything out or to add anything or to change anything . . .
> (*t. Megillah* 3:41 A–C)[17]

---

17. Translation by J. Neusner, *The Tosefta* (6 vols.; New York: Ktav, 1977–86).

Again we read:

> "The secret things belong unto the Lord our God; but the things
> that are revealed [belong] to us and to our children forever" (Deut.
> 29:28). Each of the letters that spell out the words "to us and to
> our children" and the first letter of the word "forever" have a dot
> over them. Why? Because Ezra said: If the prophet Elijah comes
> and asks me, "Why did you write it thus" I will reply, "But I did put
> dots over the letters [to indicate my uncertainty about the text.]" If,
> however, he says to me "you wrote out the text accurately," I will
> remove the dots. (*Avot of Rabbi Nathan* 34)[18]

And finally:

> A man is required to have a scroll of Torah written with good ink,
> a good quill, by competent scribes, on good sheets of parchment
> made out of hides of deer. He is then to wrap it in beautiful silks,
> in keeping with "This [is] my God, and I will glorify him" (Exod.
> 15:2). (*Soferim* 3)[19]

Such examples of the care given in translating or copying and preserving the law are typically found in ancient Jewish sources, but
they are not in much evidence in the early centuries of the Christian
practice of copying the Scriptures, even if there are examples here
and there of well-copied papyrus manuscripts, especially from the
Alexandrian family.

There appears to be little correlation between the accuracy of
ancient biblical manuscripts and the recognition of their sacredness.
After their recognition as Scripture near the end of the second century and following, those involved in copying the New Testament
writings were still largely literate novices without special training.
There are exceptions to this, of course, but the Christian community was generally not as careful in transmitting their Scriptures as
were the scribes in the rabbinic tradition. For example, manuscripts
in the Western Text tradition that are among the earliest of the

---

18. Translated by Wm. G. Braude in *The Book of Legends, Sefer Ha-Aggadah* (ed.
H. N. Bialik and Y. H. Ravnitzky; New York: Schocken Books, 1992), 444, #406.
19. *Book of Legends*, 448, #443.

manuscript traditions are also commonly known for their poor transmission practices.

Metzger and Ehrman have observed, "the chief characteristics of Western readings is fondness of paraphrase. Words, clauses, and even whole sentences are freely changed, omitted, or inserted. Sometimes the motive appears to have been harmonization, while at other times it was the enrichment of the narrative by inclusion of traditional or apocryphal material."[20] The chief representatives of this family, which were also used by Marcion, Irenaeus, and Tertullian, include $\mathfrak{P}^{48}$, $\mathfrak{P}^{38}$, Codex Bezae (D), and Old Latin versions. Metzger and Ehrman conclude that the manuscripts of the first two centuries show considerable proneness to error. They write:

> The earliest copyists would not have been trained professionals who made copies for a living but simply literate members of a congregation who had the time and ability to do the job. Since most, if not all, of them would have been amateurs in the art of copying, a relatively large number of mistakes no doubt crept into their texts as they reproduced them. It is possible that after the original was placed in circulation it soon became lost or was destroyed, so all surviving copies conceivably have derived from one single, error-prone copy made in the early stages of the book's circulation.[21]

On the other hand, the later Alexandrian text family is known for its greater precision and consciousness of care in copying manuscripts with accuracy, which probably reproduces the earliest and most reliable text of the New Testament that is possible. The chief witnesses to this family include $\mathfrak{P}^{45}$, $\mathfrak{P}^{46}$, $\mathfrak{P}^{66}$, $\mathfrak{P}^{77}$, Codex Vaticanus (B), and Codex Sinaiticus ($\aleph$).

What often appears strange to biblical students today is the scarceness of references in the Christian tradition that describe the care for the accuracy of the transcription of Christian sacred literature. There are relatively few ancient texts that reflect an awareness of the diversity in the texts of the New Testament writings circulating among the churches. Irenaeus, for example, when discussing the number 666 in the book of Revelation (13:18)

---

20. Metzger and Ehrman, *Text of the New Testament*, 276–77.
21. Metzger and Ehrman, *Text of the New Testament*, 275.

acknowledges both the absence of the original texts of the New Testament and the problem of errors among the existing copies of the texts. He writes: "Such, then, being the state of the case, and this number [666] being found in all the most approved and ancient copies" and adds in support of this number, "I do not know how it is that some have erred following the ordinary mode of speech, and have vitiated the middle number [6] in the name. . . ." He goes on to say that he is "inclined to think that this occurred through the fault of copyists, as is wont to happen, since numbers are also expressed by letters; so that the Greek letter which expresses the number of sixty was easily expanded into the letter Iota of the Greeks." Irenaeus explains how this may have come about, but warns those who deliberately change the sacred texts adding that, "there shall be no light punishment [inflicted] upon him who either adds or subtracts anything from the Scripture" (Irenaeus, *Against Heresies* 5.30.1 [*ANF* 1:558]). This passage reveals the absence of any original text to appeal to and how variant readings were already present in the early church ca. 170 CE.

Eusebius informs us later that Irenaeus also reminded those who will copy his work that they should take extra care in doing so. At the end his treatise *On the Ogdoad*, Irenaeus felt obliged to write the following colophon: "I adjure thee, who shalt copy out this book, by our Lord Jesus Christ, by his glorious advent when he comes to judge the living and the dead, that thou compare what thou shalt transcribe and correct it with this copy whence thou art transcribing, with all care, and thou shalt likewise transcribe this oath and put it in the copy" (Eusebius, *Ecclesiastical History* 5.20.2 [Lake, LCL]). Origen was also interested in establishing an accurate biblical text when he produced his Hexapla (or six-columned Old Testament) in the third century. He included critical marks to say what should be omitted and what should be included in the translation, which was his attempt to revise the Septuagint (LXX) from the Hebrew text. Later, Jerome was also aware of deliberate and accidental changes in the biblical texts and sought to correct them; but Jerome did not have a lot of company, and there is little indication that the early church as a whole took serious steps to deal with the errors that had crept into and were perpetuated in the biblical manuscripts.[22] Until the time of Erasmus in the sixteenth century, there was no comprehensive editing project undertaken to create a critical recension of the New Testament text.

Metzger observes that until the fourth century when Christianity received official sanction from the Emperor Constantine, those who copied the Scriptures were often less trained and worked too fast to ensure accuracy in their copies. He further adds that because the Christian community continued to spread rapidly in its first few centuries and had need of more copies of its Scriptures, those that were produced were often copied in haste and were prone to error. In regard to the production of translations, he cites Augustine, who reflected on the inaccuracies in the biblical manuscripts saying wistfully: "anyone who happened to gain possession of a Greek manuscript and who imagined that he had some facility in both Latin and Greek, however slight that might be, dared to make a translation" (*On Christian Doctrine* 2.11.16).[23]

This all seemed to change in the fourth century and later when it became more common for the church to use professional scribes to produce copies of the Christian Scriptures. The cost of producing both the Old and New Testaments by professional scribes was approximately 30,000 denarii, or roughly four years' salary by a legionary some 100 years earlier. The commercial places for literary productions were called scriptoria. Great care was given in the scriptoria for such productions, but in the Byzantine era the task of producing copies of the Scriptures was often given to monks in the monasteries who produced individual copies of the Scriptures. Errors continued to appear in biblical manuscripts throughout this process of transmission and some difficulties in transcription were

22. See B. M. Metzger, "Explicit References in the Works of Origen to Variant Readings in New Testament Manuscripts," in *Biblical and Patristic Studies in Memory of Robert Pierce Casey* (ed. J. N. Birdsall and R. W. Thomson; Freiberg: Herder, 1963), 78–95; repr. in *Historical and Literary Studies: Pagan, Jewish, and Christian* (Leiden: Brill; Grand Rapids: Eerdmans, 1968), 88–103; idem, "St Jerome's Explicit References to Variant Readings in Manuscripts of the New Testament," in *Text and Interpretation: Studies in the New Testament presented to Matthew Black* (ed. E. Best and R. McL. Wilson; Cambridge: Cambridge University Press, 1979), 179–90. Cf. M. Holmes, "Textual Criticism," in *New Testament Criticism and Interpretation* (ed. D. A. Black and D. S. Dockery; Grand Rapids: Zondervan, 1991), 101–34.

23. Metzger and Ehrman, *Text of the New Testament*, 24–25.

compounded by the weariness of posture necessary to make such copies in these less-than-comfortable places. With the use of an ink pen, such copying required a fresh dip in the ink well after every four to six letters. One can only imagine the difficulty in producing such manuscripts and the sheer effort in maintaining attention to detail while at the same time sitting in cramped positions that strained the muscles of the body. As the body would weary and tire, many mistakes crept into the copies, whether prepared in the scriptorium or the cell in a monastery.[24]

Use and Recognition of Writings

The value and importance of the New Testament writings for mission, worship, and instruction were perceived early on in the church, and in several cases the writers intended that their works be circulated among the churches (see Gal. 1:2; Col. 4:16; James 1:1; 1 Pet. 1:1; 2 Pet. 3:15–16). Because they told the story of Jesus, the earliest and most important canon of authority in the early church, the Gospels certainly had an authority attached to them almost from the beginning of their circulation in the churches; however, they were not generally called Scripture until the end of the second century. But not all of the writings of the New Testament received that status at that time, and the early church fathers did not initially acknowledge the sacredness of the same books. The processes that led to the writings being assigned to a fixed list of sacred Scriptures took more than 150 to 180 years longer, but even then there was little interest in promoting a single textual form of the New Testament writings in the early church. Students of the Bible who are familiar with the variety of textual variants noted at the bottom of the pages of their Greek New Testament know that there are many instances when the issues surrounding textual variants are sufficiently complex that accurate decisions cannot be made about the authenticity of a particular text.

24. Metzger and Ehrman, *Text of the New Testament*, 25–27, have provided an excellent background on the processes employed in copying Scripture in antiquity. Given the circumstances of the times, it is amazing that there were not many more mistakes made in transcription.

The early church recognized the value of Christian writings for their worship, mission, and catechetical instruction, especially the canonical Gospels and Paul's writings. Because the Pauline letters emphasized the importance of the death and resurrection of Jesus, and because of their relevance for perpetuating both the theology and ethical practices inherent in the reception of the church's good news about Jesus, many churches also saw great value in using and circulating the letters of Paul. His letters were present and circulating in many churches by the end of the first century if not sooner. It is quite possible that early followers of Paul collected and circulated his letters among the churches he founded.[25]

In the fourth century, after Constantine embraced Christianity he requested that Eusebius of Caesarea produce with special care fifty copies of the Christian sacred Scriptures for use in the churches in the New Rome, or Constantinople. The report of this request and the production of those copies are described by Eusebius as follows:

VICTOR CONSTANTINUS, MAXIMUS AUGUSTUS, to Eusebius:

"It happens, through the favoring providence of God our Saviour, that great numbers have united themselves to the most holy church in the city which is called by my name. It seems, therefore, highly requisite, since that city is rapidly advancing in prosperity in all other respects, that the number of churches should also be increased. Do you, therefore, receive with all readiness my determination on this behalf. *I have thought it expedient to instruct your Prudence to order fifty copies of the sacred Scriptures,* the provision and use of which you know to be most needful for the instruction of the Church, *to be written on prepared parchment in a legible manner, and in a convenient, portable form, by professional*

---

25. I object here to David Trobisch's view that Paul himself collected, edited, and circulated his writings in the churches. There is virtually no support for this supposition, and those scholars who have cited the work as evidence for this have failed to examine Trobisch's support for his position. What could have happened is not evidence that it in fact did. See L. M. McDonald, review of David Trobisch, *Paul's Letter Collection: Tracing the Origins, CRBR* 8 (1995): 311–14, but also the more lengthy and detailed review of that work in S. E. Porter, "When and How Was the Pauline Canon Compiled?" in *The Pauline Canon* (ed. Porter; Pauline Studies 1; Leiden: Brill, 2004), 113–27. See also Porter's essay in the present volume, "Paul and the Process of Canonization."

transcribers thoroughly practiced in their art. The catholicus of the diocese has also received instructions by letter from our Clemency to be careful to furnish all things necessary for the preparation of such copies; and it will be for you to take special care that they be completed with as little delay as possible. You have authority also, in virtue of this letter, to use two of the public carriages for their conveyance, by which arrangement the copies when fairly written will most easily be forwarded for my personal inspection; and one of the deacons of your church may be entrusted with this service, who, on his arrival here, shall experience my liberality. God preserve you, beloved brother!"

Such were the emperor's commands, which were followed by the immediate execution of the work itself, which we sent him in *magnificent and elaborately bound volumes of a threefold and fourfold form [trissa kai tetrassa]*. (Eusebius, *Life of Constantine* 4.36–37 [*Nicene and Post-Nicene Fathers*, Series 2]; emphasis mine)[26]

The detail that was followed here is representative of the best copying of the day, as the emperor requested. Some scholars have speculated that Codex Vaticanus (B) and or Sinaiticus (ℵ) may be examples of these fifty copies, but that is uncertain. They are similar in style and precision to what Constantine requested of Eusebius and reflect careful copying in the Alexandrian tradition.

Which Text Is Authoritative?

Our discussion to this point raises an obvious question: Which biblical text is the authoritative text of Scripture for the church today? It is more than likely that all of the biblical manuscripts that have survived antiquity were accepted as sacred texts in the ancient communities of faith, but they are not exactly the same. There is historical precedence in trying to find the earliest sources that describe and proclaim the Christian faith. The author of the Muratorian fragment, for example, argued against public reading of the *Shepherd of Hermas* in churches because it was written after

---

26. For our purposes the italicized words in this last paragraph are crucial. Do they refer to making three or four copies at a time or to three or four columns per page? Scholarship is divided over the matter, but the words may also refer to the sending of the copies "three and four at a time." For a more detailed discussion of this text, see G. A. Robbins, "Fifty Copies of the Sacred Writings," *Studia Patristica* 19 (1989): 91–98, here 93–94.

the apostolic age (Muratorian fragment 73–80). From the time of Irenaeus (*Against Heresies* 3.1.1; 3.11.8–9), the early church emphasized the importance of an apostolic witness (especially Matthew and John) and accepted materials into its Scripture collection that were believed to be contemporary with them, namely Luke and Mark.

As translators of the New Testament know, the first difficulty is discerning what the most reliable or authentic Greek text is and consequently which manuscript evidence supports that text. Most seminary students, and even most biblical scholars, rely heavily on the most recent publications of the Greek New Testament, namely the Nestle-Aland editions of *Novum Testamentum Graece* or the United Bible Society *Greek New Testament*, but those who regularly examine the variety of Greek texts that support a given reading know that determining the earliest and most reliable biblical text is complex and not an exact science. Consequently, students of the Bible rightly must listen to the experts in textual criticism for the most likely conclusions about the text. Textual scholars recognize that the oldest existing manuscript may not be the most reliable. Many factors are involved in the establishment of a reliable Greek text including discerning not only the most ancient witness to a text, but also the competence of the copiers or transcribers of those texts. It is quite possible to produce a very good translation of an inferior Greek text of the New Testament, as we see in the case of the King James Version.

Erasmus of Rotterdam produced a Greek text of the New Testament in 1516 that was based on relatively late manuscripts (none dating before the tenth century CE and several dating much later), and he depended on the relatively few manuscripts that were available to him (approximately five or six). His Greek text also included a correction of several Latin translations in Jerome's Vulgate. Erasmus's first edition was revised several times and finally by Theodore Beza, whose work was the foundation for the King James translation. Beza's Greek text became known as the Textus Receptus or "received text," and for generations biblical scholars based their translations and exegesis on it. While little of substance is lost in the King James translation, and nothing of significant theological matter is changed by it, it is nonetheless an inferior version in that it does not reflect the earliest biblical text of the church. It is now fair to say that most biblical scholars prefer the Alexandrian text family, earlier called the "Neutral Text" by Westcott and Hort, over the Textus Receptus Greek text which is much later and less accurate than manuscripts from the Alexandrian family. Scholars know that many biblical texts were altered in transmission and translation, and following tireless comparisons of ancient texts they have almost universally abandoned the King James Version as the most reliable English translation of the Greek New Testament. Many textual scholars today have also abandoned hope of ever recovering the "original text" of the New Testament, but by careful sifting and analysis of the surviving ancient biblical texts they believe they have come closer to the elusive original manuscripts than was possible earlier. Other scholars, however, continue to affirm the pursuit of the original text even if some believe that they are now about as close to such a text as they will ever get.[27]

New text-critical finds have been incorporated in recent editions of the standard English translations, but no textual critic today says that we have discovered or discerned all of the original words of the literature that make up the New Testament. The ancient church, apparently, never decided which textual form of Scripture was sacred and which was not. In the older designations of families of manuscripts (namely, Western, Alexandrian, Neutral, Byzantine), textual scholars found a multitude of variations in the texts. It is even stranger to modern readers that little attention was given to this important detail in antiquity. The books of the New Testament were first written, preserved, circulated in the churches, and copied. In time the originals were worn out, lost, or destroyed, and the same things happened to the copies. While some of them were discarded, some burned by the church's enemies, some destroyed in natural disasters such as earthquakes, fires, and floods, still others were preserved in a variety of ways. Several thousand still exist today, and their recovery allows textual critics to make better informed decisions on the most likely original text of the Bible than was possible just a hundred years ago.

27. E. J. Schnabel, "Textual Criticism: Recent Developments," in *The Face of New Testament Studies: A Survey of Recent Research* (ed. S. McKnight and G. R. Osborne; Grand Rapids: Baker Academic, 2004), 75, makes this observation.

Over the last century, thousands of Greek manuscripts and fragments of manuscripts of the New Testament writings have been
recovered, and they continue to be investigated. Roughly only 8
percent of these manuscripts cover most of the New Testament;
the vast majority contain only small portions of the New Testament writings, and those are often only in fragmentary condition.
In 1994 at the official registry of biblical manuscripts, the Institute
for New Testament Textual Research located in Münster, Germany,
there were some 5,664 Greek manuscripts of the New Testament
listed (some include the Old Testament or portions of it). The number of New Testament papyrus manuscripts that we now possess
stands at 117, the number of uncial manuscripts (or texts using
capital letters without spaces between the words and written on
parchment—the next oldest category) is now listed as 306, the list
of minuscule (lowercase-lettered) manuscripts now is at 2,812, and
the register of Greek lectionaries (selected portions of Scriptures
that were read in churches) now stands at 2,281 manuscripts.[28]

While copyists of the New Testament manuscripts no doubt
tried to be careful in their transmission of the biblical text, they
still made mistakes by adding or omitting letters, words, or lines. By
and large, they did not prepare literary documents at first because
of the considerable cost involved,[29] which may also indicate that
these documents were not generally recognized as Scripture until
the end of the second century CE. Some of these copiers of the

28. This information is supplied by Schnabel, "Textual Criticism: Recent Developments," 59–75. The figures change almost annually as more manuscripts are found or placed
in the public domain. For example, P. D. Wegner, *The Journey from Texts to Translations:
The Origin and Development of the Bible* (Grand Rapids: Baker Academic, 1999), 207–12,
observes that there were 5,400 New Testament manuscripts of which a little more than 100
were papyrus manuscripts, 266 were uncial manuscripts, and 2,754 minuscule manuscripts,
and the rest lectionaries. By the time of this writing, the papyri manuscripts have climbed
to 117 and more are likely. The numbers are not that far apart, and both were probably
correct when published.

29. Scribes in the ancient world were paid well, namely some 750 denarii per year plus
the scribes' regular maintenance (home, etc.). For a discussion of this, see B. M. Metzger,
The Text of the New Testament: Its Transmission, Corruption, and Restoration (3rd ed.;
New York and Oxford: Oxford University Press, 1992), 15. That amount was more than
double what the average workman received. The church did not regularly employ such
persons of careful skill until the fourth century and following, and the lack of skill in
transmission is often seen in the earlier papyrus manuscripts.

New Testament writings made not only inadvertent mistakes, but also deliberate changes in the texts in which they tried to clarify the meaning or make it more relevant to their own communities. These changes were passed on for centuries in subsequent copies. Many of the changes were undoubtedly intentional, even though there are plenty of unintentional variants in most manuscripts of the ancient world.[30]

Metzger argues that most of the changes in the biblical texts occurred in the early decades of transmission where words and entire lines were omitted and outright mistakes in copying occurred. As noted above, Metzger suggests that many errors may be attributed to amateur copyists who were simply literate members of the church, and many of the later manuscripts may be copies of these early, error-prone texts.[31] For a variety of reasons, changes in the texts took place. Some students of the Scripture saw that certain manuscripts differed not a little from the ones with which they were most familiar, and they or the copyists made what they thought were corrective changes in order to improve the text of Scripture before them. Not all such changes were caught, however, and numerous questions about the authentic (original) text of the Bible continue.

Codex Vaticanus—a mid-fourth-century CE uncial manuscript mostly in three columns per page produced quite possibly in Alexandria, Egypt, as its text type suggests—is often acknowledged as the oldest codex manuscript containing both the Old and the New Testaments. Its beginning is fragmentary with some forty-five

---

30. The most common types of errors are put in two categories: unintentional and intentional. In the former category, these include a misreading of letters that look alike, substitution of similar sounding words (homophony), omission of a letter or word (haplography), repeating of a word (dittography), reversal of two words (metathesis), incorrect word division that results in two words joined as one (fusion), incorrect word division that results in one word written as two (fission), omission because of two words or phrases that sound alike (*homoioteleuton*), and omission because of two words or phrases that begin the same (*homoioarchton*). In the intentional kind, there are changes in grammar or spelling, harmonizations between passages, adding of words that naturally go together, clearing up of difficulties, conflation by combining two or more readings, and theological changes. See K. Aland and B. Aland, *The Text of the New Testament* (Grand Rapids: Eerdmans), 282–316, and Metzger, *Text of the New Testament*, 186–206. These are also summarized with illustrations by Wegner, *Journey from Texts to Translations*, 225–26.

31. Metzger and Ehrman, *Text of the New Testament*, 275.

chapters of Genesis missing. At the other end of the volume, the original hand breaks off mid-word (*kathariei*) in Hebrews 9:14, and the rest of Hebrews and Revelation were supplied by a later hand. The Pastoral Epistles are missing, and it is unlikely that they were ever included. On the other hand, 1 and 2 Maccabees were intended but strangely were not included. Several other so-called apocryphal books were included, however. While Codex Vaticanus is one of the most important ancient New Testament texts surviving antiquity, it is nevertheless an edited text and a partial or defective one at that. If this is one of the best and most reliable manuscripts of the New Testament—as well as the Greek Bible—available today, it is safe to say that there is much we simply do not know about the original text of the New Testament writings or the books contained in it even as late as the fourth century. As yet, as Schnabel observes, we also do not have "a coherent view of the transmission of the text."[32] Only a few papyri date from the early to middle second century, namely two fragments of the Gospel of John ($\mathfrak{P}^{52}$, ca. 125 CE,[33] and $\mathfrak{P}^{90}$, ca. mid-second century), but most of the manuscripts originate from the end of the second century and later. The absence of an understanding of the text's sacredness may have contributed to the frequent lack of careful transmission of the New Testament texts, which in turn must have considerably affected their subsequent transmission.

Helmut Koester reminds textual critics that the most significant corruptions of the texts came during the first and second centuries,[34] and we repeat that this took place when their canonical status was not yet fully established in the church. As noted by Koester and implied by Metzger and Ehrman, many, if not most, textual variants in the New Testament manuscripts occurred

32. Schnabel, "Textual Criticism: Recent Developments," 69, 73–75.

33. The letter P followed by a number identifies various papyrus manuscripts and indicates the order in which these papyrus manuscripts were found and so identified not in terms of their date of composition. Some papyrus manuscripts have a higher number, but date earlier than others with a lower number. In a later example, for instance, $\mathfrak{P}^{45}$ is listed before $\mathfrak{P}^{46}$, but was likely produced at least some fifty years or more after $\mathfrak{P}^{46}$.

34. H. Koester, "The Text of the Synoptic Gospels in the Second Century," in *Gospel Traditions in the Second Century: Origins, Recensions, Text, and Transmission* (ed. W. L. Petersen; CJA 3; Notre Dame, IN: University of Notre Dame Press, 1989), 37.

before the year 200.[35] The fact that there were so many variants initially strongly suggests that the later views of the inspiration that focus on the inviolability of the biblical text were not yet in place. This coincides with the fact that while several New Testament writings were read and cited by the second-century church as frequently as many Old Testament texts, they were still not generally called "Scripture" much before the late second century.

In modern times, and with the discovery of many more manuscripts of various text types, scholars have, by detailed comparison and with what is called either "reasoned eclecticism" (Michael Holmes) or "thoroughgoing eclecticism" (J. K. Elliott), sought after the most reliable texts from all of the manuscripts that are available to make more informed decisions about what the original or earliest attainable biblical text said.[36] In many instances, however, one still cannot be certain of the original reading. For our purposes, namely canonical inquiry, this investigation raises many questions about which text of the Bible is the authoritative text for the church or believing communities.

The wide diversity among ancient New Testament texts is also evidence that for centuries the church's primary focus in canon formation was on the books that comprised the Bible and not the integrity of the text of the Bible. More recently scholars of the church have sought to establish a more reliable and stable text of the church's sacred Scriptures. It is important to remember that the vast majority, if not all, of the 5,700 plus New Testament manuscripts were likely acknowledged as Scriptures in the churches that preserved and copied them and were used in the church's worship, mission, and instruction for Christian living. What was it that brought these texts that had a variety of changes and interpretations into a manageable collection? Undoubtedly the church's view of orthodoxy had a major part in the process. The diversity of books and even texts were held

35. Koester, "Synoptic Gospels in the Second Century," 37; Metzger and Ehrman, *Text of the New Testament*, 31.
36. These scholars' positions are explained in M. Holmes, "The Case for Reasoned Eclecticism," and J. K. Elliott, "The Case for Thoroughgoing Eclecticism," in Black, *Rethinking New Testament Textual Criticism*, 77–100 and 101–24, respectively.

in check by the canon of faith, or the *regula fidei*, that was operative in the greater church during that period. It is also quite likely, as Bart Ehrman has shown, that loyalty to the church's orthodoxy also affected the transmission of the biblical texts.[37] He concludes his investigation of the ancient biblical manuscripts as follows: "This is exactly what the scribes did: they occasionally altered the words of the text by putting them 'in other words.' To this extent, they were textual interpreters. At the same time, by *physically* altering the words, they did something quite different from other exegetes, and this difference is by no means to be minimized." Only from a distance, namely ours, Ehrman says, can "we evaluate the causes and recognize the effects of these kinds of scribal modifications, and so designate them 'the orthodox corruptions of Scripture.'"[38] There was surely acceptable diversity in the early church, but there were also boundaries imposed on such diversity. The church's vigorous challenge against "heresy" in the second through the fourth centuries, and to some extent thereafter, testifies to the limits that were acceptable.

Most biblical scholars today are not yet ready to ascribe sacred authority to any particular text of the Bible, but, as we noted above, they are more involved in seeking an eclectic text that appears to be the construct derived from a careful examination of many ancient texts. This does not specifically answer our question, however, and so we pose it again: Which text of the Bible is authoritative for the church today? There has been little change in the basic Greek texts of the UBS and Nestle-Aland editions in recent years, and this has prompted Ehrman to conclude that "at this stage, our work on the *original* amounts to little more than tinkering" with the text rather than significantly altering it.[39] He suggests that the task now before New Testament textual critics is to write a history of the development of the biblical text asking how the various social influences impacted its transmission. Eldon Epp similarly concludes that we are—

37. Ehrman makes a strong case for this in *The Orthodox Corruption of Scripture*.
38. Ehrman, *Orthodox Corruption of Scripture*, 280.
39. B. D. Ehrman, "*Novum Testamentum Graece Editio Critica Maior*: An Evaluation," *TC* 3 (1998), http://rosetta.reltech.org/TC/vol03/Ehrman1998.html, §20.

barring an unforeseen discovery of the autographs, or original manuscripts—about as close to the original text of the New Testament as we can get.[40]

Helmut Koester reminds us that the earliest existing text of a writing is not necessarily the original, authorial form of the text. As noted above, he states that the most serious changes to the texts occurred in the first two centuries of the church and cites the Synoptic Gospels as primary examples. The earliest form of the canonical text of Mark's Gospel, Koester argues, is not what was used by Matthew and Luke, and the earliest form (the so-called Ur-Mark) is now lost.[41] The point that Koester makes about the canonical Gospels, Metzger and Ehrman also make in regard to Paul's writings, as noted above. They question further whether we can get back to the oral dictation of Paul and behind the amanuensis that Paul used.[42]

Again, the question here is: Which form of the text should function as the canonical biblical text for the church today? Should biblical scholars argue that the latest edition of the Nestle-Aland and UBS Greek texts—there is essentially no difference between the two texts, but the footnote apparatus differs—is in fact the authoritative text of the church? It is difficult to get beyond this question since all scholars acknowledge that we do not have the originals but we are substantially closer than we have ever been before. There is very little hope, however, of recovering the originals and eliminating all of the ambiguities in the present texts, and so further revisions of them are likely. The answer to the question posed above may be that the real authority here is not in the text after all, but in the One who comes to us in the text and to whom the texts point their readers.

---

40. E. J. Epp, "The Multivalence of the Term 'Original Text' in New Testament Criticism," *HTR* 92 (1999): 245–81. See also E. J. Epp, "Decision Points in Past, Present, and Future New Testament Textual Criticism," in Epp and G. D. Fee, *Studies in the Theory and Method of New Testament Textual Criticism* (SD 45; Grand Rapids: Eerdmans, 1993), 17–44; idem, "Issues in the Interrelation of New Testament Textual Criticism and Canon," in McDonald and Sanders, *Canon Debate*, 485–515; idem, "Issues in New Testament Textual Criticism," 70–76.

41. Koester, "Synoptic Gospels in the Second Century," 37.

42. Metzger and Ehrman, *The Text of the New Testament*, 272–73.

Translations

As all theological students soon learn, the first translation of the Hebrew Scriptures (or the First or Old Testament) was a translation of the Law or Pentateuch into the Greek language in the early part of the third century BCE (281). At the request of Ptolemy II of Alexandria, his chief librarian compiled the largest library in the ancient world with estimates of up to 450,000 volumes. According to the *Letter of Aristeas*, the chief librarian, Demetrius of Phalerum, also requested that the king include a copy of the Jewish Scriptures, but it would need to be translated by competent persons and placed in the sacred "Museum" (or royal library) in Alexandria. Although according to this account the Jews did not initiate the translation, they subsequently made considerable use of it. The initial translation, which was later expanded to include the rest of the Old Testament literature as well as other Jewish writings that were not eventually included in the Hebrew Scriptures, is generally known as the Septuagint, or LXX. [43]

The use of the LXX continued variously throughout Jewish history, but in the second century CE the Jews were making other Greek translations of their Scriptures (one produced by a certain Aquila), but most of the Christians continued to use and reproduce the LXX even if a few used two other new Greek translations by Theodotion and Symmachus. Some portions of the LXX were eventually "corrupted" with a Christian bias. This translation, in whatever state or condition it was in the first century CE, became

---

43. It is commonly believed that the term *Septuagint* derives from the tradition passed on in the *Letter of Aristeas* that there were seventy-two translators (six from each of the twelve tribes of Israel) who worked on the translation. The number seventy-two could have been simply rounded off to seventy, hence "Septuagint" (from the Latin for "seventy"), but it is also quite possible that the number LXX derives from the tradition of the seventy elders of Exod. 24:1, 9 who accompanied Moses to Mount Sinai when he received the Law from Yahweh. If this is the case, then the use of the term *Septuagint* by the Jews is likely an acknowledgment of an early Jewish and Christian belief in the divinely inspired status of the translation, that is, that it authentically and faithfully conveyed the full intent of the Law given to Moses. Again, the tradition related to this translation and the term *Septuagint* technically should only be applied to the Greek translation of the Pentateuch and not to the rest of the OT Scriptures, though the term eventually came to refer to these other books as well. By ca. 130 BCE the Prophets and other sacred Jewish writings were likewise translated from the Hebrew into Greek.

the Bible of the early Christian community, as is apparent by the quotations of the Old Testament Scriptures in the New Testament. Although there are many legitimate challenges to the veracity of several claims of the *Letter of Aristeas*, most scholars conclude that it does have several elements of truth in it, for example, that it is likely true the translation came about not as a request from the Jews but rather from Demetrius himself, who weighs prominently in the *Letter*.[44] The point here is that the precedent of a translation of the Scriptures was well established before the time of Jesus, and as we will see, it has continued to the present.

By the year 2000, there were 6,809 known living languages and dialects in the world, and the whole Bible has been translated into 371 of them. Portions of the Bible have been translated into 1,862 other languages and dialects.[45] By the early seventh century, the Scriptures of the church existed in Greek, Latin, Gothic, Syriac, Coptic, Armenian, Georgian, Ethiopic, and Sogdian. By the year 1456, when the Gutenberg printing press and moveable type for printing were invented, only about thirty-three languages had portions of the Bible.

At the conclusion of this section we will once again ask the question: Wherein lies authority? Is there an authoritative translation of the Bible that reflects the full intent of the original biblical text? What translation of the Bible is authoritative for the religious communities of faith that read it?

Early Translations of the Bible

The first translation of the Hebrew Scriptures was the LXX and the second was the Aramaic targums[46] that date roughly from the first century CE to the Middle Ages. An early example is a targum on Job discovered at Qumran that dates from the first century CE. Later, from the seventh or eight century, a targum on Esther was

44. Collins, *Library in Alexandria*, 115–83, makes a cogent argument in favor of Demetrius implementing this project.

45. These figures come from B. M. Metzger, *The Bible in Translation: Ancient and English Versions* (Grand Rapids: Baker Academic, 2001), 8–9.

46. The word "targum" comes from an Aramaic word meaning "translation." A targum is essentially an ancient paraphrase or interpretive translation of the Hebrew Scriptures into Aramaic.

discovered containing lengthy homilies on that book. While it is largely in Aramaic, it also contains many Greek words and had a probable Palestinian origin. The two most complete targums contain all books of the Hebrew Bible except Ezra, Nehemiah, and Daniel. There were reportedly two translations of the Pentateuch initially made in the second century CE, one by Akylas (Aquila) and the other by Onqelos, but the latter may well be a corruption of the name Aquila, who made a Greek translation of the Hebrew Scriptures and then subsequently one in Aramaic. *Targum Onqelos* is sometimes referred to as the *Babylonian Targum* since it reflects some of the social conditions in that region and was adopted by the Babylonian Jews. The other prominent targum is the *Targum Pseudo-Jonathan*, attributed to Yonatan ben Uzziel (cf. *b. Megillah* 3a), which contains the Law, the Prophets, and part of the Hagiographa and reflects a Palestinian origin. There is also a targum known from a single manuscript, Vatican Neophyti 1; discovered in 1956, it has a Palestinian origin and contains the Torah. The Palestinian targums are more paraphrastic and some include homiletical interpretations. The producers of targums were less concerned about expansions of the text than we find in the transmission of the Hebrew text.

There are a number of early Christian translations that illustrate what the translators thought was important, if not sacred, literature and help textual critics piece together the earliest text of the New Testament. From the end of the second century CE, the Christians freely translated their Scriptures (and the Old Testament) into several languages, the earliest of which included the Old Latin and the Syriac versions, especially the Syriac Peshitta, and the Armenian translation. When the Christian writings were translated, it may be assumed that their sacred status was either already recognized by those who translated them or that recognition was well on its way. Also it is fair to say that what was translated formed something of a canon of sacred Scripture for the community for which it was translated. Of the New Testament translations that have significance for the early development of the Christian biblical canon, the following are the earliest and most important.

(1) The Old Syriac version. Although only the four canonical Gospels are preserved in two fragmented manuscripts of this trans-

lation that date from the fourth or fifth century, the translation probably originally dates to the end of the second or beginning of the third century. The eastern church fathers also refer to Acts and the letters of Paul, but the Old Syriac manuscripts of these writings have not survived.

(2) The Peshitta (or Syriac Vulgate, designated Syr[p]) likely comes from the beginning of the fifth century and contains twenty-two of the New Testament books (it omits 2 Peter, 2 and 3 John, Jude, and Revelation).

(3) The Philoxenian version (perhaps produced in the early sixth century) is largely known through the Harclean version (named after Thomas of Harkel, who revised the Philoxenian text in the early seventh century). For the first time in this translation the minor Catholic Epistles and Revelation were added to Syrian churches' Scriptures.

(4) The Palestinian Syriac version (ca. fifth century). Only a few fragments of this translation exist, which include the Gospels, Acts, and several (not all) of the letters of Paul.

(5) The Old Latin versions (ca. third century). There were a number of Old Latin manuscripts produced during the third and later centuries, and they fall generally into two categories: African and European versions. The surviving fragments include portions of the four canonical Gospels, Acts, and portions of Paul's letters, along with a few fragments of Revelation.

(6) The Latin Vulgate version produced by Jerome in the late fourth century. There are a good number of surviving copies containing the whole Bible, and two codices (Codex Dublinensis, ca. eighth century, and Codex Fuldensis, ca. sixth century) that also contain the apocryphal letter of Paul to the Laodiceans.

(7) The Coptic Versions (ca. beginning of the third century), primarily the Sahidic and Bohairic dialects. The contents of the surviving manuscripts include the four Gospels, Acts, and the Pauline letters.

(8) The Gothic Version (ca. middle to end of fourth century). Among the manuscripts that survive, the four Gospels and some Pauline letters were included, along with a portion of Nehemiah 5–7. Acts, Hebrews, the Catholic Epistles, and Revelation are missing.

(9) The Armenian Versions (late fourth and early fifth centuries). The fifteen hundred or more copies that remain are much later (eighth century and later). Some have all, others only part of the current New Testament.

(10) Georgian Version. It is possible that the origin of this version goes back to the fourth or fifth century, but the oldest manuscripts date from the ninth century. All four Gospels and some other New Testament books, mostly Pauline, are included.

(11) The Ethiopic Version (ca. as early as the fourth or as late as the seventh century). Most of the surviving manuscripts of this version date after the thirteenth century and include both canonical and noncanonical writings.

Other later and, for our purposes, less important translations include the Arabic Versions from the eighth century to the nineteenth century, the Sogdian (or Middle Iranian) Version dating from the ninth to the eleventh century, and the Old Church Slavonic Version during the ninth century which was important especially for the Bulgarians, Serbians, Croats, and eastern Slavs. Around the sixth century some churches were planted in Nubia, but when the Arabs to the north essentially cut them off from the rest of Christendom, they declined and eventually disappeared. The Nubian Version of the Bible was produced sometime between those two time frames, but it is not clear exactly when.[47]

What is clear from an examination of these translations, or the portions that remain of them, is that none that date earlier than the fourth century contain all of the writings that we currently have in our New Testament and few after that time do. Some of these versions later expanded to include other canonical and noncanonical books. The same could be said of the oldest Greek manuscripts that have survived the ravages of time. While Codex Sinaiticus contains part of the Old Testament and has a complete copy of the New Testament, it also contains some noncanonical books (the *Epistle of Barnabas* and a fragment of the *Shepherd of Hermas*). None of them contain the exact collection of New Testament books that are now in the Christian Bible. Whatever else the various catalogue lists or collections of books that date from

---

47. See Metzger, *Bible in Translation*, 25–51, for a brief summary of these versions of the Bible.

the fourth and fifth centuries tell us, they clearly identify which writings were received, used, and transmitted by the churches as authoritative books.

Modern Translations

Most modern translations of the Bible, beginning with John Wycliffe's English translation of the Bible in 1380 until the first part of the twentieth century, were based on the Greek and Latin manuscripts from the tenth to the fourteenth centuries. The King James Version was based on these later manuscripts, but at that time this was the best English translation of the Bible ever produced. As we observed earlier, the KJV was also based on manuscripts that are inferior to and later in origin than those now available, and which contained many mistakes and corruptions of the text.

Because of the work of many textual critics, a significant number of translations have emerged that are on the whole much more accurate than the older KJV, and indeed, the most recent ones are more accurate than the translations before 1950. Important ancient manuscripts have been found over the last 150 years or so that take us much closer to the original texts, in some cases as much as one thousand years closer to the originals. As a result, the more modern translations of the Bible are generally more accurate and faithful to the original text than earlier editions. The discoveries of earlier New Testament manuscripts have had a positive effect on all modern translations produced. Those translations produced before 1950 are essentially out of date and do not accurately reflect the earliest text of the biblical manuscripts.[48] We hasten to say, however, that even the earlier manuscripts that we now possess do not take us back to the first century when the New Testament writers wrote; therefore, some ambiguity and uncertainty still remain in all Bible translation.[49] Some modern translations, such as the Cotton Patch Version and The Amplified Bible, do not improve our understanding of the text and meaning

48. Similarly, the discovery of the Dead Sea Scrolls has advanced knowledge of the Old Testament text by over one thousand years!

49. A useful listing of the translations in English in the last century (up to 1996) is found in P. D. Wegner, *Journey from Texts to Translations*, 394–95.

of the New Testament writings and are not serious candidates for replacement of older translations.

Finally, as was true of specific texts of the New Testament writings, as noted above, the ancient greater church never suggested that only one translation of the Bible was inspired and all others were not or were less authoritative. For example, the Syriac Peshitta was Scripture to those Christians who used it. They did not conclude that their Bible was less inspired than the one used by Greek-speaking or Latin-speaking Christians. The Ethiopians had their own translations, as did the Copts, but none of them treated their translations as if they were inferior to the Hebrew or Greek Scriptures. Early Christianity, that is up through the fourth century and through the later seven ecumenical councils, never suggested that only one or no translation was inspired, even though at various times the Greek translation of the Old Testament and the Latin Vulgate came close to that status in the church. In terms of the contemporary church, a similar situation is present. Although most Christians could not hope to read their Bibles in the original languages of Greek, Hebrew, and Aramaic, they nonetheless believe that their Bibles, in whatever translation they have, are sacred and have their origins in God.

Among the most recent English translations, are there any that are authoritative for the church today? The question seems strange given that many conservative Bible scholars want to anchor their faith in a biblical text that exists in the original languages of Hebrew and Greek. There are no perfect translations, however, and those who produce translations rely heavily on textual critics to tell them which biblical text or reading is most reliable. Nevertheless, no credible biblical scholars today argue that any particular translation of the Bible, and only that translation, is authoritative for the church, even though several scholars have tried to produce a translation that garners widespread support by the evangelical churches. The most common translation in the evangelical community is the New International Version, and many other Christians prefer the New Revised Standard Version or the New Jerusalem Bible. These and a few other translations are generally reasonably good, though scholars debate many of the details and all who have been involved in these projects confess that they have not produced the perfect translation.

To have a perfectly reliable translation, we would, of course, need to have a perfect text from which to produce a translation, but that also does not exist. There are no manuscripts that we can appeal to that give the exact original wording of the biblical text. The Nestle-Aland and UBS Greek texts are perhaps as close to the original texts as one could hope for, but that is not the same as saying that we have the original text. This brings us back to the question of which, if any, translation of the Bible is authoritative in the church today. While preachers cannot discontinue their preaching until we find the perfect text or perfect translation for them, that does not make the question of translations unimportant. Frankly, the differences in all of the most recent competent translations of the Bible are not that essential, and most translations reliably tell the story of Jesus and call for an obedience of faith in God. The authority of the text has not significantly been altered by the fluidity within it. Is it possible that the terms *original* and *perfect* are not applicable to the inspiration and power of the text to transform lives? Few can question the authority and inspiration that the Bible has brought to persons of faith, and yet no responsible person can demonstrate that we have a perfect original text of Scripture or a perfect translation.

Conclusion: Wherein Lies Authority?

So back to our earlier question: Wherein lies authority? If we carefully interpret the earliest Christian communities correctly, the earliest canon of faith for the church was Jesus. All Scriptures are, of course, a derived authority. Jesus indicated that "all authority" was given unto him (Matt. 28:18), and Christians know from experience that the Word of God remarkably comes to us in a variety of translations, not all of which are of equal value and technical quality. Jesus and the gospel he proclaimed are at the heart of the Christian message, and we would do well not to place a written text with numerous variables in his place. The Scriptures are always a derived authority, but the final authority for the church is Jesus Christ.

While some translations are more faithful to the earliest biblical manuscripts than others, the people in our churches depend on translations of these Scriptures for their worship and instruction. The authoritative base of the church has from its beginning been more legitimately placed in a person rather than in the variety of books, texts, and translations that it has produced. I am not convinced that anyone will go too far astray regardless of which translation that he or she prefers. I often encourage churches to adopt two translations, namely one for reading in church and another for study purposes (Today's English Version plus the New Revised Standard Version, or some such combination). Often one translation helps interpret the other. For those without skills in the original languages, this is not a bad practice.

Even for those with sufficient skills in Hebrew, Aramaic, and Greek, the problem remains that we still do not have an established authoritative text that all Christian biblical scholars have adopted. Likewise, we do not yet have one universally accepted set of books that all Christians acknowledge as divinely inspired, and there is no single text or translation of the Bible that garners the full support of the Christian community. The history of the Bible's development teaches us that it is very difficult to establish hard and fast rules that apply in every situation. That was true in antiquity and is still true today. In the midst of some of the uncertainty that we have shown, wherein lies authority for the church? Jesus himself said that all authority has been given to him (Matt. 28:18), and he did not speak of transferring this authority to a particular collection, text, or translation of books to rival his authority in the church.

While it is true that we cannot know who Jesus was in historical and theological context apart from the ancient biblical texts that speak of him, still those texts and the translations of them do not stand in the first place in Christian faith. Remarkably, the various translations and biblical canons present in churches today (Greek Orthodox, Roman Catholic, Ethiopian, and Protestant) all reflect the message and identity of Jesus the Christ as well as the obligation of the church for worship and mission. Most of the major teachings of the church are not seriously challenged by the variables in the biblical text and, indeed, in most of the translations used in churches today. Final authority for the church resides in the One who comes to us through the biblical text, but not in the text itself. This conclusion does not make the various doctrines of inspiration easier to articulate, but perhaps scholars and church leaders should consider statements of faith that are more reflective of the actual state of canonical inquiry, textual investigation, and translation practice.

8

Canon and Theology

What Is at Stake?

JONATHAN R. WILSON

Many years ago a journal published back-to-back essays on biblical authority and interpretation by a theologian and a Bible scholar. The Bible scholar, who happened to be an evangelical New Testament scholar, began his article by noting that to move from the theologian's account of the authority and interpretation of the Bible to the real world of biblical scholarship was like moving into another universe. At the time that I read this remark, I was struck by its perceptiveness. This New Testament scholar accurately describes a situation that many have worked to rectify in recent years as both biblical scholars and theologians are striving to overcome the dichotomy between their disciplines.[1] This commitment does

1. As an example, consider the two commentary series that have begun to overcome this dichotomy. Bible scholars are writing theology in the Two Horizons Commentary

not mean that the work will be easy, but the situation has been recognized as a problem and several research projects are underway to solve it. However, one area that I still find insufficiently acknowledged and addressed by theologians in relation to biblical scholarship is the notion of canon.[2]

If one moves from most theological accounts of the concept and function of "canon" to accounts of the historical formation of the canon, one moves into another universe. From a kind of hermetically sealed purity of concept, one moves to a politically charged history. From a tidy, antiseptic ideal, one moves to a messy reality.

One could argue that it is a good thing, this difference between a theological account of canon and a historical account. While we cannot avoid the messiness of politics and history, we also need an alternative. So, the argument goes, theology moves in the realm of conceptual clarity while history (and biblical scholarship) moves in the realm of contingent events. Putting it this way, of course, reveals the mistake—theology (and here I have in view Christian theology) betrays its subject when it prescinds from history. Any Christian theology must be rooted in the history of Israel and the belief that Jesus of Nazareth is Israel's Messiah and Savior of the world. His identity and his work is historical. Any denial of history, formally or informally, is a denial of the Christ.

Of course, this has not prevented Christians from making this mistake. This propensity to seek escape from historical and material contingency started almost at the beginning, perhaps in the super-apostles who seem to be Paul's opponents in Corinth and certainly in the proto-gnosticism that may already be presaged by contrary teaching in New Testament texts such as 1 John. The temptation will always be with us, but we must not succumb. So, one thing that is at stake in canon and theology is the congruence of theology with its subject, that to which it must submit itself.

series, edited by J. Green and M. Turner (Eerdmans), and theologians have begun the Brazos Theological Commentary on the Bible series, edited by R. R. Reno (Brazos).

2. This essay was originally presented at a conference devoted largely to biblical scholarship and concerned to engage in conversation with those scholars; it is not, then, a contribution to the promising dogmatic sketches of canon that may be found in recent works such as J. Webster, "The Dogmatic Location of the Canon," in *Word and Church: Essays in Christian Dogmatics* (Edinburgh: T&T Clark, 2001), 9–46, and R. W. Jenson, *Systematic Theology*, Vol. 1, *The Triune God* (New York: Oxford, 1997), 26–33.

But there is more at stake here. Because theology shapes and is shaped by its community, the way that theology understands its relationship to canon reveals something about the community to which theology responds. The question for theology then becomes: Which community? Is theology responsive to the church? If so, which church, and what is the nature of theology's responsiveness—as guardian, as guide, as judge, as servant? Is theology responsive to academe? If so, where do we locate theology within academe? Whose interests does theology serve?

At stake, then, in the discussion of canon and theology are two issues that I will explore here: the nature of theology and its location in community. But of course, the most basic question is the nature of "canon." To this point I have been writing "canon" as if it were an obvious and unproblematic word with a clear denotation. But a closer examination reveals that "canon" is fraught with complexities. Those complexities go beyond the simple list of books that varies among Christian traditions and even beyond the historical messiness of the formation of the canon. Indeed, the complexity extends beyond the canon to canonicity itself.

This complexity can be best identified and described through an investigation of three notions of canonicity that John Howard Yoder labels "high Protestant scholasticism," "high Tridentine Catholicism," and "high modernism."[3] For the sake of clarity and brevity I will shorten these to "Protestant," "Catholic," and "Modernist," intending always to keep in mind the narrower historical reference of these labels to specific instances. These three do not come close to exhausting the possibilities, but they do provide three different ways of understanding canon, community, and theology in actual practice. Once we have investigated these and seen their shortcomings, I will propose an alternative account of canon, community, and theology.

In high Protestant scholasticism, as in each of these, the notion of canonicity and the canon are so deeply intertwined that it is unproductive to try to untangle the line of dependency—that is, which comes first: the canon or the concept of canonicity? My

3. J. H. Yoder, "The Authority of the Canon," in *Essays on Biblical Interpretation: Anabaptist-Mennonite Perspectives* (ed. W. Swartley; Text-Reader Series 1; Elkhart, IN: Institute of Mennonite Studies, 1984), 265–90.

concern instead will be the interdependency of these in the mature, "high" practices of this tradition. In the Protestant tradition, the canon is the result of a historical process guided authoritatively by the Holy Spirit. In the midst of the power struggles that are shaped by political, ecclesiastical, cultural, social, and even doctrinal commitments, we confess the sovereignty of God in the process that led to the canon. In their controversy with the church in Rome, the Protestants separated this canon from the church and asserted its uniqueness as a body of literature. The canon is not dependent upon the church, but the church upon the canon.

In this way, then, canonicity also becomes separate from the church and located in a body of literature, a set of books whose boundary is carefully identified. Thus canonicity, as authority, becomes located textually. This served the Protestants well in their controversies with Rome. It also set up an understanding of theology that continues to mark the Protestant tradition today.

If the canon is separated from the life of the church so as to be its foundation, and if authority is located textually, then theologians too become separated from the life of the church and are defined primarily by their relationship to the text rather than to the community. Certainly, the Protestant scholastics continued as faithful churchmen, but they did so as people primarily responsible to this text, the canon. This conviction may be seen in practice in the form that theology takes—as an extraction of propositions from Scripture and the logical ordering of those propositions.

The relationship between high Protestant scholasticism and high Tridentine Catholicism is historically complex. Perhaps the best way to describe it is to recognize that what was established at the Council of Trent adopts what is already present in Thomas Aquinas, but does so as a polemical response to the Protestant challenges to that earlier tradition. So we have an early account of canon and canonicity in Thomas that the Protestants must overcome in their controversy with the church in Rome. Their attacks generate the position of high Protestant scholasticism, which further develops in controversy with high Tridentine Catholicism, itself a development of the earlier Thomistic tradition as a polemical response to the Protestants. As we have seen above, these traditions, arising in polemical situations, continue beyond those situations to shape the trajectory of their theology.

In high Tridentine Catholicism, "the canon" becomes clear, but it is also placed within the larger context of a canonicity that claims the canon for the church. Catholicism did this by asserting that God provided two traditions for the guidance of the church—written and oral. At any time in history, the church may, in submission to the guidance of the Holy Spirit, draw on the oral tradition as an authoritative guide. This is further developed in the assertion of the Magisterium of the church.

Thus, for Catholicism, the work of theology is located not so much textually as institutionally. Theologians identify themselves, their work, and their responsibility in relation to the church's structures and interests. This produces a very different theological tradition from the Protestants, which could be illustrated extensively from Catholic works that follow in the wake of Trent. It is particularly evident in the resistance of Catholicism to modernity and in one area of development for the Catholic tradition—moral theology, the theology that guides the practice of hearing confession.

In this polemical context, clarity was a virtue and unclarity a vice. Without reducing the canon and canonicity in Catholicism and Protestantism to historical and political motivations, we can nevertheless see the attractiveness of what developed. For Protestants, the clear boundaries of the canon, the perspicuity of Scripture and the exegetical and theological method of Protestantism, promise clarity, certainty, and authority for Protestant claims. For Catholicism, the teaching office of the church, her Magisterium, with its access to the whole revelation of God and its unchanging tradition, guarantees clarity, certainty, and authority for Catholic claims.

In both cases, it is especially important to note that any uncertainty about the history of the formation and recognition of the canon disappears with the closing of the canon. Neither the Catholic nor the Protestant position in the end admits to real messiness or uncertainty in this history. Each sees it under the providential guidance of the sovereign God. So in both the canon and canonicity, these historical instances become traditions that prescind from the contingencies of historical and material situatedness.

This denial of our situatedness no longer became tenable to a large number of people as a result of the set of developments that we gather under the term *Enlightenment* and the rise of modernity. These developments gave rise among many Protestants to an erosion of confidence in the clarity, certainty, and credibility of the Protestant account of the canon and canonicity. (An early-nineteenth-century foray of modernity into Catholicism was repulsed; the next significant invasion came in the latter part of the twentieth century and succeeded.) The rise of modernity and the loss of confidence in the Protestant account is interwoven with the development of the high Modern account of the canon and canonicity. This Modern account seeks a replacement for the ground of canon and canonicity articulated by high Protestant scholasticism.

For modernist Protestants, this search took two different paths, roughly speaking: the rationalist and the romantic. The rationalist account subjects the canon to the standards of canonicity established by reason. This path is identified by Gotthold Lessing: "the accidental truths of history can never become proof of the necessary truths of reason."[4] The accidental truths are the content of the canon—that historically contingent account of historical events. Its content is "canonical" only when it is made to conform to the necessary truths of reason. While Lessing identifies the rationalist path of modernity, Immanuel Kant actually walks it in *Religion within the Boundaries of Mere Reason*.[5]

The romantic path of the Modernist account of canon and canonicity also follows from the loss of confidence in high Protestant scholasticism. Here, the romantics abandon claims about God's sovereignty in the historical process of the formation and recognition of the canon. They also, in the immediate aftermath of the devastating wars of religion, abandon any claim to the perspicuity of Scripture and the reliability of exegetical and theological

4. G. E. Lessing, *Lessing: Philosophical and Theological Writings* (Cambridge Texts in the History of Philosophy; trans. H. Nisbet; Cambridge: Cambridge University Press, 2005).

5. I. Kant, *Kant: Religion within the Boundaries of Mere Reason; And Other Writings* (Cambridge Texts in the History of Philosophy; trans. A. Wood and G. DiGiovanni; Cambridge: Cambridge University Press, 1999).

method. In place of these, the romantic Modernists turn inward. This turn is brilliantly argued and asserted by F. D. E. Schleiermacher in his *On Religion: Speeches to Its Cultured Despisers* and *The Christian Faith*.[6] Here the canon becomes a record of earlier Christians' inner life that is subject to our experience of the inner life of faith today. Thus, the canon is subject to the canonicity of our contemporary experience of faith—or absolute dependence, as Schleiermacher would have it.

So in high Modernity the canon is explicitly subject to the canonicity of reason or of experience. In the rationalist turn, theology becomes the discipline of conforming the teaching of Christianity to human reason. Thus, theology locates itself within the context of some account of reason that is justified on grounds other than Christian faith. The canon becomes the source of those ideas that must be conformed to the "necessary truths of reason." In the romantic turn, theology becomes the discipline that investigates and explicates religious experience. In high Modernity that experience was seen as having a universal quality. Theology thematizes that experience and reflects it back to particular cultures in a way that demonstrates the core, universally true religious experience. For romantic Modernity, the canon becomes a collection of various cultures' accounts of religious experience that conceal this universal experience. The task of theology is to peel away the layers of concealment to reveal that religious experience at the core.

In high Modernity, then, we see a new turn in the relationship between the canon, canonicity, and theology. In the Protestant tradition, the canon is dehistoricized and the work of theology is timeless. In the Catholic tradition, the church is dehistoricized and the work of theology is timeless. In Modernity, the canon and the church are historicized and humankind is dehistoricized, either by an appeal to "the necessary truths of reason" or to universal religious experience. Theology then becomes the mediator between a historical faith and a timeless human essence.

In our final episode of this historical account, high Modernity develops into late Modernity. Here, everything becomes histori-

6. F. Schleiermacher, *On Religion: Speeches to Its Cultured Despisers* (trans. J. Oman; Louisville: Westminster/John Knox, 1994); idem, *The Christian Faith* (ed. H. R. Mackintosh and J. S. Stewart; Edinburgh: T&T Clark, 1999).

cized and localized. We have lost confidence in the claim of high
Modernity to give an account of timeless human reason or universal religious experience. Indeed, we have become amodernists—
unbelievers in Modernity, which is why accounts of late Modernity
are nearly indistinguishable from accounts of postmodernity. (I am
still in favor of retaining both terms, reserving "late Modernity"
as a description of a condition that had not yet been fully recognized for what it was, and applying "postmodernity" to the fuller
recognition and thematization of that condition.)

In late Modernity, human reason becomes historicized and localized. The "truths of reason" are no longer "necessary." Like
historical events and identities, reason is now also "accidental" (or
contingent). Likewise, human experience is no longer universal,
it is now local and contingent. Thus, various understandings of
reason must be applied to the canon to produce a theology fit for
that account of reason—and no claim can be made to universal
validity for that theology. Likewise, various communities of experience read "the canon" to create various canonical accounts
of theology.

In late Modernity, all theology now moves in the realm of
contingency and particularity; nothing is necessary or universal.
Everything can be and is otherwise: canon, church, reason, experience. Of course, all of these earlier movements are still with
us and resist in various ways the challenge and encroachment of
late Modernity and postmodernity. The problem with all of these
resistance movements that have their roots prior to late Modernity
is that each seeks in some way to deny historicality to that which
is historical. High Protestant scholasticism denies the historicality
of the canon. High Tridentine Catholicism denies the historicality
of the church. High Modernism denies the historicality of human
existence. Then comes late Modernity and its denial of the reality,
the possibility, or the necessity of redemption in history.

What we need is a faithful and credible account of canon and
theology that begins and ends by recognizing the historicality of
the good news of God's redemption in Jesus Christ. It is not simply
that this good news is communicated to historical reality or that
it is accomplished in history; rather, the historical redemption of
creation is this good news. Protestantism and Catholicism treat this

good news as historical up to the moment of "canonization," then immediately move to theology and practices that deny the continuing historicality of that redemption by removing the closed canon from history (Protestantism) or by removing the church from history (Catholicism). High Modernism acknowledges the continuing historicality of the closed canon, but immediately moves to purge that historicality by means of ahistorical reason or universal experience. Late Modernity historicizes everything, but has no place for redemption in the contingencies of history. What is needed, then, is an account that thoroughly embraces our inescapable historical particularity and affirms the reality of redemption in that particularity. To make the point one more time: in the past theology has treated God's work of redemption as historically particular up to the coming of Jesus, after which time this work passes into a realm of timelessness no longer marked by particularity.

In contrast to this, our understanding of the canon and of theology must arise from and be responsible to the recognition that what began in historical particularity continues in historical particularity. Apart from the Christian conviction that the work of Jesus Christ continues today, we would be reduced to the post/late/modern conviction that all we have is historical flux. But in the conviction that the kingdom of God that has come in Jesus Christ continues its work today in the flux of history, we have more than historical flux, we have historical redemption (not as past eras would have it, a "redemptive" escape from history).

This recognition of the continuing work of redemption tells us that the canon, as a body of texts formed in history and bearing always the marks of that historical particularity, is precisely the body of texts that we need as witness to that redemption. If we seek to remove the historicality of the canon by means of a faulty doctrine of inspiration, ecclesiology, or anthropology, then we remove its power to participate in God's work of redemption and to bring us into that historical work. Of course, if that work of redemption does not continue today in historical particularity, then admitting the intractable historicality of the canon would also remove it and us from that work—unless it is removed from history, as in the traditions that we have examined. One can imagine that just such convictions may have motivated the earlier attempts to remove the canon from its historicality or to remove historicality from the canon.

If the work of redemption is historical from beginning to end, then it must have some presence in history today. Here, the canon in all its ineradicable historicality is joined by the people of God in all their historicality. It is in a particular people, located in space and time, or better, throughout space and time, that God's work of redemption continues. It is this people whose life is bound up with the canon, as the community that participates in God's work of redemption.

Here we encounter a problem that is profound, illuminating, and often deeply tragic. Who is this people of God? The history of redemption, in which the canon participates and to which it bears witness, is grounded first in the people of God called Israel. Most of us who are the church are latecomers, the wild branch grafted in, Gentiles whose claim to participate in this redemption and to become "canonical" people depends upon God's faithfulness to Israel and upon our conviction that Jesus of Nazareth is the historical culmination of that work of redemption. For too long, theology has neglected the responsibility to engage in gracious, humble controversy with the people of God called Jews.

Is this an issue really related to canon and theology? Absolutely. Up to this point I have deliberately concealed the importance of recognizing that the deepest and most illuminating debate about the canon is whether the New Testament is canon for the people of God. That is, the most difficult canonical question is not the differences between the Orthodox, Protestant, and Catholic canons, but the difference between the Jewish and Christian canon. Denying the historicality of the Christian canon has obscured and even concealed this critically important question. If we admit the historicality of both the canon and the community, then we must engage in this controversy until the Messiah comes—or returns.

But if we locate the canon and the community within the flux of history, what happens to canonicity? All of the earlier positions establish canonicity by locating it in a timeless universal. And the one tradition that denies any timelessness or universality—post/late/modernity—also denies canonicity. Here we must retrieve the claim with which I began my account of this alternative understanding of canon, community, canonicity, and theology. All are located within the historicality of God's work of redemption in Christ. In shorthand, then, we may say that canonicity is located in the kingdom of God. We believe that the kingdom has come, that it has come in Jesus as the Messiah, and that we are participants in that kingdom by faith in him.

So the kingdom of God is "canonical." But, then, let the arguments begin. We must resist our desperate but misguided desire for timelessness and for certainty that we can control. Canonicity is not something that we can have, it is something to which we must submit—and how we are to do so is a matter for constant discernment.[7] This account of canonicity is congruent with and may be extended by considering once again "the canon." This collection of books is precisely that—a collection. These books are themselves part of the ebb and flow of history. They arose in the midst of controversy and argument, and we must not flatten that reality.

At the same time, some available texts were excluded from the canon. So the recognition of the canon—a set of texts with boundaries—also represents the recognition and submission of the church to "a rule derived from the apostolic age. This 'standing under a rule' is not a statement about the event of inspiration or the uniqueness of the authorship of certain texts. It is a statement about the accountability of the Christian community as a movement within history, whose claim to be faithful to historical origins in the midst of historical change obliges it to identify the criterion of that accountability."[8] Moving beyond this assertion, I would add that the church's recognition of the canon acknowledges that the church itself is not "canonical."

But if the church is not canonical, neither is the canon. That is, the existence of the church tells us that "the canon" is not canonical. This body of texts is itself received by a community, and it is within that community that the canon has life. So the canon and the community are bound together in their participation in the kingdom of God. And canonicity is located neither in the canon

---

7. See R. Hütter, *Suffering Divine Things: Theology as Church Practice* (Grand Rapids: Eerdmans, 2000).

8. Yoder, "The Authority of the Canon," 274–75.

nor in the community but in their participation in the kingdom of God. That assertion, of course, does not settle any arguments; it simply tells us which arguments we should be having and how we are to engage in those arguments. But that is precisely what we should expect if we are caught up in the history of redemption.

This leads us then, finally, to theology. What becomes of theology on this account of canon, community, and canonicity? That question requires an extensive answer that I can only point to here; it is best answered by the practice of theology, not by an account of the practice of theology. Nevertheless, something may be said even in this context.

On this account of the historicality of the gospel, theology becomes a guide to the continuing arguments about the presence of the kingdom today—what does it look like, where is it at work, how may we participate, how are we failing to participate? In this way, theology enters into the lively arguments of the community that form its life and extend its understanding of the gospel of the kingdom. Theology is that office, role, or calling in the life of the church that has special responsibility for knowing, guarding, and making available to the community the rules that the community has developed over time for its life and thought.

Theology must practice wisdom in its work—not every rule (doctrine) is applicable in every circumstance. Sometimes a rule may be precisely the wrong rule to apply in a particular circumstance ("grace," Rom. 6). Sometimes a circumstance may require the retrieval of a forgotten rule (e.g., justification by faith) or the development of a new rule that emerges out of the history of redemption (e.g., the Trinity). Some rules are so well developed that they require little argument today. In all of this, the responsibility of the church is to engage in reading the canon and to listen to one another in the community so as to discern and participate in the work of the kingdom today.

One final word: This essay is, in reality, an essay on the Holy Spirit, though I deliberately set myself the task of writing the paper without reference to the Holy Spirit. Now, let me make that explicit. It is the work of the Holy Spirit that extends redemption in the world today. It is the Holy Spirit who worked in history and guided the writing of Scripture and the formation of the canon.

It is the Holy Spirit who called into being the church and gathered a people for God in Christ. And it is the Holy Spirit who leads us today into discerning the kingdom and living in it. Why did I not make that explicit in the beginning? Because the Holy Spirit does this work in a way that grants us no special privilege or claim. The Spirit's work is concealed and revealed in our ordinary humanity in the same way that God is concealed and revealed in Jesus of Nazareth. It is our calling to be faithful disciples of this Messiah who came to us in history and is himself the meaning and end of history. Let us walk in this way.

Index of Scripture and Other Ancient Writings

255

Index of Subjects and Names

Printed in Great Britain
by Amazon